1 *Homage to the Square: Into the Open*, 1952. Oil on wood composition board, 21 × 21 in.

11 *Homage to the Square: Guarded*, 1952. Oil on masonite, 24 × 24 in.

111 *Homage to the Square: Renewed Hop*e, 1951. Oil on masonite, 24 × 24 in.

IV *Study for Homage to the Square*, 1968. Oil on masonite, 24 × 24 in.

v *Study for Homage to the Square: Dimly Reflected*, 1963. Oil on masonite, 24 × 24 in.

VI *Study for Homage to the Square,* 1965. Oil on masonite, 24 × 24 in.

Charles Darwent

Josef Albers
Life and Work

 Thames & Hudson

First published in 2018 in the United States of America by Thames & Hudson Inc., 500 Fifth Avenue, New York, New York 10110

www.thamesandhudsonusa.com

Library of Congress Control Number 2018932309
ISBN 978-0-500-51910-3

Printed and bound in China by C & C Offset Printing Co. Ltd

Preface

Like many educated Germans of his day, Josef Albers had a visceral mistrust of history. With this went another of self-expression. These twin distastes, together, made him a very particular man. To locate Albers in time was to incur his wrath; so, too, to attempt to analyse his motives or influences. His vision of himself was as *ex nihilo*, born of nothing. 'I came,' he said, 'very much from my father, and from Adam, and that's all.'

This makes him an uneasy subject for biography. In a long and very public life, Albers managed to remain inscrutably private. He kept no diary, and batted away questions about his emotions or past. What mattered was his art, which was inexplicable by his life. Piecing together this last has to be done against the wishes of the man who lived it. If the Josef Albers who emerges from these pages seems inconsistent, then that is how the evidence suggests him. As I finish this book, I feel a certain sympathy for the trial judge who, at the end of a long summing-up, sighed to the lawyer F. E. Smith, 'I have listened to you for an hour now, Mr Smith, and find myself none the wiser.' 'None the wiser, perhaps, my lord,' Smith purred, 'but certainly better informed.'

Like any biography, this one is partisan. For that, I make no apology: I took Josef Albers as I found him. It is also necessarily partial. Among other things largely missing from it are the story of Anni Albers *née* Fleischmann, a fascinating artist in her own right, and her working partnership with her husband. These require books of their own; I look forward to reading them. Josef Albers' teaching, too, gets relatively short shrift, although he was arguably the most important teacher of art in the 20th century. My reason for this is that pedagogy tends to be a specialist interest, and this book is aimed at the informed but general reader. In any case, an excellent book on Albers' teaching already exists, namely Frederick A. Horowitz and Brenda Danilowitz's *To Open Eyes*.

In researching this biography, I received the material and moral support of the Josef and Anni Albers Foundation in Bethany, Connecticut. I really can not thank my friends there enough for their tireless good humour and intelligent help, or for their patience. You are too numerous to name, but you know who you are. My particular thanks go to Jeannette Redensek for her capacious mind; to Anne Sisco, for being Anne Sisco; Brenda Danilowitz, for not pulling her punches; and to Fritz Horstman, for teaching me Albers' colour course and moseying over for drinks. Michael Beggs is no longer at the Foundation, but remains a source of dispassionate good sense. I wish I could have thanked Fred Horowitz in person, but, alas, he died in 2013. His unpublished essay, 'Squares: Form, Colour, and Meaning in Josef Albers's *Homages*', was a revelation. His interviews with Albers' ex-students, of which he himself was one, inform the last half of this book.

Beyond these, my profound thanks are due to the specialists who agreed to read it in manuscript in its various sections. In chronological order: Professor Marjorie Lamberti; Magdalena Droste; Heather South and Dr Eric Bentley (the latter the last surviving of Albers' colleagues at Black Mountain College); Dr Eeva-Liisa Pelkonen and Frances Morris. Half a century ago, Margit Rowell spent a year's worth of Saturdays travelling by train from New York to New Haven to interview Josef Albers in his basement. All too typically, Albers fell out with her. The material Rowell gathered should have appeared in her own book; instead, she generously allowed me to use it in mine. Thank you, Margit.

Finally, my great gratitude to the following: in Germany, Drs Heinz Liesbrock and Ulrike Growe at the Josef Albers Museum in Bottrop; Heike Biskup and her colleagues at the Bottrop city archive; Peter Ennemoser at St Michael's church; the archivists of the Stadtlohn, Büren, Dülmen, Essen and Münster archives, and of the State Archive of North Rhine-Westphalia; the Klassik Stiftung Weimar; the Stiftung Bauhaus Dessau; the Bauhaus-Archiv, Berlin; to David Hamann, for deciphering and transcribing Albers' unreadable early hand; to Prof. Dr Ursula Frohne, for tea and support; and to Joachim Driller, for sharing his essays on the Essen *Kunstgewerbeschule*. In America: the librarians and archivists of the Archives of American Art, Smithsonian Institution, Washington, DC; the Western Regional Archives, State Archives of North Carolina, Asheville, NC; the John Hope and Aurelia E. Franklin Library, Fisk University, Nashville, TN; the Guggenheim and Museum of Modern Art Archives in New York; the Stirling Memorial, Robert B. Haas Family and Beinecke Libraries at Yale; Michelle Cotton, manuscripts archivist at the Corning Museum of Glass in Corning, NY; the Avery Architectural and Fine Arts Library at Columbia; Brothers Alan Reed OSB and David Klingeman OSB at St John's Abbey, Collegeville, MN; and Ken and Gail Resen. In England: Sophy Thompson, Camilla Rockwood, Jo Walton and Kate Edwards, who had the wearying tasks of publishing, editing and illustrating this book for Thames & Hudson; to Kate Burvill, who inspired and publicized it; Gordon Wise, my agent at Curtis Brown; and Josephine Grever, for patiently correcting my German. In Paris, Michael Smith. Last, to the friends and strangers who have put up with me for these three years, thank you.

Introduction: *Homages to the Square*

Art is there lest we perish from the truth.
Friedrich Nietzsche

Art must do more than Nature. That's why it's art.
Josef Albers

He liked the square for its simplicity. It was like a self-portrait.
When you saw that square looking at you, it was Albers looking at you.
Richard Anuszkiewicz

In the summer of 1950, while teaching a summer school at Harvard, Josef Albers made a painting he would call *Homage to the Square*. It was not to be the last of the name. By the time of his death a quarter of a century later, he would have painted more than two thousand *Homages* – roughly a hundred a year, or one every four days. In a single year, 1961, he painted more than two hundred of them. If, as Albers said, he destroyed more work than he kept, then the numbers will have been unknowably higher. It was a series that would define him as an artist, and a late flowering. In 1950, when he made his first *Homage*, Albers was sixty-two years old. He would carry on painting them until his death, in 1976, at the age of eighty-eight.

Like Albers himself, the *Homages* were, problematically, both old and new. In terms of his oeuvre, they appear out of nowhere. Albers had, since the mid-1920s, been making art that was both abstract and geometric. In the years immediately before 1950, this had increasingly been made in series – latterly, one of vaguely architectural-looking blocks of oil paint on hardboard, another of linear graphics etched on laminate. The first explored how colours worked in proportion and juxtaposition; the second, how the eye reads one etched angle as parallel to the picture plane but another as recessive to it. Between these series and the *Homages*, though, there is nothing – no visual stepping stones to the work that would occupy Albers for more than a quarter of a century; no false starts.

This, of course, is not the whole story. There may have been no obvious antecedents to the *Homages* in Albers' work, but there were many, and compelling, claims to their paternity elsewhere. It was impossible to make a painting called *Homage to the Square* in 1950 without conjuring up that *ur*-square of modernism, painted by Kasimir Malevich in 1915: the so-called *Black Square*. That same square had stalked the Bauhaus when Albers had studied and taught there in the thirteen years from 1920. Paul Klee, Albers' colleague at the school, had painted squares; so, with concentric circles in them, had Wassily Kandinsky. 'Three days in Weimar and one can never look at a square again,' one critic had groaned. 'Malevich invented the square a decade ago. How fortunate [for the Bauhaus] that he didn't patent it.'

If, in 1950, these historical squares suggested that Albers' *Homages* were re-fighting a battle fought long ago, then other more modern squares would be just as misleading. Paintings of squares had been common enough in 1920; by 1950, they were thin on the ground, particularly in America. Fifteen years later, they had come into American vogue. The young Americans Frank

Stella, Ellsworth Kelly and Barnett Newman, mustered under the crisp new flag of post-painterly abstraction, all painted squares of one sort or another. One of their band, Sol LeWitt, would be Albers' keenest apostle. His twenty-part *Wall Drawing 583* (1988) differs from the *Homages* in being painted on the wall rather than hung from it, but the work's palette and interests – the way colours can be made to recede or advance in relation to each other – are an homage to the *Homages*. LeWitt made no bones about it: three decades after his mentor's death, he co-titled *Wall Drawing 1176, Seven Basic Colours and All Their Combinations in a Square within a Square: Wall Drawing for Josef Albers*. Twenty years before that, LeWitt's influential manifesto, 'Paragraphs on Conceptual Art', had been written with his future dedicatee in mind. Its imagining of an art of 'millions of variations', in which 'all of the planning and decisions are made beforehand', made a low bow to the *Homages*; so, too, its call for the 'eliminat[ion of] the arbitrary, the capricious, and the subjective' in art. And yet the most famous of LeWitt's edicts, that 'the idea becomes a machine that makes the art', bears little relation to the reality of Josef Albers' work. Le Witt was making an early fist at defining what he called 'conceptual art'. There was no room in this for 'the skill of the artist', nor for 'emotional kick', both of which, quietly, are at the heart of the *Homages to the Square*.

Given the push and pull of these conflicting histories, it is not surprising that it took a decade for Albers' late, great series to begin to be understood. So, too, Albers himself. He was over seventy before he began to gain wide recognition as an artist, at least in part because, as a survivor of the Bauhaus, he had come to be viewed as an artefact. 'I was in awe of him just for his living history,' one wide-eyed Yale student would say. Albers was variously an oxymoron: an old man making new art that was old-fashioned or, possibly, worryingly modern; an artist whose work was European in its moderation and scale, but made in America; a contemporary and a forerunner at once. Taste and the art market are conservative things, placing a premium on clarity. Albers, in historical terms, was unclear. Even more so were his *Homages to the Square*.

What were these pictures? For works made in thousands of iterations over a quarter of a century, there can clearly be no single answer. Despite their obvious likenesses, *Homage to the Square (A)* – the first, painted at Harvard in the summer of 1950 – and the work catalogued as 1976.1.524, finished in

1 *Homage to the Square (A)*, 1950. Oil on masonite, 30 × 30 in.

2 *Homage to the Square*, 1976. Oil on masonite, 24 × 24 in.

the weeks before Josef Albers' death, are emphatically unalike (figs 1, 2). The point of Malevich's square was to close down debate, to be a *terminus ad quem*. It was an art-historical full-stop: after it, art would be forced to start again. The black square at the centre of *Homage to the Square (A)* has precisely the opposite meaning. Albers' working method is often likened to that of a scientist, his precisely organized, artificially lit studios to laboratories. These are neat analogies, but not wholly satisfactory ones. The point of scientific experiment is to reach a conclusion; of the *Homages to the Square*, to generate questions – ever more of them, exponentially, as Albers grew in experience and deftness, as 'his nerves [became] still more sensitive'. 'Malevich had painted a full stop,' wrote one critic. 'From this full stop Albers...developed a whole alphabet.' As to the artist himself, he said, 'All my painting is actually study. The longer I do it, the more and more it is endless.' Malevich's zero became Albers' starting point. He made something out of nothing.

This chapter has assumed the *Homages* as paintings, although, for reasons of number and price, they will be familiar to many more people as silkscreened prints. There was, in Albers' mind, no difference in status between the two mediums: they were simply separate. 'Usually, I do not try to do reproduction, because the[y] are so different,' he said. The prints *Tenuous* and *Equivocal* (1962) (figs 3, 4) are works in their own right, being neither studies for, nor facsimiles of, paintings. Albers' insistence on exactness meant that *Homage* prints were technically very difficult to make. It was only in 1962, when one of his ex-students found a way of producing chalky saturations of colour in ink, that the *Homages* began to appear regularly on paper as well as hardboard, more than a decade after *Homage to the Square (A)*. Another student recalled Albers expressing a preference for print over paint, 'because the paintings were too much about the hand and the mark, but the silkscreens were more just about the eye'. One can only guess at why, or whether, Albers might have said this. It is, among much else, the painted *Homages'* lack of control, their materiality, that makes them so compelling.

One such is the small work, eleven inches by eleven and in grey, white and blue, painted by Albers in 1951 (fig. 5). Various things mark this as an early *Homage*, its odd-number dimensions among them. By 1960, Albers had settled on a fixed repertoire of sizes for his squares, starting at sixteen by sixteen inches and working its way up, in mostly even-numbered increments,

3 *Equivocal*, 1962. Screen print, 16½ × 16½ in.
4 *Tenuous*, 1962. Screen print, 16½ × 16½ in.
5 *Homage to the Square*, 1951. Oil on masonite, 11 × 11 in.

to forty-eight by forty-eight, the largest width of masonite available. On these last and largest, destined for museums and his best collectors, Albers lavished particular care. Only three known *Homages* are eleven inches square, all of them painted in 1951 – a fecund year, from which around sixty works survive. This one is also unusual in having a fruitwood box frame, made by Albers himself. Later *Homages* would mostly be framed in thin steel. The surround of this small picture had been made for an earlier painting and cut down to size: handwritten dimensions on the wood read 26⅜ × 15½. The panel, too, has been re-used. Just visible through the white paint on its reverse is an incised pattern rather similar to the Arp-like lithographs Albers had made in Mexico twelve years before.

For all its unorthodoxies, this small, early *Homage* is typical of the series. Its composition is the first of four types that Albers would eventually come to use, one of nested squares of four colours, three of three. Here, the three outer squares share the same proportions – their bottom edges are half as deep as the side ones are wide, one-third as deep as the top ones. The fourth, central square is four times the width of one side edge. Much has been written on the precise optical effect of these arrangements, although to suppose that they were intended to provoke a uniform reaction, visual or psychic, is to miss the point of the *Homages*. Albers' aim in using a fixed set of templates is not to impose sameness, but to set us up for difference. A formula that would guarantee an identical response in all viewers would have appalled him. As *Newsweek* perceptively put it, 'The Albers square is not self-defined: each man who looks at it defines it in a different way.'

Before considering this small *Homage*'s front, though, it is necessary to look at its back. Since Alberti's *De pictura*, the cloth or panel support of a painting had been assumed as a *finestra aperta*, an 'open window' through which the world of the artist's imagination might be seen. Open windows do not, by definition, have backs: that paintings had an obverse had become a dirty secret in art. Dutch Baroque painters, ever subversive, played on this illicitness by making *trompe l'oeil* paintings of the backs of paintings, their aim being the proto-postmodern one of puncturing Albertian illusion. Albers' intention is different from theirs, although not entirely so. From the 1940s on, he recorded what he called the 'recipes' for his pictures on their reverse sides – the colours he had used and colourmen who had made them, their undercoat and varnish. In finished works, this information might be recorded three times: written in a (relatively) clear hand, neatly indented and in plain sight in the centre of the back of the panel; inscribed again, less neatly, around the edge, eventually to be covered by the frame; and logged a third time in a notebook. On the back of this small, blue, early *Homage*, Albers has written:

Ground: several coats of casein and some linseed oil.
Varnish transparent.

Painting: colours used (from centre):
Mixture of Permanent blue Pretested + zinc white (Sargeant)
Cerulean blue shade [?] (Pretested)
Reilly's Grey No. 8 (Grumbacher)

---

all in one coat + no additional painting

Varnished with Eonite.

At the top is the painting's title, and below, its maker's name and the year of its making: *Albers 1951*.

In 1951, Josef Albers had not long been a professor at Yale. His previous teaching had been at experimental schools in Germany and America. Although the point of hiring him had been to loosen up Yale's art and design curriculum, the university remained academically rigorous. The first *Homages* were made at a time when Albers was systematizing his thought to cope with the new demands made of it; this would culminate, a dozen years later, in his great publication, *Interaction of Color*. There had never been much separation in his mind between the teaching of art and the making of it, both being grounded in repetition and experience. The lists of materials on the reverse of the *Homages* are there in part as teaching aids; although, of course, the audience for them would necessarily be small.

Why else, then? This particular *Homage* is both typical of its series and not. It was among the last to be painted on the smooth, rather than the textured, side of hardboard, Albers noticing early on that his grounds tended to flake from a shiny surface. Not long afterwards, he switched to painting on the rough, more adherent side, so that for the next twenty-five years it was the backs of his paintings that would be smooth. In this 1951 picture, he solves the problem of writing on a knobbled surface by painting it gloss white. This, later, would land conservators with another problem, namely that hardboard sealed with paint on both sides is prone to warp. For the moment, though, a painted obverse had the added advantage of evening up the status of the two sides of his work. Among other things, the *Homages* are acts of rescue, or, perhaps, of redemption: of unglamorous colours, cheap materials, workaday techniques. Albers extends this impulse to the side of a painting normally disregarded. This taste for completeness, the whole picture, for embracing the dark and the shadow, had been core to the teachings of Gestalt psychology, which had swept the Bauhaus in the late 1920s. It was also at the heart of Roman Catholicism, the faith in which Josef Albers had been raised.

The backs of paintings were more than just a handy place for taking notes. The striking thing about the recipes on the *Homages* is their resemblance to Albers' poems, begun when he was in his twenties. At seventy, he published a collection of these, interspersed with drawings from a series of etched laminates – the *Structural Constellations* – on which he had recently been working. The connection between word and image in the book is both allusive and clear. Like any German of his day, Albers had imbibed Nietzsche at the cultural knee. As that tireless cosmopolitan Count

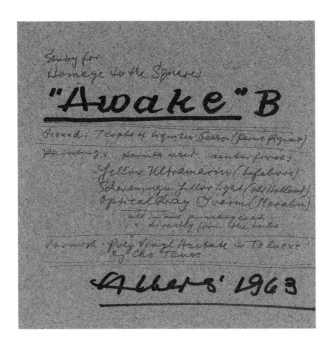

6 Detail, back of *Study for Homage to the Square: Awake B*, 1963.

Harry Kessler wrote, to belong to the Nietzschean generation was 'to *be* something new, to *signify* something new; to *represent* new values'. To be new, of necessity, meant doubting the old: not for nothing is Nietzsche classed, along with Freud and Darwin, as a master of suspicion. Among other assumptions questioned by Albers' *Poems and Drawings* is that of the self-evident difference between word and image, the visual and verbal. If his graphics call out for verbal reasoning, his poems are strongly plastic:

> Keine Zeit ist – niemals
>   niemals sowie überall
>   überall ist immer
> keine Zeit   ist immer

(No-time is – never/never but also everywhere/everywhere is forever/ no-time is forever)

They are ideograms, imparting their meaning both through words and their visual arrangement. Even non-German speakers could recognize the columnar stacking of the first and last phrases, the growing gaps between them. 'Keine Zeit' is made up of solid and void, what is there and what is not – a rectangular rebus of word-patterns, of which some are present and others absent. That paradoxical balance of existence and nothingness is, both visually and verbally, the poem's subject.

The resemblance of these ideograms to the writing on the backs of *Homages* is more than coincidence. Both are attempts to pin down qualities that interest Albers in their instability. In the recipes, you sense his fascination with the poetic vocabulary of colour; so, too, with its inadequacies. For iron oxide reds alone, there were a dozen variant names: Venetian Red, Persian Red, Indian, English and Pompeian Reds, Spanish Red, Mineral Rouge, Terra Rosa, and so on. It wasn't only names that were fickle. A cerulean blue from the Dutch brand Rembrandt and another from the American Grumbacher might differ radically from each other in appearance. Albers, intrigued at the gap between word and image, made several three-square *Homages* using a different make of Naples yellow for each square (fig. 7).

As ever, each was applied straight from the tube, unmixed and thinly spread and varnished in the same way. The result was three squares of three different colours. Even paints by the same manufacturer might change

7 *Study for Homage to the Square*, 1971. Oil on masonite, 24 × 24 in.

over time as their constituent pigments grew more or less easy to find. Albers' habit of date-marking the hundreds of tubes of paint in his studio (III.8, say), was an attempt to get around the problem; although even this method proved not to be foolproof, quite possibly to his delight.

In 1953, five years before *Poems and Drawings* and back in Germany for the first time in two decades, Albers had met Eugen Gomringer. Gomringer was an intriguing young man, the Bolivian-born son of a Swiss father, working as secretary to the artist Max Bill. The next year, he would publish a volume of ideogrammic poems in German, English and Spanish, of which this, called 'Schweigen' (Silence), is one:

schweigen   schweigen   schweigen
schweigen   schweigen   schweigen
schweigen   schweigen
schweigen   schweigen   schweigen
schweigen   schweigen   schweigen

The book in which the poems appeared was called *Constellations*, an echo of Albers' etched laminates; in exchange, Gomringer's influence on Albers' verse was clear. If, as language artists or concrete poets, the men met unannounced on the backs of the *Homages*, it was on the front of the paintings that Gomringer's admiration for Albers was spelled out. In the year the older man turned eighty, Gomringer published the first full-length monograph in English on his work. This set out its stall as a critical history, although it was in reality no such thing: correspondence between author and subject shows Albers' close watch over the book's contents. For all that, Gomringer's remarks on the *Homages* remain acute. While he notes that, as the late children of constructivism, they seem to be aesthetically antithetical to the then-voguish Pop Art, he recognizes that both are 'general[ly] subject...to the primacy of colour'.

If the notion of a kinship between the *Homages* and Roy Lichtenstein's *Whaam!* seems far-fetched, Gomringer's claim is perceptive. Like that of the Pop artist, Albers' colour was grounded in everyday life. The squares of the *Homages* may trace their fine-art line back via the Bauhaus to Malevich, but their palette had been worked out in the graphic and product design studios of the Bauhaus, in advertising and architecture. Teaching colour in America, Albers had had his students work from Lucky Strike packets and Coca-Cola bottles. Among the *Homages*' ancestors in his own oeuvre are the set of coloured glass side tables he had made in Dessau in the late 1920s, and the walls and ceiling he had painted for the Weimar apartment of the pedagogue Wilhelm Flitner in 1923. Art, Albers insisted, stretched from the church to the plaza. The (apparent) decisiveness of early the *Homages* gives them the feel of logos or emblems, both of which Albers had designed.

In terms of technique, the *Homages* are arguably more *populaire* than Lichtenstein's paintings. Lichtenstein, in his Manhattan studio, painted upright on an easel; Albers, in his Connecticut basement, painted flat on a table. There were practical reasons for this, the most obvious being that he had abjured the brush for the palette knife. The paint of the *Homages* was spread on 'like butter on pumpernickel', as Albers was fond of saying. This would have been next to impossible to do on a vertical surface. But palette knives and masonite were themselves part of a process of renunciation, which he described to his friend and fellow artist Elaine de Kooning while making his first *Homages* in 1950: 'no smock, no skylight, no studio, no palette, no easel, no brushes, no medium, no canvas; no variation in texture...no personal handwriting, no stylization, no tricks, no "twinkling of the eye"'. The series was a whittling away of art, a paring down.

Albers was not the only modernist to paint on a table – Mondrian, one of the few of his contemporaries he confessed to admiring, did so too – but he was unusual in working in this way precisely because it struck him as workmanlike. The rejection of so-called 'easel art' was one thing; the insistence on painting on a table because it seemed a practice more typical of an architect or designer is quite another. This was part of a broader imagining of modernism on Albers' part. In a letter about his *Homages* to the critic Lucy Lippard, he wrote:

> The now popular concept of serial production...is a product of an industrial age when the perfect repetition of an element presents a new insight into human experience. There is an excitement in being able to repeat precisely, with none of the little aberrations typical of Gothic architecture, for example, in which the windows were supposed to be all the same but were actually a little different.

Working on a table made for a table aesthetic – what the critic Leo Steinberg called 'the flatbed picture plane [with] its symbolic allusion to hard surfaces such as tabletops, studio floors, charts, bulletin boards – any... surface on which...information may be received'. The artwork and the means of its making became conflated. In this regard, the *Homages* and the floor-made drip paintings of Jackson Pollock may be counted as part of the same tendency, even if Pollock was one of many of his contemporaries for whose work Albers retained a deep loathing. If the seriality of the *Homages* – more than two thousand of them, made over a quarter of a century – has tended to be compared with scientific method, another analogy is with mass production. An industrial aesthetic had been central to the Bauhaus. Albers himself had made paintings on glass, sandblasted in a commercial studio. And yet there is an obvious problem with Albers' own explanation of his *Homages*. Had 'perfect repetition' been his main ambition for them, then he had chosen an odd way of realizing it. While mechanically produced screen prints are free of the maker's mark, the painted *Homages* are just that: painted – in artists' oils and by an artist's hand, even if that hand had held a knife rather than a brush.

In 1962, the year of the first prints, Albers made *Homage to the Square: Study for Autumn Sound*. Painted, like all *Homages*, from the middle out, its squares are increasingly scraped away from centre to edge. There are several results of this. First, although in terms of area of paint *Autumn Sound* is a brown picture, its focus shifts to the yellow central square. Second, Albers' exposure of the knobbled white undercoat of the outermost square rewards an ill-used dull brown colour by making it glow like gold. Last, that same outer square, its remaining paint thin and uneven, looks as though it has been scumbled, a technique more typical of classical painting. Albers' scari-fied surface would not look out of place in, say, Jacques-Louis David's *Death of Marat*. For an insistently modern work, *Autumn Sound* is both romantic and painterly. So, too, its title, typically given to it after it had been finished. As with all of the *Homages*, the power of *Autumn Sound* lies in a nesting of paradoxes.

Given that every one of the two-thousand-odd *Homages* contains squares in its composition and title, it would be reasonable to assume them as the series' subject. But here, too, the works are paradoxical. In an interview in

8 *Study for Homage to the Square: Autumn Sound*, 1962. Oil on masonite, 18 × 18 in.

1966, when Albers had been at work on the *Homages* for nearly two decades, he made a surprising observation: 'I'm not paying "homage to the square"!' he chortled. 'It's only the dish I serve my craziness about colour in.' Why he chose the name – as opposed to, say, *Homage to Colour* – one can only guess. On his choice of the square as a vector for colour, Albers was clearer. An initial attraction had been a belief that squares did not occur in nature. When he discovered that they did (in rock salt crystals, for example), he decided to carry on anyway. What he liked about the square, he said, was that it 'has a seat. It sits. A circle can not sit. It also does not reveal whether it rotates around its centre or not.' And yet stability, in the *Homages*, exists to be destabilized. Given the right conditions, even the most four-square of squares might be made to move about. It could even, as Albers delighted in noting, be made into a circle:

> Cartier Bresson, the well-known French photographer, once...
> referred to one set of my squares and said, 'Oh, I mean that circular
> square of yours.' 'That is a wonderful contradiction,' I said. 'That
> excited me. What do you mean by circular square?' He answered:
> 'Yesterday, you showed me two *Homages to the Square* in which the
> central square no longer seemed bounded by straight lines and
> 90-degree angles.'

As well as stability, squares, unlike other geometric shapes, had an unvarying orientation and proportions. (Albers' friend, the Gestalt psychologist Rudolf Arnheim, described them as non-human, where rectangles might be tragic or comic.) Everything was set up for sameness. Albers' emphasis on the 'sitting' of squares, on their solidity to the ground, suggested weight, which implied gravity. The squares of the *Homages* are not arranged concentrically but appear to sink towards the lower edge of the painting or, conversely, to rise towards the top. Rather as with the Doppler effect and sound, the lower edge of each middle square thus tends to read as darker than the rest and the upper as lighter, as though weight has transformed into luminance. The picture's vanishing point, shifted from its expected place in the centre of the composition, dematerializes across the middle square. Caught in this gravitational back-and-forth, lateral edges disembody, so that adjacent colours define themselves by their neighbours, reading differently with proximity or distance. The effect overall of the *Homages'* composition

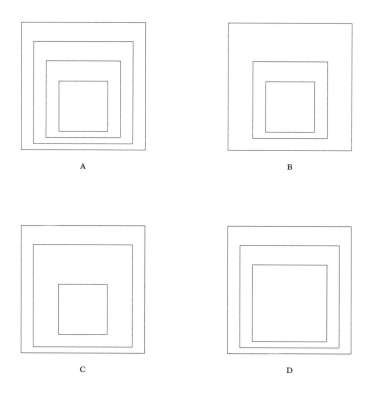

9 The four pattern types of Albers' *Homages to the Square.*

is of slight instability (or, perhaps, possibility), born of that most stable of things, the square.

This much, at least, is true of all the *Homages,* although the mechanics of uncertainty vary with the four pattern types. Type A works – the earliest, of which the small 1951 *Homage* is one – tend to be more *mouvementée,* the recessionals from the four corners to their vanishing point the most heavily implied.

These act as perceptual axes or rails along which the picture's four sliding planes can recede or advance. The figure-ground paradox – the effect by which the warriors on a frieze can appear by turns raised or incised – had been a source of fascination to Albers since his days at the Bauhaus, part of the so-called 'Gestalt shift' memorably illustrated in the Duckrabbit (fig. 10). In a given Type A *Homage,* any of the four squares may occupy any of the four possible positions for it – uppermost, lowermost, or either of the

Welche Thiere gleichen einander am meisten?

Kaninchen und Ente.

10 Kaninchen und Ente (Duck and Rabbit), 1892.

two in between – propelled there by the interaction of its own colour with the colours of the squares around it (figs 11a, b, c).

In Type D compositions (figs 12a, b, c), the drama transfers from the wings to the stage. Here, the kinetic force of perspective dissipates across the large central square, so that its colour becomes spatially unknowable, like a James Turrell lightwork. All four compositional types, though, have one thing in common: they are made without overpainting. The belows and on-top-ofs of Albers' squares, their apparent transparence or opacity, is entirely perceptual. Each square sits on the white ground, its edges pushed up against those of its neighbours by Albers' palette knife.

Clearly, one of the extraordinary things about the *Homages to the Square* is their robustness as a series. The first of the works and the last are remarkably similar; but they are also remarkably different from each other. This is as you might expect of a series of so many iterations, produced over so long a period of time, and whose aim was in part a refining of the eye. While Albers wrote and spoke about the *Homages* extensively, he seldom mentioned the arc of their history. He had a Nietzschean mistrust of what he termed 'retrospection', applied either to his life or his work. Nonetheless,

11a *Study for Homage to the Square: Amplified*, 1957. Oil on masonite, 24 × 24 in.

11b *Study for Homage to the Square: Tranquil*, 1967. Oil on masonite, 32 × 32 in.

11c *Homage to the Square*, 1971. Oil on masonite, 40 × 40 in.

12a *Homage to the Square*, 1963. Oil on masonite, 18 × 18 in.
12b *Homage to the Square: R-1 c-4*, 1968. Oil on masonite, 16 × 16 in.
12c *Study for Homage to the Square*, 1973. Oil on masonite, 16 × 16 in.

the *Homages* are both paintings and historical objects, shaped not just by their number but by the time they were made.

One similarity of the early and late paintings is that both come from classical periods in the series, times when Albers painted with something like certainty. Certainty, like history, was not always welcome in modern painting. In Albers' first year at the Bauhaus, André Gide had written of classicism as the enemy of romanticism, a thing of order, antithetical to experiment. The first *Homages* have a smoothness that is not just to do with the side of the masonite (figs I–III). They are often very beautiful, but with a beauty that is lapidary: theirs is a drama of the surface. It is as though Albers is recalling the lustre of the glass paintings he had made at the Bauhaus, and trying to recreate it. If the colours he uses in the early *Homages* are strong (at times gaudy), their interactions tend to be lateral, across the picture plane – one colour, or pair of colours, forcing another to change its identity. A dull yellow may be made to shine, a bright one to fade. Any colour, denatured by its fellows, may revert to grey, although Albers' greys are far from null. Later, in the early sixties, he would begin to paint *Homages* entirely in shades of grey, their own interactions at least as dramatic as the eye-popping ones that had preceded them (figs IV–VI). Parleying between themselves, greys might become blue or violet, or even red. 'That same grey is here violet is here bluish and the same is here greenish,' Albers enthused of one of these works. 'Don't you think it's wonderful? It's not art – *nein*, it's not art, it has nothing to do with art. It is just a demonstration how colour can cheat me, deceive me, and out of this I make an new experience that I can tell my grandmother: such things I have never seen before.'

It is only in the *Homages* of the late fifties that Albers begins to explore in paint another quality of glass: its translucence. If the surface of the early paintings tended to be impenetrable, that of the works post-1957 becomes increasingly nebulous. At eighty-one, filmed in the suburban basement that did service as his studio, Albers recalled his move towards thinness, championing the luminosity of his late paint as the equivalent of Turner's or Bruegel's. Painting, now, was as much about subtraction as addition. With their oils applied and scraped back, the squares took on a new dimension. Where before they might lie below or above each other, they could now be seen *through*. An ugly colour – Albers denied that such a thing existed – was made to glow as if starlit: the sludgy dross of aureolin yellow could be alchemized into gold (fig. VII). More and more, the *Homages* had become about redemption. The composition of the later paintings takes on a depth that no longer comes from implied linear perspective, but from colour itself. It was Albers' mastery of this new translucence, sometimes hard-won, that would end in the *Homages'* second classical period, in the last decade of his life.

It had not always been easy. 'Often I have to paint a picture ten different times before I reach a realization,' Albers grumbled to an interviewer, a decade into the *Homages*. In visual articulation, he said, there was never a final solution; only endless experiment. Not all of these ended well. Albers was a remorseless editor of his own work – after he and his wife, Anni, moved house in 1970, he 'destroyed a hundred paintings', he said. It was not the only occasion. 'When I destroy,' he went on, 'I feel better than after an operation or Confession. I feel clean.' From as early as the mid-fifties, he had added to the four variants of nested squares. Infrequently, but over twenty years, he painted so-called 'mitered' *Homages*, the opposite sides of their outer squares perspectively bevelled (figs VIII–IX). Occasionally he divided a central square laterally, so that it looked like a landscape with a skyscape above it (fig. X). In 1957 came two rectangular works, one vertical and one horizontal, each with two squares on each panel (fig. XI).

In the early sixties, Albers painted his only diptych, *Homage to the Square: Despite Mist*, bought by the actor Maximilian Schell. But these compositional experiments remained oddities. The great variance of this great series lay not in form, but in colour.

Seen side by side, a group from the early years of the *Homages* and another from the last are surprisingly unalike (figs XII–XVII). The traffic-light colours of the first telegraph their difference: their job is to work against each other. By contrast, the colours of the late works both differ and collude, to the point where they may, without close examination, seem monochromatic. It is tempting to anthropomorphize this change, to see the early *Homages* as a tale of struggle and the late ones of resolution. In a series as long-lived as this one, and with so many iterations, there can be no single work that marks this change exactly; but the year 1961 – an especially fecund one in Albers' basement studio – seems to have seen the necessary shift of gear. It is after this that the focus of the *Homages* begins to change from difference to kinship, from strangers to siblings. In 1962, there is a suite of all-green *Homages*, followed by another in yellows (figs XVIII–XXIII). Both colours would periodically recur, in family groups, for the rest of Albers' life. The suite of red paintings begun in 1966 marks the beginning of the *Homages'* second classical period. If the first had been driven by a need to make work that looked traditional, *richtig*, the second threw caution to the winds. Albers now had the ease that comes with mastery. Colours, he said, appeared to him in the moments before sleep. Interviewed at home shortly after his eightieth birthday, he was all mirth and excitement:

> When you go downstairs [to the basement] and see – I am now in my red period. I was for years in the yellow period, you know. But now I am with the reds, it was hard for me to get into the reds. Very hard, how I am tickled to death to make more reds. Which one is the best I don't know. But this is to show why I am promoting serial image. Because like Cézanne has demonstrated it, like Picasso has said it, 'We don't get what we want.' And therefore we continue.

One of the more mundane mysteries of the *Homages to the Square* is their price. Even with recent successes in the saleroom, the paintings fetch less than those of Albers' Bauhaus contemporaries Klee and Kandinsky, or students such as Robert Rauschenberg. Possible reasons are suggested earlier in this chapter. Superfluity, too, may have played its part: had Rauschenberg made two thousand red or black paintings, their unit price might have been lower. But the *Homages* were also dogged, during Albers' lifetime and to an extent since his death, by doubts as to their nature as art.

Even critics who might have been expected to understand the *Homages* failed to do so. One was another of Albers' Bauhaus colleagues, Herbert Bayer. '[Albers] came to the square...a very simple construction for a very pleasant position of the square within the square,' Bayer condescended. 'And then he varies it to push, without end, really, in showing the relativity of colour. If yellow is on green, it's different than on blue, and so on....' He paused, then burst out: 'A person like Albers, I absolutely can not understand how he could have done that, how he could have lived and done that. I mean, you are going like a horse through life.'

Albers, to an extent, colluded in this misapprehension. His jocular playing down of the *Homages* – '*Nein*, it's not art, it has nothing to do with art' – did not help, although this was the same teasing Albers who named his series *Homage to the Square* and then denied that it was. When a student translated a passage from a French magazine opining that the *Homages* were not works of art but perceptual exercises, he was surprised by Albers' delighted response: 'Wonderful! They got it!' That he took them seriously in spite of this is clear enough. His comparison of the seriality of the *Homages* to that of Cézanne's Mont Saint-Victoire paintings shows that. Cézanne was Albers' god in art. His name was not taken in vain.

Perhaps the problem of the *Homages* is the very thing that makes them great: they are unknowable. Their paradoxes – figure/ground, front/back, soft-edge/hard-edge – are there for all to see. But beyond these again is a meta-paradox to which these lesser ones contribute. Albers' reticent, wordless works are stories, or rather fables. Their absolute simplicity – three or four squares, their colours and means of making all neatly written down – alerts us to the fact that nothing is simple. 'I lead the spectator from "to glance" to "to notice",' Albers said. 'To see, in the sense of the German word *Schauen*.' That the arc of the *Homages*' history takes us from conflict to collaboration was a fact not lost on Albers. As a young man at the Bauhaus, he had written of the link between geometric simplicity and moral philosophy: 'We believe...that [the] desire for the simplest, clearest form will make people more united and life more real, that is, more essential.' Now, as an old man in America, he said:

> He who sees better, who discerns more clearly, recognizes the relativity of facts, and knows that there is never just one solution for visual formulations, will then change his way of thinking about other formulations; most importantly, he will become both more precise, and more tolerant.

This was Albers writing for an audience. Face to face, down in his basement, his explanations were earthier: 'You may buy here brown and I sell you red – I always want to cheat you if you are my customer, but it is cheating for a good reason,' or 'Colour is fooling us all the time. All the time, like women do, you see? Life is interesting.' That Albers spoke of his art in the language of a *bonhomme* or the Brothers Grimm only tells us that he was a man of his time, place and class; where he had come from. It does not explain what he became, which is the purpose of the book that follows.

1   *Am Anfang*

What difference does it make if I was the son of a blacksmith, a professor, a businessman? Who I am is what I am today.

Josef Albers

Josef Albers was born on 19 March 1888 in Bottrop, a small country town in Westphalia. It was the Feast of St Joseph: as was customary, Lorenz and Magdalena Albers' first child was baptized in the saint's honour, Franz Joseph. The first part of the name seems soon to have been dropped; it appears in no documents after the record of the child's birth. The spelling of the second would be changed, unofficially, from Joseph to the more usual Josef, by the age of eleven. Like many Westphalians, the Albers were Roman Catholics. The Prussian-dominated German Empire, then just seventeen years old, was openly anti-Rome: laws aimed at suppressing the Church had led to a so-called *Kulturkampf*, or 'culture fight', in places such as Bottrop. That the Albers' son bore the name of the Catholic Emperor of Austria rather than of Germany's Prussian Protestant Kaiser – Frederick III had come to the throne ten days before the boy's birth, and would die eighty days after it – seems something more than accident.

It was a usual birth at a highly unusual time. Known as *das Dreikaiserjahr*, the Year of Three Emperors, 1888 marked the transition from the conservative reign of Wilhelm I to the reactionary one of his grandson, Wilhelm II. This change mirrored, but did not explain, vast shifts in German society as a whole, and in that of the industrial Ruhr in particular.

Lorenz Albers had arrived in Bottrop a year before his son's birth, on 15 March 1887, from Bödefeld in the Sauerland, in the east of Westphalia. He had been born in 1859 in Heinrichsdorf, a village ruined by the failure of its zinc mine three years before. Lorenz's father, a carpenter, also named Lorenz, had taken his family to nearby Bödefeld, a pretty place five hundred metres up on the Hunau ridge. He had connections there. It was isolated, though: Dortmund, seventy kilometres to the north-west, was the nearest town of any size. Today, Bödefeld is a small but lively ski resort. When the younger Lorenz Albers was growing up, there would have been little to do there and scant opportunity for work. There had been Albers in the village since 1670 and likely before; there still are. The local inn, now as then, is called Gasthof Albers. It was no place for a young man (fig. 1.1).

A hundred kilometres to the west, things were different. In 1849, a decade before Lorenz Albers' birth, Germany's first coke-fired blast furnace had been built in Mülheim, in the Ruhr. Burning coke rather than coal made for bigger smelters and cheaper steel; all that was needed was a supply of iron ore to feed them. Troublesomely, local Ruhr ores suffered from impurities of phosphorus. In 1879, English engineers had found a way around this problem by lining their smelters with basic limestone rather than acidic silica. Now steel could be made with low-grade ores: by the end of 1879 a new smelter had been built in Hörde, south of Dortmund. By 1884, more than half of the world's steel was being made in Germany, most of it in the Ruhr.

More steel meant more coke, which meant more coal, which meant more men to dig it. In 1850, 1.5 million tonnes of Ruhr coal had been extracted by 12,000 miners. In 1890, when Lorenz and Magdalena Albers' first son turned two, 128,000 miners dug 33 million tonnes of coal. Much of this came from a pair of mines, Prosper I and Prosper II, near Bottrop, west of Essen, where the Albers had moved in 1887. These mines would be joined by others during their son's youth – Rheinbaben in 1896, Prosper III (1905), Arenberg-Forsetzung (1909), Vereinigte Welheim (1913) – each with its own matching wave of immigration. The pit heads and slag heaps of the mines loomed over the town; their shafts and terraces spread for kilometres, tunnelling out towards Essen and Oberhausen and back under Bottrop itself. The town's air was thick with coal dust. 'Even my spit was black,' Josef Albers would say in old age.

1.1 Photographer unknown, Lorenz Albers, Josef Albers' father.

The effect of its coal boom on the town's population had been seismic. In 1875, Bottrop, a bucolic place, had just over 6,000 inhabitants, a working windmill and a four-hundred-year-old horse market. By 1899, the population had grown fivefold, to 30,000. By 1915, the year Josef Albers would come home from Berlin as a fully-fledged art teacher, it had more than doubled again, to just short of 70,000. By far the greater part of the influx was made up of Poles from the East Prussian provinces of Masuria and Silesia, dismissively dubbed *Ruhrpolen*. The town was not alone in experiencing this surge: the population of nearby Essen grew from 9,000 to 295,000 in the fifty years from 1860. What made Bottrop unique was that Ruhrpolen soon formed a majority of its population – seventy-five per cent of it by 1910, a greater proportion than anywhere else in the Ruhr. The town had grown so quickly that there had been no time to update its statutes. With a population topping 72,000, the ironically-named *grossten Dorf Preussens* – biggest village in Prussia – was finally incorporated as a city on 21 July 1919, a few weeks after Josef Albers had left home again, this time for Munich and for good. The tower of Bottrop's windmill still stands, in a municipal car park; rising buildings stole its wind in 1908, and it was later shorn of its sails. The town's ancient horse market lives cheerlessly on in the name of a pedestrianized shopping precinct, the Pferdemarkt.

For Lorenz Albers, this turmoil was good news, at least at first. The Polish immigrants had to be housed: the number of dwellings in Bottrop trebled in the three decades from 1887. Lorenz's trade is given on his resident's card first as *Dekorationsmaler* (decorative painter), then, as he grew more established, as either *Anstreichermeister* or *Malermeister* (master painter). According to his son Josef, the elder Albers could turn his hand to anything – marbling, faux-wood ragging, glass cutting, stone carving. Given the skilled nature of Lorenz's work, it seems unlikely that his clientele can have been made up of miners. A more probable market came from the growing cadre of middle-class professionals who arrived in Bottrop to service its coal boom – the managers and engineers, bankers and lawyers whose villas would soon line Randebrockstrasse, the road that now leads to the museum named for *Malermeister* Albers' first child.

At any rate, business was good enough for the Albers to have moved within a year to the house where their child would be born, on Gerichtsstrasse (later re-named Horsterstrasse). Photographs show number 18 to have been a straightforward affair of three sooty brick storeys with an attic floor, in a terrace of similar houses; it was torn down in 1972, to be replaced by a parade of shops that has itself been lately torn down. Lorenz Albers would die in the house in 1944. In 1888, Gerichtsstrasse, connecting the old centre of Bottrop to the new suburbs on the Ostring, would have been home to that respectable class of small shopkeepers and craftsmen, *Handwerker*, which formed the backbone of any middle-sized German town. Lorenz Albers was a master painter; so, too, was his neighbour, Bernhard Mengede. The house at 18 Horsterstrasse would be sold, after Lorenz's death, to Bernhard's son Wilhelm, a master butcher (fig. 1.2). Even as this class prospered, however, its place in society was slipping.

The decline had begun earlier in the century. The French victory at Jena in 1806 had seen eastern parts of Westphalia made a vassal state of Napoleon's First Empire, ruled over by his brother, Jérôme. In 1815, the Congress of Vienna handed this ersatz kingdom to Prussia, with lands to the west, including those of the Ruhr, tacked on. In the years since, society in the enlarged, strongly Catholic Westphalia had been run, to deep local resentment, by a predominantly Protestant elite appointed from Berlin. With this went a three-part Prussian division of society into an aristocracy, a bourgeoisie and a proletariat. From the mid-century, though, the industrialization of what would become the German Empire – a change vividly visible in Bottrop – had begun to gnaw at the safe edges of these divisions.

1.2 Josef Albers, Albers' family home, 18 Horster Strasse, Bottrop, Germany, 1960.

The old middle class, the *Bürgertum*, had polarized. As before, there was an upper middle class made up of non-nobles with a university education or landed property, or both. But those with lesser land or schooling now subdivided into a new, salaried middle class, the *Mittelstand*, which emerged above a *Kleinbürgertum* – a lower middle class, or petite bourgeoisie – formed of people exactly like Lorenz Albers: craftsmen, small shopkeepers, tradesmen. As Engels had predicted, this was the class that was to suffer most at the hands of modern capitalism. Lorenz may have done faux-marbling for the new Jugendstil villas on Randebrockstrasse, but he was never going to be able to live in one himself. Gerichtsstrasse, upright, solid and new on St Joseph's Day 1888, was the place for people like him. And the street slid downmarket, even as Lorenz's family grew.

This was the snakes-and-ladders world into which Josef Albers was born. Over the next sixty years, the dynamics of that world would shape the life of the child, of the man he became, of all Germans and of millions who were not. Lorenz Albers was by no means unusual in having left his village for a town: the rural population of Germany fell by a third in the years from 1858 to 1895. Where his story is untypical is that moving to Bottrop would make him a stranger in his own land.

So great and rapid had been the influx of Ruhrpolen into the valley of the Emscher – the river that runs from Dortmund to the Rhine – that it was held, by 1900, to have lost its Westphalian character entirely. In Bottrop, members of the Polish-speaking majority now agitated to have the town's council and church hierarchies made up of Poles like themselves. These incomers were politically radicalized and given to violent protest in a way that native Westphalians were not. At intervals throughout Josef Albers' youth, in 1889, 1898 and 1905, the Prosper mines would be rocked by bloody strikes: during the last, armed police opened fire on a crowd that included women and children, killing a miner. Comparisons were drawn, not entirely in jest, between the town and Dodge City, Kansas. Even in the knockabout Ruhr, the area from Bottrop to the Rhine was known as *der wilde Westen*.

For the town's native-Westphalian artisan class, or *Handwerkerstand*, the pressures were thus not just economic but tribal. Even more so than elsewhere in the new German Empire, free trade fed insecurity. The dangers were as much spiritual as financial: industrialization was an agent of 'commercial anarchy', a threat to 'the religious and moral health' of the nation. Craftsmen, well represented in Berlin, hit back. In 1881, trade guilds won legal standing; in 1897, the Craftsmen's Protection Act ring-fenced them, requiring would-be guild members to pass exclusive entrance exams. Even so, financial anxiety translated into political conservatism. The reactionary *Verein zum Schutze des Handwerks*, an umbrella Association for the Protection of Handicraft, was particularly active in Westphalia, backing the conservative Catholic Centre Party on the perverse grounds that Ruhrpolen, also Catholic, voted Social Democrat. The building trades, with their low barriers to entry, were particularly prone to political conservatism, often bordering on reaction. It was against this background that the master painters of Bottrop set up their own *Malerinnung*, the Painter-Glaziers' and House Painters' Compulsory Guild, in 1905, two years after the town's tailors and cobblers had done the same. The guild's mission, as its statutes said, was to fight for the *Ordnung und Sicherheit* – order and security – of its twenty members. At its first meeting, on 11 October, Lorenz Albers ran for chairman. He lost to Johann Lordick by three votes to fourteen. Lorenz's elder son was then seventeen.

It is fair to assume that these social currents and counter-currents must have eddied around Josef Albers' childhood. They could hardly not have done. Like most masters' households, Lorenz Albers' mixed domesticity with hard work. The house in Gerichtsstrasse was home not just to the growing Albers brood – Josef's birth in 1888 had been followed, in 1890, by that of, known as Paul; then of Magdalena (1893), Johann (born and died in 1895) and Elisabeth (1897) – but to a varying number of apprentices who slept in the attic and lived and ate with the family: Wilhelm Lauscher from Simmerath, Richard Frank from Bergedorf, and many more. Later, Josef Albers recalled something of the milieu:

> My father was quite musical; he played several instruments and directed even the little band of the firemen group....He considered music very important: for example, the apprentices lived in our house as it was at that time, you live with the master and you eat with the family, you know? They got some musical instruction – they got instruction from my father, they must play the flute or so. Some days they must make landscape drawings, and to make also some music. He wanted me to play the violin....I was not an instrumental musician, but he has tried very hard to make me do more.... He was particularly skilful at playing the zither. He played in the evening, so we were exposed to music.

In 1899, when Josef was eleven, the household was joined by Lorenz's younger brother, Max, another *Dekorationsmaler* who had also made the journey from Bödefeld. He is recorded as living *in das Haus seines Bruders* before marrying Johanne Grothe and leaving to raise eight children nearby. The status of the *Handwerkerstand* – of hand-making itself – cannot have been an abstract question for the residents of Gerichtstrasse. It was a matter of survival.

Even allowing for Albers' later dislike of retrospection, it is remarkable how little evidence remains of his childhood. The archives of the Albers Foundation in Bethany, Connecticut, show him to have been an assiduous keeper of papers, including a number that he and his wife brought to America in 1933 and preserved for five decades. Albers made carbon copies of his own letters; yet there are none in the archive either to or from his father. The only proof of Lorenz Albers' existence there is a wartime Red Cross card, addressed to Professor Josef Albers, Black Mountain College, North Carolina by his sister Elisabeth, announcing, in the twenty-five words officially allowed, that their father was dead: *Papa am 26.1.44 friedlich gestorben* – Papa died peacefully on 26 January. Josef Albers was then fifty-six. There are four letters from Elisabeth in the archive, all largely to do with business; there is one from Magdalena, written ten days before Josef Albers' death, at eighty-eight, in 1976. Other than these, there are no mementos of childhood, nothing before his late twenties; nothing at all of his family.

What are we to make of this? Albers was a ruthless editor of himself. Family letters may simply have been disposed of as unimportant in touching on sentiment rather than art, as being retrospective. The feeling persists, though, that his childhood was unhappy. Such few boyhood recollections (or retrospections) as he later allowed himself had to do with his development as an artist rather than a nostalgia for childhood. Thus, his admiration for his father, publicly unwavering, was professional rather than sentimental.

A painter like my father did everything....I worked in his workshop....
He knew the rules, the recipes, and he taught me them, too....
He installed the electricity in our house. He, himself. Could
do plumbing. He could do glass etching, glass painting, he did
everything....He was an artisan. He made soap during the war from
wax which he had formerly used to etch with. He could sandblast.
He had a very practical mind. I was exposed to many skills, which
I learned to steal with my eyes.

Later, when Josef Albers was newly arrived at the Bauhaus, he refused to go to a wall-painting workshop on the grounds that his father had already taught him all its skills.

> Gropius said, several times, 'Albers, you don't go to the wall-painting workshop.' And I said, No, I don't need it....What I learn there, I learned already in my father's workshop....I have helped him to paint stage sets, and all that which happens in a workshop of a man who does everything himself. He was painter, you see? He came from his father as a carpenter, he knew carpentry very well also. He made glass – I know all that, you see? And Gropius said, 'I have several times reminded you to go to the wall-painting workshop,' and I did. Not to submit to a dictate, but to help my friends who were in need of help, only for that reason, not for the sake of learning any wall-painting....Then Gropius said, 'Then, Albers, we will have to send you home.' And I said, OK, then I will do my best.

It is a telling story, and one often told: Josef *contra mundum*. The Bauhaus – the Building-House – was a belated outcome of that upsurge in construction that had swept Germany in the last years of the 19th century, casting architects and designers, town planners and theorists in the role of civic heroes. It was this shift that allowed the building crafts to gain a toehold in art schools, which led to the formation of *Kunstgewerbeschulen*, or applied arts schools, of which the Bauhaus was a late and radical example. And yet Albers was almost alone among the students there – and certainly among the teachers – in coming from a background in the building trades. Johannes Itten, his nemesis, was the son of a schoolmaster, Kandinsky a law graduate from a rich and vaguely aristocratic Russian family. Where Lorenz Albers played the zither in a fireman's band, Paul Klee's Swiss father was an academic musician and musicologist, Lyonel Feininger's a professional violinist and composer. Gropius himself was the upper-middle-class architect son of *haute-bourgeois* architect parents. Being taught to paint walls by men whose fathers had never done so clearly rankled with Albers. It would do for the rest of his life.

His mother, too, came from a line of craftsmen: in later life, Albers would delight in her workmanlike maiden name, Schumacher, shoe-maker. In fact, Magdalena Albers was from a family of blacksmiths from Siedlinghausen, the next village to Bödefeld. She had married Lorenz Albers there on 7 June

1.3 Eugen Josef Merten, Magdalena Schumacher, Josef Albers' Mother.

1887, her husband travelling back from Bottrop for the wedding (fig. 1.3). Their first child would be born a respectable nine months later. The young Josef would often holiday in the Sauerland with his parents, staying with his mother's family. 'They made specialty horseshoes, and the nails for them,' he later said of the Schumachers. 'As a child, my main fun was to watch others working.' A more intimate memory of his mother was of being taken by her to a bank in Bottrop, where, in middle age, Albers recalled being fascinated (and a little terrified) by the spatial ambiguities of a black-and-white marble floor – the way he had felt he was stepping *down* into the black tiles and back *up* onto the white ones; although even this recollection was told in the context of his art, a later fascination with the three-dimensional reading of two-dimensional form.

   This boyhood story has the feel of a dream or nightmare. Perhaps it was overlain by another, later memory of looking down into his mother's grave, for Magdalena Albers died on 17 February 1899, when she was thirty-eight years old and her older son not yet quite eleven. A portrait photograph, apparently signed 'L. Albers' – can Lorenz really have taken it? – shows four blond children chivvied into the poses of Victorian mourning, the two-year-old Elisabeth holding another photograph of her parents, who appear separately in yet another pair of photographs on the wall behind. To the right of the children, eloquently, is an empty chair. Paul and Magdalena look bewildered or even frightened, although they may just be frowning at the magnesium flash. Josef is expressionless (fig. 1.4).

Not quite two years later, in December 1900, Lorenz Albers was married again – to a woman called Elisabeth Funke, who was eight years younger than his late wife and from Elspe, also in the Sauerland. Lorenz's first and second mothers-in-law shared an unusual maiden name, Pieper; whether his two wives were related is unclear. He had been married to Magdalena Schumacher for nearly twelve years; his marriage to Elisabeth would last for forty-four. They were to have no surviving children. Franz, their first son, Josef's first half-brother, died in 1903 at the age of nine months; their second, Wilhelm, the day after he was born in 1906. Elisabeth Albers *née* Funke lived on until 1952, when her surviving stepson was in his mid-sixties. By then, Josef Albers was at work on the *Homages to the Square*, a series whose interrelations he would often construe in familial terms. Of a colour that did not fit in, he would say, 'This colour is not in the family. It is an stepchild in the family.' Colours that he himself excluded from his palette, he dismissed as, 'My stepchildren.' There are no surviving letters between Josef and his stepmother (fig. 1.5).

1.4 Photographer unknown (possibly Lorenz Albers), Mourning photo of Josef Albers and his siblings at the death of their Mother, 1898.
1.5 Photographer unknown, Lorenz Albers with Elisabeth Funke.

In 1963, when Albers was seventy-five, the American sculptor George Rickey would approach him for help with a book he was writing on the history of Constructivism. In a moment of rare self-revelation, Albers told Rickey a story that has about it the feel of a fable. In the summer of 1933, he says, before leaving for America, he and Anni had holidayed on the Baltic island of Hiddensee. There they had been approached by a stranger who asked to see their work. Albers wrote:

> I happened to have with me a few final cuts which I wished to show to a friend. I lent those prints to [the stranger], and he returned them the next days, telling me his conclusions from one of them. He was/ is a neurologist and now well known as a professor at the [illegible]. He concluded that I was the oldest of the four children in our family; that I liked the best the youngest of the four (my little sister); that we children felt distant from our parents (we have a stepmother); and that from the parents, the mother 'has the trousers on,' which was all very true. My conclusion to his conclusions was: 'One has to be careful, probably.'

In even older age, Albers identified the print in question as *Ründe* (Circle; fig. 1.6) (1933). Made at a time when he was experimenting with shapes that were at once abstract and suggestively biomorphic, *Ründe*'s jagged composition does battle with its tightly compressed structure. The work's subject, formally at least, is strife. Nonetheless, that a stranger could deduce from *Ründe*

1.6 *Ründe (Circle)*, 1933. Woodcut print, 13¾ × 18¼ in.

the particular dynamics of the Albers family seems extraordinary; that the family's fiercely rational elder son should have believed that he could, no less so. Next only to retrospection, Albers hated introspection. The moral he draws from his story to Rickey is that it is all too easy to give oneself away. Although the evidence is entirely circumstantial, both Albers' fable-like tale and his own interpretation of it add to the feeling that his childhood was unhappy.

The last days of the dying century must have been hard ones for the child. As well as losing a mother and gaining a stepmother, Josef changed schools – from the small, old elementary school in a house next to the family's parish church, St Cyriakus, to the new senior school on Osterfelder Strasse. This was a forbidding place, brick-built, beetle-browed, with crow-stepped gables on each of its four sides; as was the way of Bottrop, it was soon outgrown and torn down (fig. 1.7). The 15th-century St Cyriakus had itself been replaced by a bigger, neo-Gothic version in the 1860s, an early sign of the town's swelling population. Schools, too, would be outpaced by Polish immigration. In 1899, the names on the new school's register are, like Albers', all German. A year later, alongside the Brinkmanns and Borchmanns and Perdekamps are a Krakowczyk, an Adamczyk and a Bernenczyk. If the proliferation of Ruhrpolen, and of buildings in which to house and teach them, were one

1.7 Josef Albers, Catholic school, Bottrop, Germany, 1960.

sign of Bottrop's coal boom, the tenuous lives of those buildings was another. In 1904, the new St Cyriakus, where Josef Albers had been baptized just sixteen years earlier, began to sink into the ground. In time, it would settle by seven metres. Geologically as socially, the town's foundations were being undermined by the coal seams dug out beneath them.

The short lives of new civic buildings may have struck a chord with Lorenz Albers. His first son could either, like him, learn to build Bottrop's schools, or he could learn to teach in them. It is hard to gauge the prosperity of the Albers household in Josef's youth. Lorenz's name is not among the eleven *Malermeisterin* listed as having earned enough to pay tax in the 1890s; that he would spend nearly sixty years in the same drab house on an increasingly down-at-heel street suggests that he was not rich. (On the other hand, his oldest child, a millionaire by the time of his death, would end his days in a wholly ordinary house in a plain Connecticut suburb. Westphalians are not given to ostentation.) Like all Germans, Lorenz Albers would suffer in the hyperinflation of the 1920s. In a letter of December 1923, he appeals to the authorities in Münster to find a teaching job for his son-in-law, Heinrich van Bömmel, husband of Magdalena and an ex-colleague of Josef's. Lorenz cannot afford to support the Van Bömmels: he has earned a hundred million marks in the previous year, at a time when a postage stamp cost five billion marks and the exchange rate was four trillion marks to the dollar. 'I cannot cope with the burden that has been placed upon me,' Lorenz says. Even in 1900, the future vice-chairman of the Bottrop painters' guild must have known that the days of his kind were numbered. Teaching would offer a more secure future for his son. The town's population was not just growing quickly, but growing younger: by 1910, seventy-five per cent of inhabitants were under thirty-five, and the number of schoolchildren had doubled in a decade. In 1900, there had been eleven elementary schools in Bottrop; by 1918, there were twenty-seven. There were schools to be built, and there were children to be taught. Like many German fathers of his class and time, it was the second of these careers that Lorenz Albers chose for his son.

In this, as in much else, he proved unadventurous. Male elementary schoolteachers in Wilhelmine Germany were drawn from exactly the small-town *Kleinbürgertum* which the Albers had come to typify. Teaching was both a prudent alternative to house painting and a social step up – if, in the rigid class system of Prussia, not too much of a step. To teach in a *gymnasium*, the German equivalent of a grammar school, one had oneself to have been *gymnasium*-taught. Only then could one sit the *Abitur*, the examination needed for matriculation to a university. Teachers in such schools were government employees, with salaries and a social status to match. *Gymnasium* teaching was a job for boys from Randebrockstrasse, not Gerichtsstrasse. Elementary schoolteachers, by contrast, were badly paid, lowly regarded and at the pedagogic mercy of the local clergymen, who doubled as school inspectors. In choosing this modest path for his son, Lorenz Albers showed himself well-meaning but passive. He presumably cannot have known that elementary school teachers were about to be at the forefront of a revolution in German education that would lead, like the building boom, to the Bauhaus.

In an interview in 1968, when he turned eighty, Josef Albers recalled his parents' decision to turn him into a schoolteacher:

> SEVIM FESCI: You yourself wanted to become a teacher? Or was it that your family wanted it?
> JOSEF ALBERS: It was my family that wanted me to be a teacher. That was safe, you see. To be a painter was terrible. I wanted to stop really when I was in a teachers' seminary, a teachers' college as it's called now, it's called [in Germany] now a pedagogical academy. I was there. And I would like to stop, you see. Oh, boy, my parents just got mad, you see. I finished and became a public school teacher.
> SF: In Bottrop?
> JA: No, it was in Westphalia also; also in the Ruhr. I had six years to study for that affair. And then I was in Bottrop. I taught at the public school.
> SF: You taught art?
> JA: No, everything. Reading, writing, arithmetic; you see, everything. No, you see I was really trained as a teacher for all the things. And this training again was also quite Prussian; you know what that is – Prussian?
> SF: I know, yes,
> JA: You have to fulfill all the demands and obey. I liked very much to teach drawing. But I had to teach gymnastics, too, and everything. When we were in the seminary we got a stipend direct from the government and for that stipend we had an obligation to stick to our teaching job for five years. So in those five years I collected a little money so that after I could afford to go to Berlin and study.

In light of this, Albers' later idolizing of his father is puzzling. The photograph of Lorenz in a history of the Bottrop Malerinnung shows a mild-looking man with disconsolate moustaches. There is no hint of the heroic figure evoked by his son. That Lorenz could glaze, plumb and wire houses as well as paint them was hardly remarkable: so, according to the same history, could pretty well any member of the guild. Perhaps Josef's admiration was born of resentment, a sense that he had himself been looked down on at the Bauhaus despite being one of the few with (as it were) a hereditary right to be there. Or perhaps the retroactive invention of his father was necessary to his own myth of himself: one can only be godly if one is a child of gods. Albers' repeated insistence that his skills had been learned from Lorenz, and not from Kandinsky or Klee – 'I came very much from my father, and from Adam, and that's all' – puts the last two in their place while blurring the boundary between house-painting and fine art. But it also makes Lorenz a Kandinsky of sorts.

If, in later life, Albers was to emphasize the importance of lessons from his father, Lorenz's decision that his son should himself be a teacher was to prove at least as fateful. Training for elementary schoolmasters began early in Wilhelmine Germany, with a three-year course at a *Präparandenschule*, a feeder school for a teachers' training college, or Lehrerseminar. Josef Albers was fourteen when, in 1902, he set off for the preparatory school in Langenhorst, a village on the River Vechte in Münsterland, ninety kilometres from Bottrop.

It was, and is, a pleasant place. Langenhorst's St John the Baptist church is among the most remarkable of Münster's four-square *Stiftskirchen*, dating in parts from the 12th century. It is, as in Albers' day, a pilgrimage church, a stop on the Baltic road from Lübeck to Santiago de Compostela: among its treasures, then as now, are a piece of the True Cross and a set of life-sized Baroque Nativity figures in polychromed wood and plaster. Next to the church is a corn mill, its wheel fed by a pond on which, in winter, the *Präparande* could skate. Clustered around this are what would have been, in Albers' time, the house of the parish priest-cum-headmaster, Father Karl Keller, and a pleasing jumble of outbuildings from a former Augustinian convent. Seventy years later, Josef Albers would recall his hometown like this: '[Bottrop was] the Pittsburgh of Westphalia...everywhere there are mines and furnaces and metal melting there. It was loud and very dirty, and unpleasantly ugly....Except at night when you go on the train through that country the fireworks are just incredible. So that's where I came from.' Langenhorst could not have been more different.

Lorenz's choice of school may have had more to do with money than air quality: at 1.27 marks a day for board and tuition, Langenhorst was the cheapest *Präparandenschule* in Westphalia. Compared with the barrack-like buildings of others, it was also unusually intimate. Its seventy-odd pupils, divided into three classes, were taught in what had been (and is now again) a small private house. They were boarded with suitably Catholic farmers. A near contemporary of Albers' at Langenhorst recalled lodging with a family called Eiler, who, as all locals did, wore clogs. 'Children even came to school in them,' wrote Heinrich Feldmann, a wide-eyed Dortmunder, his urban sense of propriety shaken. 'They left their "holsken" in the hall and went to class in slippers. Even altar boys did this when they were serving Mass.'

This was not all that was new and strange. Münsterlanders ate black bread and black pudding, tastes that would stay with Josef Albers for the rest of his life. There were heaths of white heather and sundew, fields of buckwheat and peach trees, roads lined with sweetgale; the Vechte ran with pike and perch. Every fourth Sunday, the boys, in blue, green or red caps according to their year, were marched to confession in Ochtrup, a larger town nearby. In summer, they ate strawberries and cream at the Café Terheyden. When, fifty years later and with the Nazi *Götterdämmerung* over, Albers again began to visit Germany from America, he never failed to go back to Langenhorst.

At the heart of school life was God. Days began with Mass at seven a.m., the boys singing Gregorian chants rehearsed earlier with the chaplain, Father Linnemann. Langenhorst may have been cheap, but its academic standards were high, staff good and syllabus broad: it included, as well as the usual subjects, three hours of piano lessons a week, with compulsory violin and singing. The headmaster, Fr Keller, in his early forties, was the author of a text on the teaching of New Testament history. One form teacher, Wilhelm Dortmann, compiler of the standard mathematical textbook for southern Westphalia, had his charges recite Schiller and Goethe by heart and took them into Münster to see *Der Freischütz*. He also introduced them to art, passing around prints of the works of German masters such as Dürer, Adrian Ludwig Richter and Moritz von Schwind, which the boys were encouraged to examine and discuss 'so as to learn to distinguish the good from the bad and inauthentic'. Unusually for a Prussian-run school, they were shown Raphaels and Titians as well, to make the point that 'art was international'.

This was not the only act of pedagogic rebellion at Langenhorst in Albers' time there. A contemporary, Heinrich Mevenkamp, recalled a heated dispute between lay teachers and priests at a conference at the school in 1904 over the use of corporal punishment. Since beating was a given of Prussian school discipline, the incident is noteworthy. Teachers in *Präparandenschulen*, like those in *gymnasiums*, tended to be university graduates. Unlike their *gymnasium* colleagues, however, they seem to have seen themselves as the educators of educators, with a sense of moral purpose in their teaching of teaching. *Gymnasium* teachers, well paid and socially established, had no reason to rock the pedagogic boat. It would be elementary-school teachers such as Josef Albers who brought about the revolution that went by the name of *neue Pädagogik*, the new education.

In the last decade of the 19th century, elementary schoolteachers throughout the Empire had begun to agitate for a *Pädagogik von Kinde aus*, a new way of teaching with the needs of the child at its centre. Friedrich Wilhelm Foerster, a Berlin philosopher, published *School and Character* in 1907, when Josef Albers was in his last year at teacher's training college. This influential book argued for doing away with *Lehrnschulen* – Prussian rote-learning schools – in favour of *Arbeitschulen*, where children would learn by doing. Set texts were to be replaced by songs and games, and pupils taught things they wanted to learn. In 1912, when Albers, aged twenty-four, was teaching back in Bottrop, the new education would be officially endorsed by a congress of the elementary schoolteachers' association, the Deutscher Lehrerverein (DLV) – with three thousand chapters and 130,000 members, by far the biggest such body in Germany. Primary teachers were now a political force to be reckoned with, far more so than their opposite numbers in secondary schools. The day when could they be dismissed as 'quintessential *Untertanen*, the servile underlings of [an] imperious state' was quickly coming to an end.

These things must have echoed through Langenhorst in Albers' time there, and even more so at the Königliches Lehrerseminar (Royal Teachers' Training College) to which he moved on 21 March 1905. As at the *Präparandenschule*, the course at Büren was three years long; here, though, similarities ended. While Langenhorst's architecture was a cosy hotchpotch of periods and styles, Büren's was vast and monolithic, its range of handsome grey stone and white render buildings by far the town's most imposing. Their regal air was more than name-deep: they had been built as a Jesuit seminary on the orders of Clemens August, Prince Bishop and Elector of Cologne. (As part of the Prussian Protestant *Kulturkampf* laws, Germany's Jesuits had been suppressed in 1872.) Where the church at Langenhorst, unadorned and blocky, dated from the Early Middle Ages, the new college's chapel, Maria Immaculata, built in its royal benefactor's Bavarian taste, was a rare burst of Baroque north of the Main. There was nothing like it in Bottrop, or anywhere near. Even Münster's Barokinsel could scarcely compare. Where Albers had left Langenhorst with a lifelong taste for *Blutwurst* and black bread, he would take away from Büren a fascination for the dramatic massings of Baroque art and architecture, still visible in his postcard collages fifty years later.

For all that, his chief memory of the school, as we have seen, was of wanting to leave it. If he later ascribed this to adolescent yearnings to be an artist, there may have been more prosaic reasons. Only one of his contemporaries from Langenhorst, a boy from Bocholt called Strick, had followed him to the *Lehrerseminar*. There were twice as many students there – forty-three

1.8 Josef Albers, Jesuitenkirche (Kirche Maria Immaculata), The Albers' Opel, Büren, Germany, 1960.

in Albers' entry alone – and they lived in the school, being split up into eight dormitories of sixteen boys apiece. Not for nothing was Büren known to Albers and his friends as *der Bunker* (fig 1.10).

The regime was relentless. From Monday to Saturday, boarders were woken at half past four so that a study period could be squeezed in before lessons began at six. Breakfast and morning Mass were followed by more lessons until noon; after lunch and an hour's free time, there were yet more lessons until five, then an evening of silent meditation – *silentium* – broken by supper, homework, evening prayers, and lights out at ten thirty. There were only four hours of lessons on Sundays, but extra morning prayers and a second afternoon Mass. The food was notoriously grim – *Kröse*, a kind of skinless Sauerland haggis, and endless lentil soup – although Albers supplemented this by frying illicit potatoes in his dormitory. Half a century later, he would retain the kind of fascination for food that suggests early hunger: the colours in paintings might be compared with children or stepchildren, but they might equally be seen as old cheese, thin stew, or, at Yale, as American ham sandwiches with chocolate ice cream in them. Rules at Büren were laid out, with Prussian exactness, in a *Stundenplan*: Rule 26 forbade the 'running of races, slamming of doors, ringing of bells, shouting [or] whistling', and directed boys to keep to the right on stairs and in corridors. For all that, academic standards at Büren were poor. More than half of the students failed their qualifying exams. Albers' own record at the school was lacklustre, the

1.9 Photographer unknown, Josef Albers as a young man, 1908.

1.10 Photographer unknown, Lehrerseminar Büren graduating class, 1908.
Josef Albers in back row, third from right.

only mutedly bright spots in it being in mathematics, nature studies and drawing – a contemporary recalled never seeing him without a pencil and sketchbook in hand. His performance in singing and on the organ were particularly abject. Nevertheless, he managed to pass his teacher's exams in February 1908 with a good mark in agricultural studies and very-goods in diligence, conduct and drawing. Albers left for Bottrop to take up a job on 23 April as third-year teacher at a primary school in the new suburb of Lehmkuhle. Fifty years later, in a letter to his Büren schoolmates, he would ruefully recall a moment from his time there. 'Having criticised a girl student for her lack of cleanliness and bad smell,' he wrote, 'I received a note from her mother with the following message: "My daughter Marinka is not a flower to be sniffed at, but to be taught."' Worse was to come. In November 1909, Albers was sent as a supply teacher to Weddern, to a one-room *Bauerschaftschule* (farming community school) set in claggy fields outside the Münsterland town of Dülmen.

Fifty years later, Josef Albers would maintain that it was here he had taught himself to teach, discovering for himself that children should be listened to rather than lectured to, that education worked from the inside out.

'I found myself suddenly confronted with a so-called *einklassigen* school, all ages learning everything from religion to gymnastics in one room,' he said. Over the course of his year at Dülmen, he came to realize that successful teaching did not rely on small classes, that big classes had the advantage of 'co-operative learning'. There were other revelations – that things learned from experience stayed in the mind longer than things learned from books, that education meant self-education; that its purpose was not economic, but moral. Weddern, he said, would shape his teaching for the rest of his career, at the Bauhaus, at Black Mountain College and finally at Yale. As with the story of his learning to make art, the discoveries he made there were autonomous. If his only ancestors in painting had been his father and Adam, the *neue Pädagogik* was, in Josef Albers' telling, entirely of his own inventing.

It has to be said that there is little sign of this invention in the contemporary *Protokollbuch* – a running day-book – which, as teacher of the Boys' School, he was required to keep. In the month before Albers' appointment, the school had been short a teacher. The girls' mistress, Fraulein Orthaus, had provided cover when she could, although her gout made climbing stairs troublesome. There were eighty-three pupils in the Boys' School, divided into two classes: years one to three were taught for four afternoons a week, and years four to eight for six mornings. Education began at the age of six and ended, as for ninety-three per cent of German children, at fourteen, although older boys could come in for evening lessons in agriculture. Albers' deadpan first entry, on 19 November, concerns these: 'Classes in the Agrarian Continuing School began today. Nine pupils attend.' Lessons were in fruit farming, chicken breeding and agricultural mathematics – unlikely subjects for a young man from Bottrop. *Bauerschaftschule* teachers also acted as local land registrars, so that much of the *Protokollbuch* is given over to the minutiae of cadastral boundary changes, road improvements and the replanting of potato fields with parsnips. All are noted in Albers' schoolmasterly hand.

For a man who, a decade later, would find himself in the radical hotbed of the Weimar Bauhaus, he toes an unexpectedly royalist line at Dülmen. On 27 January 1910, there are 'birthday celebrations for our King and Emperor', with a tally of patriotic hymns sung: 'May My First Song be for the Kaiser', 'The Little Kaiser's Birthday', and the ever-popular 'Watch on the Rhine'. 'The day ended', Albers writes warmly, 'with a hearty hurrah for Kaiser and Reich, and a stirring rendition of the national anthem.' All this was part of the Prussianizing of the new German Empire, still not quite forty years old. There were other pedagogic strategies as well. By 1910, schoolmasters were spending three compulsory hours a week on geography, their charges studying from the new *Regionalatlanten* (regional atlases) produced by the Westermann publishing house in Braunschweig. Conceived as patriotic tools, the maps of these suggested Germany as a place at once imperially united and divided into independent states or *Länder*, using bright colours and oxymoronically porous borders to blur the facts. The subtleties of these maps, and their deceptions, would stay with Albers for the rest of his life.

Otherwise, his entries are as you might expect of a young urbanite mired among wet turnip fields: complaints about the weather and mud – (21 March) 'Winter is over, thank God' – and the stupidity of his pupils: (5 June) 'Franz Dieckmann, the Mevenekamp sisters and Anna Detemann [are] half-idiots....Bernh. Möllers, the Reger children and Michael Schwandkebn are no good at counting.' His warmest praise is kept for the children's 'strong bodies and clear complexions', which he ascribes to 'cheerful frolicking' in free periods and 'the hearty appetites with which they attack the best and biggest sandwiches I have ever seen'. On 1 October 1910, the Protokollbuch records that Lehrer Albers was transferred, no doubt to his relief, to a school in Stadtlohn, a nearby market town with a population of five thousand.

If his time in Weddern seems gloomier than he recalled in old age, then it may have been due to another discovery he had made in 1908. Back in Bottrop, Albers saved up his meagre teacher's salary and went, in September, to Munich. 'I sat there as long as I could in the Pinakothek and other museums, reading everything I could about the artists,' he later said. In that year, Hugo von Tschudi, director of the National Gallery in Berlin, had been sacked by the Kaiser himself for buying art that was both modern and – at least as appalling, in Wilhelm's view – French. Moving to Munich, Tschudi took over as director of the Bavarian state museums, acquiring the first works by Gauguin and Van Gogh in German public collections. But it was nearer to home that Albers was to have his first deep exposure to modernism, in the grimy Ruhr town of Hagen.

In 1902, a rich young Hagener named Karl Ernst Osthaus had opened his private collection to the public. Osthaus's initial plan had been for a gallery of natural history. In 1898, he hired Carl Gerard, designer of his father's villa, as its architect. Gerard, deeply conventional, set to work on the kind of building that Wilhelmine bankers' sons were known to like – a three-storey, neo-Renaissance palazzo, complete with a tower and dome.

With only the exterior finished, however, Osthaus – orphaned young and, in his grandparents' deadening phrase, 'prone to flights of aesthetic fancy' – read an article by the Berlin critic Julius Meier-Graefe in which Graefe took a swipe at the historicist tastes of 'our millionaires'. Osthaus, stung, sacked Gerard on the spot, hiring in his place the Belgian Henry van de Velde to finish the gallery's interior. It would prove a fateful choice.

Van de Velde's design for what was now to be called the Folkwang Museum was shocking in a number of ways. The galleries were bathed in colour, their walls grey-green, wall hangings purple and floors polychromically mosaicked. More colours filtered down from stained-glass skylights overhead. This varying palette provided the rationale for the museum's hang, which was to include Greek, Roman and Oriental artefacts alongside works of contemporary art. Where traditional collections were arranged by date and school, the Folkwang's was ruled by what might broadly be called colour sympathies, the optical blending in a painting by Seurat carried on into the decor of the room in which it was hung and so on. No distinction was made between European and non-European, ancient and modern, the applied and fine arts. Visual cues came from the works themselves, how they looked. The effect was explosive. Of a joint show of work by Kandinsky and Alexej von Jawlensky in 1909, the critic of the *Westfälisches Kunstblatt* wrote, 'The red of the flowers, the dark green of the floor and ceiling, and the lighter [hue] of its walls detonated in sequence.' If the museum's name sounded *retardataire* – Folkwang was the hall of Edda, Norse goddess of beauty – its echoes of Wagner were bang up to date. Having a building and its contents function as one made Osthaus's gallery a Wagnerian *Gesamtkunstwerk*, a demonstration in concrete form of that blurring of boundaries which lay at the heart of modernism. The Folkwang, in the soot-blackened Ruhr, was more avant-garde than its rivals in Vienna or Darmstadt. Above all, it was anti-historicist, which made it not just shocking, but Nietzschean. In the year he finished Osthaus's museum, van de Velde – appropriately, an artist, architect and designer – was commissioned by Nietzsche's sister Elisabeth to build an archive in Weimar for her late brother's papers. In 1904, he would set to work on the buildings that would house the Weimar Bauhaus.

Albers acknowledged his debt to Osthaus, if tersely: 'Coming home [from Munich in September 1908], I discovered a small private collection in Hagen – that was the Osthaus Folkwang Museum....Osthaus was a very unusual man, a tall man; he got a few Dutch people in Germany – there was [Jan] Toorop, and [Johan] Thorn-Prikker.' Typically, he says nothing specific about the impact the museum had on him, nor what he saw there. Reconstructing this last is problematic. August Macke, who also visited the Folkwang in 1908, merely said that Osthaus had 'the best of modern artists' on show, although not which. He did recall, though, that the quality of the work he had seen made him 'go *"jeck"'*, Ruhr slang for crazy.

Macke was Albers' age and, like him, a Westphalian, but he was from a cultivated Cologne family and had been taught at a *gymnasium*, studied art at the Kunstakademie Düsseldorf, seen post-impressionism first-hand in Paris and, for several months in 1907, worked in the studio of Lovis Corinth. If he was driven mad by the Folkwang, its effect on a young primary-school teacher from Bottrop can only be imagined. Among other paintings that Albers would almost certainly have seen were three by Matisse – *Still Life with Asphodels*, *La Berge* and *Bathers with a Turtle*, all bought by Osthaus in the previous year – as well as a work from Braque's brief Fauvist period (*L'Estaque, The Harbour*) and Kees van Dongen's portrait of the Japanese dancer, *Sada Yacco*. Also in 1907 had come Cézanne's *La carrière de Bibémus*, although Albers, in old age, would recall his interest in Cézanne as having been piqued in Essen. Osthaus was also an early German collector of Edvard Munch, having bought *Winter in Nordstrand* perhaps as early as 1903. The Folkwang had given the Norwegian a monograph show in 1906. Its inventory catalogue of 1912 listed sixteen of Munch's graphic works.

As we shall see, sixty years later Albers would recall having discovered Munch at the 1913 *Herbstausstellung* (Autumn Exhibition) in Berlin rather than in Hagen. This seems fair enough. Unlike August Macke, he had, by 1908, had no formal art education, and little exposure to avant-garde painting. Three years earlier, as a Langenhorst *Präparand*, 'art' had meant looking at the folkloric prints of Moritz von Schwind. The syllabus at Büren included no art education beyond nature drawing. Macke may have said that his visit to Hagen changed his style at a stroke, but Josef Albers, so far as we know, as yet had no style to change. At the same time, his first, astonishing encounter with modernist art in a modernist setting was of a very specific kind – anti-historicist, anti-hierarchical and ruled by colour harmonies. These qualities would underpin his art for the rest of his life. If, having had this revelation, Josef Albers found the turnip fields of Weddern depressing, it is not altogether surprising. A job in Stadtlohn would at least put him back among people. It was there that he began to make art.

The only good thing about Expressionists is their name.
How can purely intellectual art be true art?

Max Liebermann, letter to Max Jordan, 3 October 1913

From the window of his room in the house on Stadtlohn's Marktplatz, Josef Albers could see the steeple of St Otger's church. In July 1911, he drew it. The image – dated, signed 'Albers' and with the handwritten legend *Blick von meinem Fenster* (View from my Window) – is his earliest known drawing still extant (fig. 2.1).

Albers had visited Hagen in September 1908. A year later, he left Bottrop for Weddern, then Weddern for Stadtlohn. Elementary schoolteachers had little spare time or money. He may have been to the Folkwang again, or not. He might have seen the earliest Sonderbund exhibitions – groundbreaking shows organised by Karl-Ernst Osthaus which, among much else, introduced Picasso to Germany. These exhibitions were held in 1910 and 1911 in Düsseldorf, an easy train ride away; but nothing in their catalogues – paintings by Jawlensky, Derain, Vlaminck et al. – suggests an obvious stylistic source for Albers' drawing. Its clearest echoes are of Van Gogh. Osthaus was the first German collector of the Dutchman's works, and there were three of them in the Folkwang by late 1908. Van Gogh would dominate the greatest of all the Sonderbund shows, in 1912 in Cologne – the model for the Armory Show in New York the following year. The problem is that neither of the Van Goghs nearest in feel to Albers' Stadtlohn drawing – *The Church at Auvers* and *Church in Neunen, with One Figure* – were in Hagen, nor had they been shown in Düsseldorf. The striking, rough-tweed cross-hatching of *Church in Neunen* is particularly like that of *St Otger*. Van Gogh's drawing, like Albers', is in pen and ink.

St Otger was an intriguing image for a young man with no formal training in art to have made. When he drew it, Albers was working at the Wallschule, Stadtlohn's large Catholic primary school, with twelve classes and a dozen teachers. The room with the view of the church belonged to Werner Schöder, who had married Katharina Trah a fortnight before their lodger moved in and was, like him, a teacher. At the Wallschule, as across Germany, there were rumblings of the *neue Pädagogik*. Three years before, the school had gone co-educational. In an inversion of the usual order, it was the local school inspector, Father Wilhelm Tigges, who had ordained this revolution; the headmaster had been appalled. It was not the last time that Albers was to be in the sphere of an enlightened Catholic priest.

Nor was St Otger his only Stadtlohn subject. *Heimatkalender* – calendars whose printed months were interleaved with engravings of local scenes – were a staple of German small-town life. The 1913 and 1915 *Heimatkalender*

2.1 *Blick von meinem Fenster (View from my Window)*, 1911. Pen, ink, and white gouache on paper, 11⅖ × 8 in.

2.2 *Garden house or wayside chapel*, in *De Kiepenkerl: Westlfäscher Volkslander für 1915, ca.* 1915.

2.3 *Haus Vondern bei Osterfeld (House in Vondern, Osterfeld)*, in *De Kiepenkerl: Westlfäscher Volkslander für 1915, ca.* 1915.

for Stadtlohn included drawings signed with the stylised 'A' that would, in various forms, identify Albers' work for the next six decades; a nod, perhaps, to Dürer's famous monogram. These calendar scenes were also printed as postcards by a local bookseller, Caspar Wüllner (figs 2.2, 2.3). Accounts show payments for them to have been made to Josef Albers, Bottrop.

The *Heimatkalender* scenes are noticeably unlike the St Otger drawing. In one scene, of the same church seen in back-view across the Berkel river, there is a faint tension between the flattened frontal plane of reeds and trees and the more traditional perspective behind. The other, of a 17th-century Marian chapel on the nearby Hilgenberg hill, is wholly conventional. *Heimat* calendars and postcards were not the place for experiment. It was in private that Albers could play with the architectonic massings and croppings that push his *St Otger* drawing towards something like abstraction.

For all that, what the postcards did suggest was that there might be a living to be made from art. On 23 September 1911, Albers received a letter from the Royal Government Department of Church and Schools in Münster, appointing him to a post back home at the Josefschule in Bottrop. He took it up on 1 October, the only male teacher at the school other than the headmaster. If he made any further drawings in the next two years, they are lost. All that remains of Albers' time at the Josefschule are his entries in the school's Protokollbuch, almost parodic in their dullness. The one for 23 February 1912 concerns the picking up of greaseproof paper sandwich wrappers and the undesirability of pupils moping outside the window of Schlenhoff's bakery; the entry for 10 July 1913 records that 'Lehrer Albers has been asked to order a larger butterfly case.' Still, there was light at the end of the tunnel. On 9 September, a letter from Münster confirmed that he had been granted leave to study at the Royal Art School in Berlin, from 1 October for two years. Like all public schoolteachers in the German Empire, Albers was a state civil servant. The cost of covering his classes would be borne by himself; the letter goes on to say that his sister, Lehrerin Magdalena Albers, has been appointed in his place. He was to report back to his post on 1 August 1915.

Albers, punctilious, was always at pains to point out that the Royal Art School was not, as its name suggests, an art school. 'It is often said I studied at the Royal Academy,' he growled in his seventies. 'No, I studied at the *Königliche Kunstschule*.' The Academy taught students to be artists; the School trained them to be art teachers. If Albers later recalled having invented, *ab initio*, the pedagogy that would shape his own teaching for the next half-century, it was clearly shaped by the revolutionary methods pioneered by Philipp Franck, a professor at the Royal Art School during Albers' time there. (Franck would take over as director in 1915; the school's first director had been Martin Gropius, great-uncle of Walter.) How the students were taught to teach art and the kind of work their teachers made were entirely different things, however. If the school's *Pädagogik* was impeccably *neue*, its aesthetic leanings were not.

Franck himself was a case in point. In 1898, with his fellow Impressionist Max Liebermann, he had helped to found the Berlin Secession – a *salon des refusés* for painters whose work had shocked the official Association of Berlin Artists with its dappled Frenchness. As is the way of these things, the Secession came to be seen as reactionary by the succeeding generation of artistic hotheads. In 1910, the Secession's annual salon rejected work by a group lately dubbed 'Expressionist' by the art historian Antonin Matějček. 'An Expressionist wishes, above all, to express himself,' Matějček said, reasonably. '[He rejects] immediate perception for more complex psychic structures [spelled out in] a simple shorthand of formulae and symbols.' These new refuseniks now organised a breakaway show of their own under the name of the *Neue Secession*, the New Secession. Franck's Royal Art School was having none of it. Typical of professors in Josef Albers' day was Fritz Greve, a *pompier* academic best known for his church murals and heroic portraits of the Kaiser. Although Albers later recalled an unusually radical teacher having taught his students collage – very cutting-edge for a German institution of its day – the Royal Art School specialised in what he called 'a real training in a very old, conservative sense'. It was not a likely hotbed of revolution.

The same cannot be said of Berlin itself. At eighty, Albers would still recall the excitement of the city in his youth:

> JOSEF ALBERS: I must say also that Berlin was for me in another way very important. At the time there were all these new movements – Die Brucke. Do you know what that is?
>
> SEVIM FESCI: Yes, Die Brucke. Yes.
>
> JA: And the Blaue Reiter.
>
> SF: Oh, the Blue Rider, yes.
>
> JA: And all that, that was in Berlin all so open.
>
> SF: Yes.
>
> JA: [Herwarth] Walden of the 'Storm' Gallery. Then Cassirer who bought the Chagalls – the first Chagalls that were ever seen in Europe

were there. And there was Die Brucke. Schmidt-Rottluff, Heckel, and Kirchner. You know, we saw all that. Which was good. You see, Cassirer was then the man who bought the modern French painters. He had particularly Degas who I consider still today a very good painter, one of the best. But, anyway, in spite of my teaching, my art was my concern.

There was, as he said, a lot of other people's art to see. In later life, Albers conceived a back-dated loathing of Expressionism. In Matějček's use of the word, 'Expressionist' suggested the opposite of Impressionist, German *Ausdruck* to the French *Eindruck*. If the latter focused on the artist's perception of the external appearance of things, the former worked outwards, from a hidden (and preferably tormented) psyche. These definitions were never as neat as they claimed. It was Franz Marc, co-founder of the Blaue Reiter, who advanced the surprising view that German art since the Gothic had been 'poisoned by... the cult of the individual [which attached] too much importance to personal feelings'. By contrast, Edvard Munch, the Expressionists' Norwegian darling, declared 'Nature [to be] formed by one's state of mind' – a piece of solipsism that would have had the eighty-year-old Albers dancing with rage. Not so the young man in Berlin, however. Albers recalled his first view of Munch, at the Sturm gallery's 1913 autumn show, with untypical warmth:

> At the exhibition, there was a painting, The Rising of the Sun. It was a huge painting. It overwhelmed me. There was such a terrific glow that you couldn't look into that sun. It was so overwhelming that it put me on my knees. That is one of the greatest experiences I have ever had in modern painting.

Yet, fifty years later, he would dismiss expressionism as 'that sentimental, self-expression business...vomit, but with the elbows this time.'

As to the art he himself made in Berlin, scant evidence remains. There are five drawings which Albers dated from his time there, presumably among those *Zeichnen nach den lebenden Modell (Kopf)* – 'Life model drawings (head)' – which, on his final report, were graded a grudging *genügend* (adequate). One bears the gnomic inscription, 'trimed [*sic*] with newspaper strips because it was used as backcover for another picture – by my father'. Whether Albers meant that Lorenz had appropriated his son's drawing as backing for one of his own, or trimmed it so that Josef could reuse it, is unclear. Finally, there are a handful of gouaches on paper, also dating from the Berlin period, among them *Untitled (Still Life With Ribbon and Floral Tablecloth)* (fig. 2.4). While the handling of these is at times clumsy – the other 'adequate' on Albers' report was for his painting – their saturated, non-naturalistic colours, simplified forms and planar flattening see Albers absorbing modernism as it was being practised in 1914. Some of the paintings – the potted geranium, the bowls and a mask on an orange tablecloth – have the enamelled feel of Kandinsky circa 1909. Others – the ceramic dish on a tray – clearly respond to Matisse. Formally, the presiding genius of all is Cézanne (fig. 2.5).

If, as he said, art rather than art education was Albers' main concern in Berlin, what he learned about teaching there would nonetheless shape his life. His own synthesizing of the two – art as teaching, teaching as art – had yet to come about. The records of the Royal Art School were badly damaged in the Second World War, so that its its syllabus has largely to be imagined from Philipp Franck's book on teaching, *Das schaffende Kind*, The Creative Child. As to Albers' student life in Berlin from 1913 to 1915, that, too, has to be pieced together from clues. As often, what is most striking about his account of the time is how much it omits.

In July 1914, in the middle of his time in Berlin, Germany had gone to war with Russia, then, inevitably, with France and Great Britain. The imperial capital was plunged into a frenzy of patriotism. While Paul Cassirer's gallery carried on doggedly showing Cézanne, German dealers for the most part followed German politics and rid their shows of foreign art. The big players of the avant-garde slipped away – Kandinsky to Russia, Klee to a Bavarian flying school, Julius Meier-Graefe as a Red Cross volunteer. In September 1914, August Macke was killed on the Western Front; he would be followed, a year later, by Franz Marc. Albers, judging all this to be 'retrospection', mentions none of it in his later telling of the time. Nonetheless, the war hit home. By 1 August 1915 he was back in Bottrop, teaching at the Josefschule. The following month, his brother Paul, a soldier in the 253rd Reserve Infantry Regiment, was wounded by shellfire in the battle for Vilnius; he died a week later. Paul Albers was twenty-five. His death certificate lists his trade as *Maler*, painter, his residence as Siegen. Josef Albers, who in later life never spoke of his dead brother, was twenty-seven.

What did this death mean to him? The next record we have of Albers, the first real glimpse, comes four months later in a letter to his friend, Franz

2.4 *Untitled (Still Life with Ribbon and Floral Tablecloth)*, 1914. Gouache on paper, 12¼ × 15½ in.

2.5 *Stilleben russische Spanschachtel (Still Life with Russian woodchip box)*,
ca. 1914. Tempera on canvas, 16 × 14²⁄₅ in.

Grosse Perdekamp. The Perdekamps had been in Bottrop since before 1700. Franz's father, Theodor Perdekamp, was, like Lorenz Albers, a member of the house-painters' guild. Franz's older brother had been in Josef's class at school; the dead Paul Albers and Franz Perdekamp were born ten days apart, in January 1890. Like Josef, Franz trained as a primary-school teacher; in 1916, he was teaching in Recklinghausen while Josef taught in Bottrop. From 1921–2, when Josef was studying art in Weimar, Franz studied art history in Münster. In 1938, he became director of Recklinghausen's local museum, overseeing its post-war reinvention as a *Kunsthalle*. The links between Perdekamp and Albers ran deep. The war years apart, they would write to each other regularly until Franz's death in 1952. What is particularly interesting about the earliest of their surviving letters is its address.

When, in 1974, Albers' wife Anni went into hospital in New Haven, Connecticut, Josef remarked to an acquaintance that he had never been in one himself. Perhaps he had forgotten the six months he spent, sixty years before, looking down on Bad Honnef, a pretty village on the Rhine near Bonn. On the hill above the village was (and is) a pompous, white-painted building in French-chateau style, called Hohenhonnef. It is now a home for the disabled; in 1916, it was a tuberculosis sanatorium. In its Wilhelmine heyday, Hohenhonnef's patients had included the consumptive great and good of Europe, the Kaiser's sister, Princess Viktoria of Prussia, among them. Inevitably, Thomas Mann's *Magic Mountain* comes to mind. Since 1912, though, Hohenhonnef had been a state-owned *Lungenklinik*, a place where less well-heeled Westphalians, sickened by the filthy Ruhr air, could come to be treated and recuperate. It was from here that Albers, admitted two weeks before, wrote to Franz Perdekamp on 14 February 1916.

The talk is of hospital routine, of fever charts and white coats: also of the teaching job Albers has been offered near Bremen, 'in nice, healthy countryside – and far away from the hell of my home'. His letters to Perdekamp are often so elliptical as to have the feel of being written in code. In a later one from Hohenhonnef, Albers speaks of 'a devil from my home town re-kindling an infernal fire in me from far away', of his wish to see again the 'sweet, pretty mother-lips that have for so many years been denied me'. Paul is dead and he himself possibly dying. Even now, two decades after her death, he longs for the dead Magdalena.

Albers' attitude to Bottrop, as to many things, changed with time. Between his marriage in 1925 and departure for America in 1933, he is known to have gone home just once, and that visit was a conspicuous failure. And yet, at the end of his life, he recalled his home happily, and was proud, at eighty-two, to be made a freeman of Bottrop. For the moment, though, it was enough to be away. Hohenhonnef's medical records are lost, but it seems clear that Albers had been diagnosed with tuberculosis. He is, he tells Perdekamp, forbidden to leave the clinic's grounds for six weeks, and there is no chance of a clean bill of health before the end of July at the earliest – six months after his admission. Fifty years later, Albers would say of El Lissitzky, who had stayed with him and his wife in Dessau in 1928, 'He was tuberculous [and so] got permission to go to Davos. Since tuberculosis is out, Davos is no longer a *Kurhaus.*' Of his own time in a *Lungenklinik*, he says nothing.

As well as deferring his return to teaching, his illness meant that he could never serve at the front. Albers would be spared the early deaths of Macke and Marc, and of his brother Paul. He would also be denied their heroism, and that of Bottrop contemporaries who died in their hundreds – the elementary-school teacher Hubert Potthast, for example, who fell in March 1917 with '*die feindliche Kugel ins treue Soldatenherz*', the enemy's bullet in his true soldier's heart. Albers' official leave of absence states merely that he is *erkrankten* – 'diseased' – but not with what; he had been off work since 10 December 1915, and would be until October 1916. To Perdekamp, from Hohenhonnef, he writes of 'muddled confusion in the roof-timbers of my mind', of thoughts that are 'turned inward, and hang in the trees'. The breakdown in his health was mental as well as physical.

If his feelings were muddled, though, his thoughts on art were beginning to solidify. On 2 March, he writes to Perdekamp:

> ...the group around Giotto and the others from Siena – well, why do they have such immediate effect? Because they were technically simple. There was only tempera and al fresco, and a small number of colours. Tools had to be made by the master himself, so they were few. Look at a modern catalogue of painting equipment and ask how many hundred times smaller was the fraction that the Old Masters had? Yes, they had great spirit, but their limited means meant that they couldn't dissipate their strength. Modern art-making only leads to slickness.

That belief in the virtue of minimal means was to stay with him to the end of his life.

By late summer, Albers was well enough to leave Hohenhonnef, although not to go back to work. At the end of August, he is in Bödefeld, recuperating with his father's family. It is October before he writes to Perdekamp from Bottrop, and then with a new-found urgency. He needs 'the two portraits' at once, drawings he has sent his friend, presumably from the *Kurhaus*: he wants to turn them into prints in Essen, where they have been much admired. He had already made a linocut bookplate for Perdekamp, of a naked man, back view, kneeling in obeisance before a Gothic arch (fig. 2.6) The drawings Albers now requested were the ones shown here (figs 2.7, 2.8) of himself and Perdekamp, which, along with several other self-portraits, he made into linocuts in 1916 (figs 2.9, 2.10).

The second has the feel of the academic life studies he had made at art school in Berlin; it presumably dates from around 1914. Its direct stare suggests Edvard Munch's *Self-Portrait with Skeleton Arm*, a famous lithograph likewise made in Berlin, twenty years earlier. The side-view portrait of Perdekamp is much more expressive, in part because it is in charcoal rather than pencil and clearly made with printing in mind. Given Albers' recent equating of Bottrop with hell, the diabolical feel of this portrait is intriguing; so, too, the Bottropish material – charcoal – in which it is made. (Forty years later, teaching at Yale, Albers would have a student from Pittsburgh, the town he described as America's Bottrop. Looking at the young man's charcoal sketches, he snapped, 'You draw like a coal miner.') Not long after, Albers drew Wilhelm Kaiser, a schoolteacher who was married to his cousin, Agatha. Since the Kaisers lived in Bödefeld, the pen-and-pencil portrait was most likely made during Albers' recuperation there in August or September 1916. If so, then another drawing in the same medium and using the same frenetic cross-hatching may also be assumed to date from that time. More accomplished than the first, it shows Albers getting to grips with the two-dimensional modelling of three-dimensional space. Its subject is himself. The linocut he made from this, he called *Mephisto* (fig. 2.11).

In April 1917, Albers writes to Perdekamp about the print. On Franz's recommendation, he has been to see Reinhard Sorge's play *King David* and been swept away by it. 'I believed that I alone could play the young David, that only I was the right man for the part,' he enthuses to his friend. Sorge, younger than Albers, had been killed on the Somme the summer before: *King David* was to be his last work. His earlier plays had been strongly Nietzschean; *The Beggar* (1912) is remembered as the first Expressionist drama. The following year, though, its atheist author had converted to Catholicism.

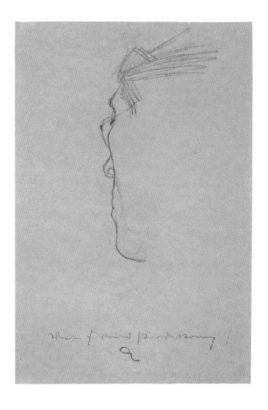

2.6 *Ex Libris Franz Perdekamp*, *ca.* 1915. Linoleum print, 7¼ × 5⅛ in.
2.7 *Mein Freund Perdekamp!*, *ca.* 1917–18. Graphite on paper, 12½ × 8½ in.

2.8 *Self-Portrait (I)*, *ca.* 1914–15. Pencil on paper, 17⅛ × 13⅛ in.

2.9 *Self-Portrait (facing front) I*, 1916. Linoleum print, 18⅛ × 11⅔ in.

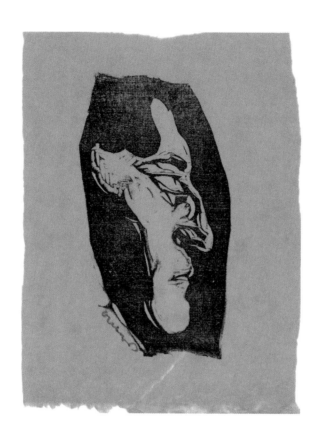

2.10. *Self-Portrait (facing right)*, 1916. Linoleum print, 12¼ × 9⅞ in.

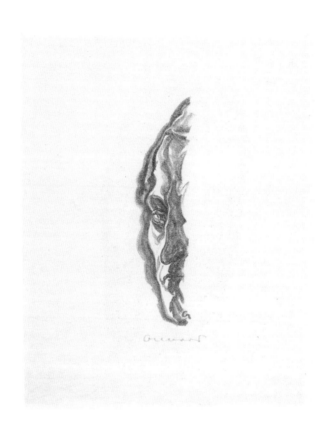

2.11 *Self-Portrait 'Mephisto'*, 1916. Lithograph, 13¼ × 10½ in.

Nietzsche had misled him, Sorge said; thereafter, his 'pen was to be Christ's'. The Expressionists, appalled, disowned him. Albers' identification with Sorge's David is intriguing. The play, he tells Perdekamp, 'made me forget my *Mephisto* – and that means a lot to me. While I am finding it so hard to escape from myself, it is hard for me to escape into other people.' *King David* had allowed him to do this. Up to this point, he says, he had identified himself with Golem, the creature from Jewish folklore recently made famous throughout Germany by a film of the same name. It may be that Albers had seen this at Bottrop's new cinema, the Lichtspielhaus, which had opened in 1911. Or the monster he had in mind may have been the one in Gustav Meyrink's book, *Der Golem*, published in 1914. The hero of Meyrink's novel suffers a mental collapse that erases all memory of his childhood. The echo of Albers' own circumstances is compelling.

For him, as for his art, 1916 stands as a year zero. From Hohenhonnef, he had sent Franz Perdekamp the drawing of a star over thin, wintry trees (fig. 2.12). This was most likely inspired by the Treysa meteorite, which had fallen with a noise like thunder in woodland near Marburg on the afternoon of 3 April 1916. Eyewitness accounts, reported at length in the German press, described the fireball as an asymmetric burning star, radiating beams of light. Like Halley's comet six years before, the meteorite was held to portend disaster. The rash of comet-related horror films that followed it only added to the German sense of doom. One film in particular, the Danish-made *Verdens Undergang* (The End of the World), gripped the country. Given Albers' own state of mind, he may have meant his star to be read as a portent of impending disaster, national or personal. On the other hand, like the star over Bethlehem, he may have taken it for a sign of salvation.

The sudden outpouring of self-portraits that begins in 1916 shows Albers looking not just at himself, but for a way of looking. What kind of artist is he to be, and what kind of man? His pen is by turns academic, Cézanne-esque, Expressionistic, classical and avant-garde; loose, tight, frenetic, studied. In the series of three *Self-Portraits with Hat*, he adds or eliminates imperceptible lines and highlights between the prints' various states, changing his expression from devilish to watchful to vulnerable with the least possible alteration (figs 2.13, 2.14). The portrait's sideways look refuses to meet its own eye – there is an odd disconnect between Albers as subject and maker, as though his own evasiveness stops him from seeing. In part, this sort of sinister self-depiction was in the air: Jan Toorop's self-portrait of 1915 has

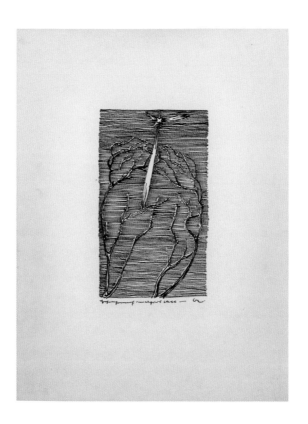

2.12 *Hohenhonnef in April*, 1916. Ink and pen on paper, 13½ × 9⅞ in.

2.13 *Self-Portrait with Hat I*, 1916. Linoleum print, 9⅛ × 11¼ in.
2.14 *Self-Portrait with Hat II*, 1916. Linoleum print, 9 × 11 in.

a similar Mephistophelean feel. But there is an intensity to Albers' search that is separate from fashion. Bound up in the kind of art he might make would be the kind of man he was. The question for both was where to start. In 1916, he was variously an outsider – a Westphalian in Ruhrpolen Bottrop, an artist in a family of craftsmen; alive when so many young men were dead. Finding himself, his *Ich-Ideal*, was a matter of urgency.

Along with the portraits are dozens of other drawings and prints, spilling from his hand in a surge of creativity, a great unlocking. There are drawings and lithographs of pigeons and horses, cows, chickens, ducks, owls and Rhinelander rabbits; many are given to Franz Perdekamp. ('My friend, Perdekamp...he might have alone a dozen [drawings] by himself,' Albers said, half a century later. 'But he is dead already.') There are quick pen and ink sketches of a boy and girl at the Glückauf Schule, where Albers taught after his illness. In 1971, one of his pupils there, Broni Molitor, identified the drawings' subjects and brought her old teacher news of them. Molitor's letter suggests something of the hardships of life in working-class Bottrop. The girl in the sketches, Antonie Altenkamp, had died of tuberculosis at the age of fifteen, her younger sister of the disease later the same day. The rest of the family perished soon afterwards, after which their house was torn down. More brightly, Molitor recalls Albers' lessons – 'drawing from 2–4 in the afternoon, and one hour of natural history....The walls of your classroom were butterfly cabinets, with all the species, from the most ordinary to the most beautiful butterflies.'

Molitor's recollections locate Albers as both a teacher and an artist. In 1905, Ludwig Zimmer had published his reformist *Heimatkunde für die Schulen der Rheinpfalz* (Local Studies for Schools in the Rhineland Palatinate), much read by *Volksschule* teachers in neighbouring Westphalia. Zimmer held looking at the world around them to be the most important skill an elementary schoolchild could be taught. The schoolroom was merely the pivot of a compass pointing outwards to the surrounding streets and, beyond those, to the *heimatlich* fields and wilds, to the butterflies and rabbits and owls that lived in them. Direct observation was everything. In the place of book-lessons on natural history would be walks, *Naturstunden*, drawings made on the spot – what another pedagogue, Heinrich Wolgast, called 'learning to see'. This new, democratized way of seeing would have social ramifications as well. Instead of history being taught as a procession of kings and conquests, it would start from the everyday truths of the city and land;

2.15 *Duck*, 1916. Lithograph from stone, 16⅞ × 11¼ in.

2.16 *Rabbit (facing right)*, 1916. Transfer lithograph, 10¼ × 13⅛ in.

rather than emphasizing their individuality, children would be redefined as social beings. Politics, economics and nature were to make up a single pedagogic whole. In 1912, the Deutscher Lehrerverein unanimously endorsed teaching through *Heimatkunde*. With many school administrators off fighting in the trenches from 1914 on, *Volksschule* teachers were left to act on that endorsement at will.

If Molitor's drawing lessons and butterfly cases conjure up Albers in the classroom, they also shed light on his art. As he teaches, so he learns. Reform pedagogy stressed the importance of the *Heimat* as a thing to be observed, painted, drawn, photographed; what it was less clear about was precisely what a *Heimat* was. It had always been a slippery word, capable of embracing a homeland on any scale, from the vastness of the German Empire to the smallest Münsterland hamlet. Given widespread resentment of Prussian rule in the non-Prussian *Reich*, *heimatlich* attachment to a province such as Westphalia might be anti-patriotic, at least in the sense of being anti-Imperial, against the cosmic dreams of the Hohenzollerns. However variable the word's political meaning, though, one thing was clear. Art that concerned itself with the *Heimat* – the drawings Josef Albers had made for the Stadtlohn *Heimatkalender*, for example – was hopelessly provincial. That long-held view, too, was changing.

In 1908, the Jugendstil artist August Endell had declared the natural *Heimat* of modern art to be no longer the Empire or *Land*, but the city. Along with this, Endell championed a new kind of art, 'neither representing anything, nor resembling anything...getting as deep into our souls as only music can do'. The metropolis and abstraction – the new homeland and a new way of representing it – went hand in hand. Out went distant vistas of spires and meadows, to be replaced with what the Expressionist painter Ludwig Meidner called 'our city world! The wild streets, the elegance of iron suspension bridges, gasometers hanging in white cloud-mountains, the roaring colours of buses and locomotives, the rushing telephone wires.'

In Amsterdam, Piet Mondrian agreed. 'The truly modern artist sees the metropolis as abstract life made manifest,' he wrote. 'It is closer to him than nature, and likelier to stir in him a sense of beauty.' In soot-choked Bottrop, this new definition of the *Heimat* must have come to Josef Albers as a kind of salvation.

In 1915, Albers had drawn the railway overpass between Bottrop and Essen (fig. 2.17). He did so, he said, 'with the feeling of Van Gogh standing

2.17 *Construction of railroad overpass on the road from Essen to Bottrop*, 1915.
Ink and brush on woven paper, 13¼ × 15¼ in.

behind me'. One wonders if he can have seen the Dutch artist's drawing *The Langlois Bridge*, which had entered Paul Cassirer's collection in 1910. That Albers had discovered Van Gogh in Berlin is clear. As he recalled in his eighties,

> Philip Franck, a friend of Max Liebermann…showed us one morning Dutch photographs of Van Gogh's charcoal drawings. He put them all on the wall. And I was always tempted to get a little charcoal off. They were so marvellously reproduced – you know, this marvellous, powdery effect from charcoal strokes. Every morning, I looked around to see if anyone was watching me. I knew they were photographs, but I had to feel them to be convinced it was not charcoal.…There was born my great admiration for Van Gogh. The strokes of Van Gogh…they always go with the form, the lines go with the form. I tried indirectly to do something similar. It was unconscious: it was not until afterwards that I realised I was doing what Van Gogh did.

It is in printing even more than in drawing that Albers' excitement shows. With notable exceptions – the aforementioned overpass, three brisk, vivid sketches of a telephone lineman (fig. 2.18) – he keeps his pencil for traditional subjects and genres: portraits, cathedrals, Sauerland pine woods, the castle at Würzburg. By 1916, he had decided to be an artist. His Berlin certificate qualified him to teach at a *gymnasium*, but he stayed on at his elementary school, as its half-day timetable would leave him time to make prints. Cassirer's new magazine, *Der Bildermann* (The Picture-Man), had recently made the aesthetic case for printing. 'Twice a month, *Der Bildermann* will publish lithographs by masters,' Cassirer wrote in its first issue. 'Lithographs are originals. In them, the photographic process does not intervene between the artist's drawing and its reproduction; a lithographic line is as alive as the line of a sketch.' Then there was the question of money. Contemporary prints had found a new respectability, working their way into even such stuffy collections as that of the Dresden Kupferstich-Kabinett. As a result, they had become very much more marketable: by 1914, it was estimated that Philip Franck's friend, Max Liebermann, was making eighty thousand marks a year from print sales alone. Kollwitz, Nolde, Schmidt-Rottluff, Corinth and Kirchner had all set up as printers, the last among the first German painters to make his own lithographs. If Albers was to survive as an artist, then printing was

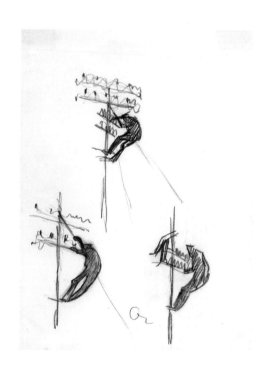

2.18 *Electrical Repairmen, ca.* 1918. Pencil on paper, 11⅛ × 8³⁄₁₀ in.

as good a place as any to start. It would also introduce him to the emerging modernist creed of working in series.

Neither art history nor commercial logic alone explains his prints of 1916–19, however. That Albers embraced the idea of an urban *Heimatkunst* so early and so vigorously is remarkable. While Die Brücke, for all its experiments with colour and form, remained at heart an art of fields and trees, Albers' eye was drawn to streets, suburban housing, open-cast mines. The lithographs he made of these, mechanically-produced images of a mechanized society, were printed at the *Handwerker- und Kunstgewerbeschule* (Trade and Arts School) in Essen – half an hour from Bottrop by tram, a journey he made again and again on his four free afternoons a week. 'They had an very good lithographer at Essen, and that is why I worked with that lithographer,' Albers recalled. 'I did a series of landscapes, of miner houses – *Haus meiner Heimat*, that's a whole series – because there was a lithographer who stimulated me to do lithography' (figs 2.19, 20, 21). In later life, he forgot this muse's name – 'a nice, small man', he recalled, vaguely – although it seems likely to have been Josef Urbach, a lithographer and longtime teacher at the school. Drawing was taught by Jan Thorn Prikker, then at the height of his local fame in the Ruhr – the Dutchman's vast stained-glass window, *The Artist as Teacher of Trade and Industry*, had been installed in Hagen station in 1911 – although his lessons were too expensive for Albers. Even so, he said, the Dutchman was 'the most inspirational for me at that time'. It was to him that Albers attributed his first interest in Cézanne, which influenced the 1916 self-portrait with its 'planes that went this way, this way, this way, this way, this way, this way'. The young schoolteacher's seriousness impressed his fellows. Another student at Essen recalled Josef Albers as 'industrious, ascetic, thin, blond, grey-eyed, strict with himself'.

If he was learning to print, then Albers was also thinking through what it meant to be modern. The *Kunstgewerbeschule*, founded in 1911, was impeccably up to date in its merging of art and crafts. Karl-Ernst Osthaus – he of the Nietzschean Folkwang – had been instrumental in the school's creation. It was through him that both Prikker and the Dutch symbolist Jan Toorop had come to teach there, and Osthaus seems to have suggested Alfred Fischer as its first director. Fischer, then relatively unknown, had taught alongside the radical architect Peter Behrens at the Düsseldorf *Kunstgewerbeschule*. If Düsseldorf's was a proper art school, though, Essen's was more like a modern community college. Its remit was to prepare students for external guild exams;

2.19 *Ostring IV, ca.* 1917. Transfer lithograph, 10½ × 16¼ in.

2.20. *Nordring I*, *ca*. 1917. Transfer lithograph, 12¼ × 19 in.

2.21 *Empty End*, *ca*. 1917. Transfer lithograph, 10 × 19 in.

many, Albers included, attended evening classes. This made attracting staff difficult. Fischer's initial attempts to lure well-known teachers from Vienna and Stuttgart failed, and he was thrown back on hiring locally. Josef Urbach, Albers' probable lithography instructor, was typical both in coming from Neuss and in being an ex-Düsseldorf student. The school's already rickety faculty was badly hit by the First World War, Fischer himself being called up in 1915. Thorn Prikker's visits dwindled after 1914, and ceased altogether in 1917. By the time Albers began at the school, it was run by a skeleton staff.

In any case, his ambitions ranged far beyond Essen. In a postcard to Perdekamp from a trip to Berlin in 1917, Albers writes that he has been to see a Max Reinhardt production of Strindberg's *The Father*, and to the annual Secession show. 'It is good to breathe new air again,' he says. Inspiration came from everywhere, in the most improbable of guises. The sand pits on the outskirts of Bottrop offered a particularly rich seam, Albers mining them even as they were mined. As he explained fifty years later:

> My home town, Bottrop, has a very rare deposit of what is a
> mixture of clay and sand, the right mixture for making cast iron:
> a very rare combination of clay and sand in the right proportion.
> It was a source of wealth for a few people at home. That was for me
> interesting....It looks like a quarry. There was a shuttle down, and
> there you see women putting the sand into the wagons, because
> that was during the war and there were not the men....I have a few
> with figures also.

In the *Sandgrube* linocuts, Albers plays around with detail, form, viewpoint, focus (fig. 2.22); even with colour, in a painting of the pit (fig. 2.23). *Sandgrube I* (1916) clearly inverts the composition of Van Gogh's drawing *La Roubine de Roi, with Women Washing* (1888) – the likeness is too close for coincidence. These works are the nearest Albers gets to Expressionism, although the echo of Van Gogh in *Sandgrube I* also suggests that its ambitions are different from the Dutchman's. A comparison of the painting with comparable scenes by paid-up Expressionists – Erich Heckel's *Straight Canal* (1915), say – highlights Albers' unusual interest in the tension between two and three dimensions, and in resolving this tension through abstract pattern. The other notable thing about the *Sandgrube* linocuts is the early interest they show in working in series.

2.22 *Sandgrube I (Sandmine I)*, 1916. Linoleum print, 13⅞ × 11⅞ in.

2.23 *Sandgrube (Sandmine)*, *ca.* 1916–17. Tempera on canvas, 25⅖ × 26⅘ in.

At least part of Albers' growing aversion to Expressionism seems to have stemmed from an un-German dislike of groups. In a poem to Perdekamp, 'Everything is hovering (The Mosquito Swarm)', he gently mocks Franz Marc's assertion that the movement would end in a new Gothic age:

> I see so many people, many ways.
> A ceaseless to and fro
> and up and down,
> but never moving forward.
> Each sets his place by his neighbours' place;
> But he who wants to move on, he cannot follow
> the others:
> He, unlike they, must go ahead.
> He is likely to be alone;
> but out there, even if it means his death,
> he may feel the free infinity of space.
> Might the others follow some day?
> This cannot trouble him.
> Maybe a later swarm will get
> – without knowing it, without crediting him,
> as if blown there by the wind –
> to where this lone one is, or at least along the way;
> and maybe they, too, will feel new air.

For a man not yet thirty, with little formal art training and no reputation as an artist, Albers' belief in himself is striking. Even so, his work shows precisely that tendency to locate itself by reference to others which he had mocked in his Expressionist mosquitoes. The clumsiness of his prints of the Bottrop militia – he was finally passed fit to serve in this non-combat troop in March 1917 – suggests that he had seen Matisse's *Dance* at the 1913 Berlin Secession, and thought, mistakenly, that its form might usefully be applied to a military subject (fig. 2.24). Albers' 1918 lithographs of workers' houses in Bottrop, in the *Haus meiner Heimat* series, take him down new roads figuratively as literally; but where these will lead is uncertain. The 1917–18 prints define themselves as much by what they are not as by what they are – not the explosive fragmentation of Expressionism, nor the grim, potato-eating realism of Van Gogh; certainly not the *flâneur*'s happy ambling prescribed

2.24 *Two Men Pulling off Boots*, 1917. Transfer lithograph, 8½ × 11⅛ in.

by Baudelaire. But what, then? For an answer to that, Albers would have to look beyond Essen.

Before leaving Bottrop, though, he was to make his first public commission. First mention of this comes, as so often, in a letter to Franz Perdekamp. After telling Perdekamp that he cannot afford to repay him the twenty marks he has borrowed – neither the loan nor the failure to repay it an unusual occurrence in their friendship – Albers complains of the return of his narcolepsy; this, presumably, a symptom of the depression he had suffered since leaving Hohenhonnef. He speaks of being surrounded by 'an oppressive, dark mass, crying out for form'. Then he ends the letter with the mysterious line, 'I shout, glass window "rosa mystica ora pro nobis"' – 'mystic rose, pray for me'.

The Mystic Rose, or Maria Rosa Mystica, is one of many personifications of the Virgin Mary, in this case wedding her flower-like purity to the thorniness of her suffering. Her veneration in Germany went back to at least the 12th century; praying to the Virgin as Maria Rosa Mystica was believed to bring hope to the hopeless. Whether Albers himself suggested the iconography of his first stained-glass window, or whether it was demanded by his patron, Father Bernhard Hugenroth, is unclear. Either way, the symbolism of Rosa Mystica cannot have been lost on the despairing young artist *manqué*. Hugenroth, nine years older than Albers, had been appointed first parish priest of the new church of St Michael, built in 1912–14 to serve the miners' housing around the Ostring. Albers taught Broni Molitor at the Glückauf School, opposite; Father Hugenroth was the school's chaplain. That the priest asked an unknown and unproven artist to take on this commission – the church had been given a thousand marks for the window by a rich donor – says much for his far-sightedness.

This is all the more true given the highly publicized case of Albers' hero, Johan Thorn Prikker. In 1911, another adventurous priest, Father Joseph Geller, had invited Prikker to make a suite of nine windows for the Three Kings church in Neuss, birthplace of his Essen colleague and Albers' lithography teacher, Josef Urbach. Geller had gone ahead with the commission without first submitting Prikker's designs to the church authorities for approval – 'I thought it wiser to place the order in secret, ecclesiastical circles at that point having no experience of modern art,' he would later reason, Jesuitically. The first window was shown, to wide acclaim, at the 1912 Sonderbund exhibition in Cologne. The city's Catholic archbishop did not share in the general adulation, however. Geller was forbidden to install the remaining eight of Prikker's windows, which languished in a church basement until 1927. In 1913, the priest was rewarded for his avant-garde leanings by being banished to a parish in Duisburg. It took courage for Hugenroth to commission *Rosa Mystica*, and for Albers to make it.

Albers' letters to Gottfried Heinersdorff at the glass-making firm of Puhl & Wagner in Berlin are full of the fretfulness you might expect of a young artist at work on his first public commission. Heinersdorff, a member of the Deutscher Werkbund and one of the most famous glass technicians in Germany, had made Prikker's ill-fated Neuss windows. The scandal of those must surely have been in Albers' mind as he worked on his own. In February 1918, he apologizes to Heinersdorff for being a self-taught glass-maker, and thus for the probable shortcomings of the sketch that accompanies his letter. Nonetheless, his vision for the piece is notably clear and specific. The rose, the window's central motif, must have 'a restrained inner glow', the ruby-like cut-glass stones on its petals be sharp-edged, bright and outlined in black. The rose must oscillate against a background of the strongest blue imaginable – 'something at the far end of the spectrum' – which must be particularly vivid between the letters of the Marian prayer. Albers asks when the window will be ready, *Herr Rektor* Hugenroth being anxious to know. The priest, meanwhile, had written to Heinersdorff himself, querying the new price he had been quoted – *Rosa Mystica* was now to cost fourteen hundred marks rather than a thousand – and complaining that he would have make up the difference from his own pocket. The window was finally installed, to only minor grumbles from Albers, on 16 July 1918.

It is an arresting work, far from the comforting image its name suggests (fig. 2.25). The window's feel is not so much Expressionist as Vorticist – it calls to mind a work such as C. R.W. Nevinson's *Bursting Shell* (1915), although Albers cannot, of course, have seen this. The mystic rose of the title may be meant to symbolize an emollient Mary on a field of Marian blue, but it explodes towards the viewer as if smashing through the glass, rays shining from it like the fireball that had landed on Treysa. Given this, the words *Ora pro nobis* read less as a supplication than as a cry of despair. How the work was received at the time is not known. In July 1918, Bottrop's newspapers were too full of the obituaries of dead soldiers and instructions to citizens on where to find rationed bread to run reviews of stained-glass windows.

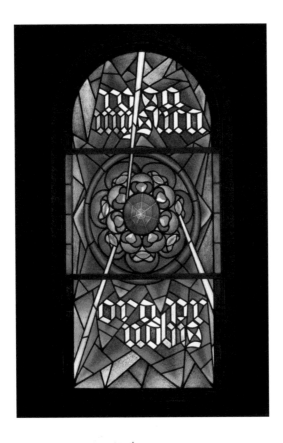

2.25 *Rosa Mystica Ora Pro Nobis*, 1918 (destroyed; replica, 2012). Glass window.

It was two and a half years since Paul Albers had been killed by a bursting shell, two years since his older brother had been sent to the clinic at Hohenhonnef. Josef Albers' letters to Franz Perdekamp in 1918 are still feverish in their language, and the behaviour they describe, too, is febrile. In one, dated 26 March, Albers writes of a drunken night that had ended with him in the bed of a man called Winkler, and a Dr Brinkmann threatening to break his windows 'if I did not accept him'. In April, Brinkmann invites him to the Mostert, then Bottrop's best hotel. Albers does not go; Brinkmann sulks; Albers, witheringly, tells him that he 'does not feel the need to reveal [his] inmost thoughts to any man'. One sees again the closed face of the boy in the photograph taken at his mother's death two decades before (fig. 2.26).

It would be a year before he wrote to Perdekamp again, and then from Munich (fig. 2.27). Why Albers had chosen to study at the city's Royal Academy of Fine Arts remains a mystery. If the Bavarian capital had been the epicentre of German avant-garde art in 1900, it was certainly no longer so by 1919. As with other Secessions, Munich's had become first established and then reactionary. In 1906, its annual *salon* rejected all nine works by a Russian painter called Wassily Kandinsky; in 1914, the Secession declared itself 'a bulwark against ultra-radical thought'. In that same year, Kandinsky's Blaue Reiter group – the ace up Munich's avant-garde sleeve – was dissolved. Going to the Bavarian capital to learn modernism in 1919 was like moving to New York in 1970 in the hope of becoming a new Jackson Pollock.

2.26 Photographer unknown, Josef Albers, Bottrop, Spring 1919.

2.27 Josef Albers, Academy of Visual Art, Munich, Germany, 1955.

What makes Albers' choice particularly puzzling is that the hotbed of new German art was half an hour's train ride away from Bottrop, in Düsseldorf. Düsseldorf's *Kunstakademie* had played a central role in the various Sonderbund exhibitions, its students gaining the kind of broad and immediate exposure to Munch, Van Gogh, Cézanne and Picasso that their counterparts in Munich could only dream of. In 1919, the Düsseldorf Art Academy was also at the centre of the Young Rhineland movement, later re-dubbed the Rhenish Expressionists. Members of this included Heinrich Campendonk and Max Ernst; involved, too, were Alfred Fischer, Jan Thorn Prikker, their joint ex-student Josef Urbach, and the ubiquitous Karl-Ernst Osthaus. Given the links of all these to Essen's *Kunstgewerbeschule*, Albers might reasonably have been expected to study in Düsseldorf. Perhaps he was put off by the Rhenish Expressionists' mosquito-like swarming. Then, too, the Ruhr had been a hotbed of revolution in the Spartacist uprising of January 1919, a general strike among coalminers being ruthlessly put down by the mercenary *Freikorps*. Most likely, though, the problem was Düsseldorf's proximity to Bottrop. Had he gone to the *Kunstakademie*, he could have commuted daily from home; and, by 1919, that was the last thing he wanted to do.

His letters to Perdekamp from Munich are as elliptical as ever. Despite the men's shared interest in art, Albers says nothing of his studies at the

Academy. Nor does he mention showing his etchings in the autumn exhibition of Hans Goltz's famously avant-garde gallery, a show in which two future Bauhaus colleagues, Lyonel Feininger and Paul Klee, both also took part. Unusually, though, he does describe the history going on around him.

On 25 October 1919, there is talk of Munich's trams stopping from dusk to dawn, of gas cut off each evening and a lack of coal. The city's brief role as capital of a breakaway Socialist Bavarian republic had been brought to a bloody end by the German army five months before, and the harsh terms of Versailles were beginning to bite. Albers has, he says, been back to the Pinakothek: Grünewald's *Isenheim Altarpiece* is gone, returned to Colmar – a symbol of Germany's post-war humiliation. He speaks of lodging with a baroness and dining with a count – not his usual milieu, and presumably code-names for people known to Perdekamp. He also writes of 'Mama' being with him, although it is hard to imagine Elisabeth Albers accompanying her thirty-year-old stepson to Munich. This, too, must be an alias. He is, as before, overwrought, 'a string about to snap'.

A month later, he writes from 95 Turkenstrasse, student digs across the road from the Academy. As in the last letter, there is mention of Friedel, identified as Frieda Karsch, a woman from Münster three years younger than Albers and to whom he was apparently close. As ever, there are complaints of poverty. He estimates that he has sixty-one marks to live on for the coming year; Perdekamp, predictably, rises to the bait. On 12 December, 'Jupp' writes to thank him for his generosity in sending money, adding that it will be good to be able to help out 'poor Friedel'. He is only allowed to bring coal as far as her door, he says, to walk with her on Sundays and to whistle under her window at night.

Of life and lessons at the Royal Academy, though, Albers says not a word. One reason for his choosing this august if hidebound place might have been that Kandinsky and Klee had both studied there before him, and under his own professor-to-be, Franz von Stuck. The avant-garde pair had been at the Academy two decades earlier, however, in 1900–1, when Stuck was at the height of his fame. In any case, Albers did not know they had been Stuck's students until he met them at the Bauhaus in the 1920s. Another inducement might have been that the princely Stuck – the equivalent of a knighthood in 1906 had allowed him to assume the aristocratic 'von' – came from stock as humble as Albers', and had, like him, been trained at a *Kunstgewerbeschule* rather than an art school. Then, too, Stuck was prodigiously hands-on: before

2.28 *Photographs of Josef Albers, Germany, ca.* 1915–55. Photocollage:
silver gelatin prints mounted on cardboard, 8¼ × 10⅘ in.

becoming an Academy professor at the age of thirty-one, he had specialized in drawing covers for menus and cartoons for newspapers. Even after his startling rise to stardom, he remained proudly *Kunstgewerblich*, making his own frames by hand and designing not just the regal Villa Stuck but all of its furniture and fittings. One wonders if he might not have served as the model for Albers' later recollections of his father.

By 1919, though, Stuck's star was in steep decline, and has remained so since. As early as 1900, Henry van de Velde had dismissed the 'false, tasteless luxury' of the master's villa. In the day of New Objectivism, his creepily erotic, Böcklin-esque art had come to look camp. Later, his reputation would be helped by his having been the favourite painter of a young Adolf Hitler. Nonetheless, Stuck was more than just a purveyor of sadomasochistic allegories. Hugo von Hofmannsthal noted his ability 'to see things as forms, irrespective of what they actually were'. This tendency to abstraction had been spotted, too, by Kandinsky and Klee, who recognized in Stuck's flattened, frieze-like Greek paintings a tension between two- and three-dimensional space that held unexpected echoes of Cézanne. It was Stuck who advised Kandinsky to concentrate on form by working only in black and white, sparking an interest in positive and negative space that would occupy the Russian for the rest of his life. Even at the Bauhaus, when it was unfashionable to do so, Klee would defend his old master, saying, 'No, I learned from Stuck.'

Albers, typically, was less kind. Going back to the academic drawing-board must have been frustrating for a man who, in Essen, had been feeling his way towards modernism, and convincingly enough for his prints to have been shown by Goltz. Asked later about a portrait sketch of a woman's head in pencil, ink and charcoal (fig. 2.29), he sniffed, 'The one with that funny hair? That's a Jugendstil coiffeur – this was my examination piece at Stuck. When I wanted to enter the Stuck class, he put a model in front of us and said, "Do what you can and see if you can get into my advanced class or not."' After a pause, Albers added, 'There was in that time the belief that drawing was the basis of painting. It is nonsense, of course.' Nonsensical, too, was Stuck's idea that artists had to paint 'in cold and warm...that cold was here and warm was there', although Albers did at least concede that his master may have been right that 'light was cold and shadow was warm.... It's true, I believe it's true.' For Hans Hofmann, whose private Munich art school he attended in the evenings, Albers conceived a lifelong dislike. Hofmann had made the mistake of criticizing his work. Worse, he would arrive in America the

2.29 *Woman (I)*, *ca*. 1914. Pencil on paper, 9⅞ × 13⅖ in.

year before Albers, be taken up by the king-making critic Clement Greenberg and, until late in the two men's careers, be by far the better known.

Albers' recollections of a blimpish Royal Academy seem caricatured. Another student, Hans Purrmann, remembered the school's syllabus including such admirably modern things as compulsory lessons on faux-wood finishes and marbling. Stuck insisted that students paint shadows and dark passages *lasierend durchsichtig* (with a transparent varnish), the mixing of white with other colours being restricted solely to areas of light, and then only sparingly. These ideas might have appealed to Albers; as a mature artist, his own views on varnishes and the mixing of paints certainly chimed with them. Nonetheless, it was Max Doerner and not Stuck who he recalled as his great Munich teacher, who would earn the ultimate Albers accolade, 'He was really competent.' When Albers was his student, Doerner was at work on his magisterial *The Materials of the Artist and Their Use in Painting*. The book's central thesis – that 'any artist who wants to use his materials correctly must know the laws that govern them' – would lead, one day, to the paint recipes on the backs of the *Homages to the Square*. So, too, would the standardization of industrially produced paint colours lobbied for by Munich's Gesellschaft zur Förderung rationeller Malverfahren (German Society of the Promotion of Rational Methods in Painting), of which Doerner had long been an active member and, from 1910, was president. Nietzsche and Meier-Graefe preached that 19th-century art had failed by separating itself from life. Albers felt that Stuck and his Academy carried on this fault. What he needed was somewhere that would bridge the gap, where he could be taught not art, but the techniques of making art. On 1 April 1919, just such a place had opened in the Thuringian city of Weimar.

3   A Man of Glass: Weimar

The Bauhaus derived its influence not from consensus, but from dissent.
Philipp Oswalt, Bauhaus Conflicts

In 1920, the Bauhaus was a year old. Its director, a Berlin architect called Walter Gropius (fig. 3.1), had chosen the school's name in echo of the *Bauhütte*, those lodges appended to German cathedrals where medieval craftsmen – gilders, carpenters, stonemasons – had all come together to work. To make the point, the cover of the Bauhaus prospectus bore a woodcut called *Cathedral* by Lyonel Feininger. Despite the concurrence of name and image, though, the school had, as yet, no clear idea of itself. As an experiment in self-invention, it couldn't. Like Germany, it was a place of mixed despair and wild hopes. There were, then, as many Bauhauses as *Bauhäusler* – a left-wing Bauhaus for Sparticists, an Expressionist one for Expressionists, a Bauhaus for followers of Zoroastrianism, one for Futurists. Albers, reading about it in far-off Munich, knew none of this. For him, the school's promise lay in its name.

As an indicator of modernity, 'Bauhaus' was a puzzling choice. Late 19th-century Germany had seen a rush to medievalize – to invent a pan-German Middle Ages where none had existed. This was part of a larger rewriting of history, aimed at providing the all-new German Empire with an ancient (and spurious) pre-Prussian unity. Church building found itself at the centre of this fiction. In 1880, after a 500-year gap, Cologne Cathedral had been hurriedly finished. The minster at Ulm found itself the world's tallest church, thanks to the addition of a 161-metre spire completed in the month when Josef Albers turned two. Whether Gropius's name and Feininger's print were responses to all this, one thing at least was clear. Building was to be at the heart of the Bauhaus project, all forms of art subsumed under it.

If *Gesamtkunstwerk* thinking been implicit at Stuck's Munich academy, at Gropius's it was spelled out. 'Architects, painters, sculptors, we must all return to crafts!' the prospectus proclaimed. 'There is no difference between the artist and the craftsman. *The artist is an exalted craftsman*....Let us create a *new guild of craftsmen*, without those class distinctions that build an arrogant barrier between craftsman and artist!' *Bauhäusler* were not to be students in the traditional sense, but apprentices. In old age, Albers recalled the impression the leaflet had made on him. 'A circular came into my hands, the first Bauhaus manifesto. A Feininger on the cover, a statement by Gropius on the inside: "Come back to the guild! Come back to handwork!"' Here, at last, was Lorenz Albers' life as a house painter raised to the status of art.

Albers' reading of the prospectus was to prove subjective. As he would discover, a return to craft was not necessarily the same thing as a return to hand-crafting. In December 1927, in the dog days of a new Bauhaus, Albers would write to a certain Wilhelm back home in Bottrop. His tone is apologetic. His father, Lorenz, is destitute. Could Wilhelm use his influence with the house-painters' guild to get him a rise? It must have been a bitter letter to write. All that his father had stood for, the *Handwerkerstand* virtues of skill and tradition, now counted for nothing. The world had moved on. Central to this change had been the Bauhaus itself. In 1920, the school had set itself up as the champion of *Handwerk*. By 1927, it had rejected craft utterly. Lorenz Albers' son had played a key role in this change. All this, though, was in the future. In October 1920, the Bauhaus of Gropius's proclamation might have been invented with Josef Albers in mind.

If Albers found the reality of Weimar disappointing, it is hardly surprising. The town was full of ambiguities, many of them shared by Gropius's new school. Germany's post-war National Assembly had convened in Weimar rather than Berlin to signal a break with the country's Prussian-led recent history. Weimar was the home of Nietzsche, the arch anti-historicist. But Weimar had also been chosen for the new Assembly for its links to Schiller and Goethe – a different history, but history all the same. So, too, with the Bauhaus.

For all the Nietzschean rhetoric of Gropius's proclamation, the school, like any other, turned out to be rife with hierarchies. If the title 'professor' had been jettisoned, it had been replaced by others just as divisive. The school's teachers were called Masters – *Formmeister*, masters of form, all painters, who led the school's aesthetic direction; and *Werkmeister*, masters of craft, who taught students how to make. Although supposedly equal in status, the two groups were anything but. *Werkmeister* were not admitted to the ruling Bauhaus *Meisterrat*, or school council, until 1922. To limit their possible influence, Gropius reduced the council to the status of a consultative body. Below the masters were *Jungmeister*, junior masters; below those, *Gesellen*, advanced journeymen, students of particular promise; below these again, ordinary journeymen who had passed the school's compulsory six-month *Vorkurs*; and below these, last and quite definitely least, apprentices, or *Lehrlinge*.

Over them all, in shaven head and scarlet robes of his own making, loomed the figure of Johannes Itten, a Swiss painter and *Formmeister* (fig. 3.2).

3.1 Photographer unknown, Portrait of Walter Gropius at the Weimar Bauhaus, 1921.
3.2 Paula Stockmar, Portrait of Johannes Itten in his Bauhaus garb, 1921.

In the first years of the Bauhaus, Gropius had his hands full. His infant son died; his marriage collapsed; Weimar's right-wing government tried to thwart him at every turn. While he dealt with these things, Itten had quietly taken over. By October 1920, he was running most Bauhaus workshops and was the sole teacher of its *Vorkurs*, a foundation course compulsory for every Bauhaus student. Then, too, Itten was leader of a group that embraced the beliefs and diet of a Zoroastrian sect called Mazdaznan. So powerful was this that all food in the Bauhaus canteen was prepared to its vegetarian requirements. Gropius's soon-to-be ex-wife, Alma Mahler, recalled the overriding smell of the early Bauhaus as being of garlic.

Half a century later, Albers still spoke of his *Vorkurs* master with dislike. 'He was always sounding off,' he said. 'Itten was a *Quatschkopf* (i.e. a bullshitter).' He was not the only target of Albers' sharpness. Friendships with schoolmates lasted until, one by one, they died; likewise, with Franz Perdekamp. With rare exceptions, though, Albers' Bauhaus colleagues were to be recalled critically. Paul Klee, said Albers, was 'a very nice man [who] loved to invite people home and cook eggs for them'. To this faint praise was added the unhappier view that Klee 'was not a particularly good teacher; he didn't care about his students....I didn't take Klee's course because there you just learned to make Paul Klees, and I wasn't interested. The same with Kandinsky.' Kandinsky, Albers allowed, was the one to whom he had been closest, quickly qualifying this by adding that '[the critic, Will] Grohmann said Kandinsky's squares came from me'. And yet the two men corresponded, warmly and often, from Albers' emigration to America in 1933 until war made letters impossible in 1940.

There are few records of Albers' life in Weimar, but it was of necessity lived on a shoestring. His income was made up of the difference between his schoolmaster's salary in Bottrop and the cost to the authorities there of replacing him. The sum that remained was meagre. Although he wrote to Franz Perdekamp, in March 1921, of rooming in 'a fine flat, but expensive', both adjectives were relative. He also mentioned having had to borrow money to eat. A year later, a whole letter would be spent agonizing over whether or not to buy a new pair of shoes. Possibly the flat was like fellow *Bauhäusler* Lydia Driesch-Foucar's, a mixture of grandeur and poverty – Driesch-Foucar recalled living in a neoclassical pavilion, but sleeping on a straw mattress on the floor. With no money to have coal delivered, students dragged it back to the Bauhaus from a mine. It was not the school's lack of comfort that bothered Albers, though, so much as its lack of respect.

The point of Gropius's project was to invent education afresh. All new *Bauhäusler*, no matter their age, had to start again from scratch. The weaver Gertrud Arndt recalled being treated as 'a zero' when she came to Weimar. She saw this as positive – 'It's what we needed.' Arndt was nineteen at the time. The Hungarian Marcel Breuer, a year younger than Arndt, arrived at the Bauhaus to find a note with his name on it pinned to a classroom door. A fellow student explained that it directed him to sweep the floor; Breuer, who spoke poor German, looked puzzled. The stranger wordlessly handed him a broom: it was Josef Albers. Albers was thirty-two: sweeping floors must have rankled. Worse, he was six months older than Johannes Itten, who was not just a master but the head of the *Vorkurs*. Albers, in old age, would repeat the story of their meeting again and again:

> So I went [to Weimar] and submitted to Itten, who was not much but somewhat younger, a few months. And then I wanted to go to the glass workshop, [which] was practically abandoned. I was the only one who wanted to go there, and I was told, no, you can't go there, it was so valuable material. And it was Itten's theory that I had no [knowledge of] colour. And I was told, if I wanted to go into glass painting, I had first to go into wall painting....

Puzzlingly, Albers' name is not on the register of the wall-painting workshop – broadly, a department of interior design – although it is on all the lists for the cabinetmaking workshop from 1920 until the Bauhaus left Weimar in 1925. He is there first as a student and then a 'visiting guest'. His earliest Bauhaus works, though, came from neither of these shops, nor from a shop at all. Early in 1921, Albers began to pick over the rubbish dumps of Weimar, hammer in hand, for fragments of broken glass. These he turned into so-called 'shard paintings', or *Glasbilder*. Five would accompany him to Dessau, Berlin, and in 1933, to America (fig. 3.3).

Albers would later maintain that Itten had insisted he attend the wall-painting workshop 'certainly to delay my study in glass'. Although the shard works were made to thwart this, they do resemble other student work from Itten's *matière* exercises. What sets Albers' *Glasbilder* apart is their professionalism. A contemporary recalled the *matière* classes: 'We made wood sculptures, we sawed the wood neatly, we sanded it, we put it together, sometimes we stuck a piece of glass or metal on it. But we were always aware

3.3 *Park*, *ca*. 1923–4. Glass, partly painted, set in lead and framed in black wood. 19½ × 15 in.

that it was senseless play, that it was nonsense.' Albers had not come to the Bauhaus to play. He had come to work in glass; it would dominate his fine-art practice for the next thirteen years. The shard paintings pick up on found ideas as well as found objects, examining, assimilating and rejecting the various art movements fighting it out in Weimar in the early twenties. The text in *Window Picture* hints at the *papier collé* of the Cubists, the goggle-eyes of *Figure* at Dada (figs 3.4, 3.5). The later Weimar glassworks pick up on the modernist grid, extrapolating an entire system of visual composition from the wire mesh of reinforced glass.

It is tempting to see this shift in Albers' work biographically. Works such as *Rhinish Legend* mark the end of a time that had begun with Paul Albers' death in 1915 and progressed, via the clinic at Hohenhonnef, to *Rosa Mystica*. Albers' interest then had been in chaos: *Grid Mounted*'s concern, by contrast, is with the rhythm of order (fig. 3.6). The wire reinforcement in the work's glass becomes its compositional key. Its gridded mount is off-the-peg steel mesh – Albers knew how to lead stained glass, but had chosen instead to use the industrial soldering he had learned at a local electrical hardware company, Elektroinstallation Oberweimar. By *Grid Mounted*, his interest was in rescue, the making of art from non-art materials.

This, too, placed him at an advantage in Weimar. Other *Bauhäusler* were appalled by the school's chronic lack of materials. Gertrud Arndt recalled asking for paper on her first day, to receive the frosty reply, 'We don't *have* paper at the Bauhaus.' Making something from nothing was, and would remain, central to Josef Albers' practice, a skill learned at his father's knee. It quickly won him recognition. In March 1921, *Meisterrat* members visited the small end-of-semester show of student work in the gallery in Henry van de Velde's main Bauhaus building. Few works caught their eye. One was a glass painting by Albers. On the strength of it, the masters voted to 'take [him] on permanently'.

If Albers made any prints between *Mein Freund Perdekamp* (1917) and *Schwarzer Kreis* (1933), they are lost. Given that he preserved so many of his pre-Bauhaus prints, it is must be assumed that they never existed. So, too, with oil paintings. Bar one known drawing, his entire fine art output at the Bauhaus was to be in glass. 'It was my dream,' he said. Links to Thorn Prikker apart, the

3.4 *Fensterbild (Window Picture)*, 1921. Glass assemblage mounted on wood, 19½ × 17½ in.

3.5 *Figure*, 1921. Glass, brass and wood particle board, 28 × 23⅘ × 2 in.

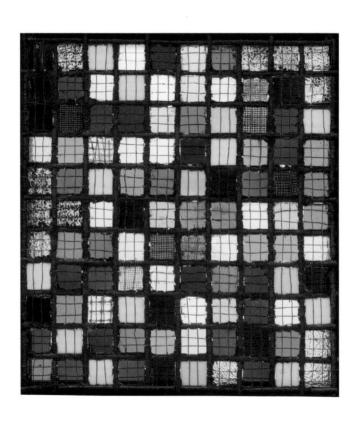

3.6 *Gitterbild (Grid Mounted)*, *ca.* 1921–2. Glass assemblage, 12¾ × 11²⁄₅ in.

material had another attraction: it was unpopular. The *Glasmalereiwerkstatt*, or glass studio, was the school's smallest. In 1919, it had had just one apprentice, Werner Gilles; Gilles soon left. Only in September 1920, three weeks before Albers' arrival, had the workshop been officially incorporated. It was given rooms in a lodge at the entrance to the Park an der Ilm – Albers recalled it having 'windows on all four sides, all a craftsman in glass needs' (fig. 3.7). The accompanying Curriculum for the Craft Training of Glass Painters listed five skills to be taught in this lodge, dubbed Workshop Seven: a) knowledge of materials and glass paints; b) stencil-cutting; c) glass working; d) the firing of glass in a kiln; and e) lead assembling. Not a single *Bauhäusler* signed up.

This was not altogether surprising. Of the disciplines taught at the Bauhaus, stained glass was the least forgiving of inexperience. The weaver Gunta Stölzl was typical in rejecting it as 'too ambitious'. Stained glass, she said, was 'an elevated field with no middle level at all, not simply a craft but rather a kind of painting'. If Albers was to make his mark, then Workshop Seven was the place to do it. He was accepted as a student there in March 1921, with Itten as his master of form and a commercial stained-glass maker, Ernst Kraus, as master of craft. Relics of the *Glasmalereiwerkstatt* are rare – a half-moon-shaped window by Johannes Driesch, three crayon studies by the

3.7 Photographer unknown, Glassmaking workshop at the Bauhaus Weimar, with glassworks by Josef Albers and others, 1923.
3.8 Photographer unknown, Josef Albers in a doorway with other Bauhaus members including Oskar and Tut Schlemmer and Gunta Stölzl.

cradle-maker Peter Keler. All extant glass works from Weimar are by Josef Albers. Many others of his pieces are lost, among them the window known simply by the descriptive name *buntes Fenster* (coloured window) (fig. 3.9). Usually dated 1923 and later destroyed, this window lived out its short life in a small room next to Gropius's director's office. This room would be a centrepiece of the 1923 Bauhaus Exhibition, its decor proof of the school's *Gesamtkunstwerk* credentials. Albers' window was not made in 1923, though, but in, or possibly before, 1922. When the Bauhaus Exhibition opened that August, it had been *in situ* for a year or more.

In 1921, before his fall from grace, Johannes Itten had been commissioned to decorate the space as a reading room. Surprisingly, given his Expressionist leanings, the modules he chose for this programme were the 'square and cube'. There were double doors by Heinrich Konrad; a handle with peculiarly sharp edges by Naum Slutzky; a carpet by Ida Kerkovius. These are listed in a letter from Oskar Schlemmer to the Swiss artist Otto Meyer-Amden, written soon after Itten's departure from Weimar in March 1923:

> What Itten leaves behind...is a space, made with pupils – a curiosity, a failed experiment. Complex sculptures fill that space, unhygienic dust collectors....A carpet so vividly black and white that it could not be walked on and had to be hung on the wall. A doorknob that bloodied more fingers than it opened doors.

And there was a window – 'A glass window [that] lets dark pink light into what is supposed to be a reading room, in which one literally cannot read, unless the window is open.' This was Albers' lost work.

No record of the reading room now exists. Itten resigned as master of the *Glasmalereiwerkstatt* on 1 February 1922; mastership of the workshop went to Oskar Schlemmer, with his older brother Carl as master of craft. The window presumably predates these appointments: the Schlemmers are hardly likely to have overseen the making of a work which, the following year, they would cite as proof of Itten's failure. The window's chequerboard pane is *gold rosa* – glass flashed with gilt. In post-war Germany this was hard to come by, and expensive. Albers recalled travelling to the glass town of Zwiesel to find it:

3.9 *Buntes Fenster/Rot und Weiß, ca.* 1922 (destroyed; replica, 2008). Coloured glass set in lead.

I was asked to get material, and I went to Bavaria, where they make materials, this antique glass, so called, in the old fashion where the glass was never even, always thicker and thinner. And I said, I want to open a glass workshop, and they were so very noble – they took me up in the attic and said, 'Select what you want.' And I found very valuable glass not even made any more, that is called 'gold rosa' – that is a pink flashed glass what is made with gold directly.

In that year, as we shall see, there had been much to occupy him.

Mention of the Weimar window is first made not by Oskar Schlemmer but Gottfried Heinersdorff, who had overseen the making of *Rosa Mystica* in 1918. In April 1921, when Albers had been a student in the *Glasmalereiwerkstatt* for barely a month, he had written to Heinersdorff to ask for offcuts of glass. The older man's reply is courteous, if exasperated:

> Your request is not as easy as you might think. Our warehouse contains more than 1,000 colours. Producing sample pieces, even were we to choose only the most important, would be very costly indeed, given today's high wages and material costs. The other method you suggest, collecting scrap pieces, is impractical because, depending on what is being cut at the moment, the combinations you receive would be random and meagre, doing more harm to you than good.

Albers was not easily put off. Later in 1922, he invites Heinersdorff to Weimar, returning the visit soon after. Back in Berlin, the master glass-maker submits notes of their meetings to the Puhl & Wagner archive. They are worth quoting in full:

> Re. Albers
> On February 19th of this year, following a telephone call, we received a visit from the painter Albers. In the year 1919 [*sic*], we realized a window, Rosa Mystica, based on his design, for the church in Bottrop.
> It so happens that Albers was the student-designer of the grand glass window I recently saw at the Bauhaus in Weimar. He came to

us with a request for our help in obtaining spare pieces for the work, which was damaged during transport. I agreed in principle, but it later turned out that only a few shards of the pink-gold glass that Albers had so abundantly used were missing, and that we had none in stock.

I was very frank with Albers and told him that I considered his work bad dilettantism. He turns out to be a 'guileless fool', a dyed-in-the-wool idealist. He is completely in thrall to Gropius and the Bauhaus, the only path to salvation for German culture....He places no value on material things, and proudly reports that his living expenses from Christmas to the present came to no more than 4,000 marks. I could only assure him that I was able to tell as much just by looking at him.

Any agreement with him on matters of principle was of course absolutely impossible. I submit this report to the archives only because in the end I told him that we would possibly be willing to take him on for some time, in order to provide him with the opportunity to create other things like that glass work of his that I saw in Weimar, and that actually do open up new, interesting and worthwhile possibilities and paths.

Although Heinersdorff had spotted the originality of the anteroom window, he missed its political explosiveness. In the month of Albers' first letter to Puhl & Wagner, Theo van Doesburg, co-founder of De Stijl, had turned up in Weimar, angling for a job at the Bauhaus. His radicalism scared Gropius, the more so when, rejected, the Dutchman opened what was in effect a competing academy to the Bauhaus a few hundred metres away.

Prominent *Bauhäusler* – among them Peter Keler, Marcel Breuer and Karl Peter Röhl, designer of the Bauhaus seal – quickly signed up to Van Doesburg's Wednesday evening lectures. Two hours long, these were held at Röhl's studio, repainted in De Stijl-ish white for the occasion. Soon, twenty-five students were on his list – a worrying figure, given that numbers at the Bauhaus were going down: from a peak of a hundred and fifty in 1921, they would fall, by 1924, to eighty-seven. One *Bauhäusler* recalled the excitement of Van Doesburg's atelier: 'Anything important and progressive, any new ideas from Holland, France, Italy, America or Russia, could be found there,' he said. The Bauhaus, cash-strapped, could not hope to compete. The school seemed parochial by contrast, old-fashioned. Van Doesburg's rhetoric grew more vicious the longer he was denied a place there, his particular venom being directed at Itten. Doesburgian students soon set themselves up in a breakaway group, called first Weimar-Stijl and then KURI. Röhl, a member of both, drew a cartoon showing Itten as a long-haired oddity clutching a thistle. Next to him was the modishly squared-off figure of Van Doesburg. The cartoon's legend read *Confrontation of Natural and Mechanical Man in Weimar, 1922*.

Van Doesburg's easy success was understandable. The first – as yet, the only – exhibition of Bauhaus work, in June 1919, had been a disaster. Gropius had shelved the idea of another indefinitely. Although his proclamation in the Bauhaus prospectus had specifically favoured building over painting, his most notable appointments to the school had been of Wassily Kandinsky and Paul Klee (figs 3.10, 3.11). Both were painters. In 1921, the Bauhaus could point to nothing in the way of *Bau*, far less to a coherent aesthetic philosophy. De Stijl, worryingly, offered students both. Like Gropius, Van Doesburg was wedded to building. Unlike Gropius, he had a number of commissions under his belt, Henri Berssenbrugge's Rotterdam studio being merely the last and most famous. The Dutchman mocked his German rival's *Bauhütte* leanings. 'It is wrong to think that the medieval craftsman's love of materials would be lost in mechanical production,' he purred. 'In mechanical production, the spiritual intention of the designer is so bound up with materials that their spirit is realized purely. That is the essence of all art – that it reveals the spirit and not the hand, the spirit's mere primitive tool.'

A month after his arrival, Van Doesburg could claim, not entirely unjustly, to have 'turned everything in Weimar on its head'. 'Each evening,' he crowed to a friend, 'I speak to students, and spread the poison of the new spirit.' By September, the victory of De Stijl was a *fait accompli*. 'What the Bauhaus in Weimar, with its internal factions, could not achieve in four years,' Van Doesburg wrote, 'De Stijl has managed in eight months. Because here was a method drawn directly from life.' Students agreed. 'We wanted [Van Doesburg] either to run a proper Architectural Department under Gropius', recalled one, 'or to replace him.' Most dangerously, De Stijl had laid claim to the square. 'What the Cross was to early Christians, the square is to us,' Van Doesburg said. As Josef Albers was himself to discover, it was the ideal form for visual experiment. It was also a summing-up in graphic form of everything the early Bauhaus was not.

3.10. *Kandinsky, Spring 1929, the teacher on the terrace with Hannes Meyer, May '30*, 1929–30.
Gelatin silver prints mounted on cardboard, 11⅗ × 16⅛ in.
3.11 *Klee in the Studio, Dessau XI 29*, 1929. Gelatin silver prints mounted on cardboard, 11⅗ × 16⅛ in.

In his magazine, *Mécano*, Van Doesburg returned, viperishly, to the fray. The so-called White Issue included a 'Bauhaus Balance Sheet', its results weighted heavily in De Stijl's favour. The Bauhaus, said the sheet, remained 'square on the outside, but Biedermeyer on the inside'. Repeating a claim made in one of Van Doesburg's lectures, the legend below read, 'Many now use the cube [*Kubus*], but few understand it.' A few students found the arrogance of this claim laughable. On the day after the lecture, some waggish *Bauhäusler* scrawled on a lavatory wall, 'Many use the *Lokus* [lav], but few understand it.' Even so, the Bauhaus was a school under siege. As Oskar Schlemmer remarked, "The Bauhaus lends itself readily to [Van Doesburg]'s rejection of it, and its masters. So far, I have been the one of whom he was most likely to approve, even though I "still" use "soft" forms.'

Itten's choice of the un-soft square and cube for his reading room's decor was a response to Van Doesburg: the Dutchman's *Kubus* jibe had been made with Itten in mind. But what of Albers' window? To make this question more complex, the work is not one window but two, or rather one window of two different halves. The colour illustration in *Staatliches Bauhaus in Weimar 1919–1923*, catalogue of the Bauhaus Exhibition and the first book produced by the school, shows a square window with panes of monochrome glass and several of flashed glass – Albers' first use of a material that would later free him from the constraints of leaded stained glass. But there is a second *Vorraum* window, below the first and half its size, known only from a photograph by Lucia Moholy-Nagy (fig. 3.12). The bottom of the first window is just visible above it; the striking thing about the second is how much more modern it looks. Its panes are larger, their disposition more open. From the flashes of overexposure on Moholy-Nagy's photo, some were of white or clear glass.

How did this mismatch come about? The lower part of the Weimar window is the replacement of an older window, the substitution dealing with both Schlemmer's complaint of lack of light and the breakage recorded in Heinersdorff's archive entry. The stylistically hybrid upper part of the window has been put together from the sample pieces Albers was given in Bavaria. It is noticeably like Peter Keler's window-sketch, mentioned above: both Keler's drawing and Alber's first window had been made between the arrival of Van Doesburg in Weimar and Itten's departure. Keler's 1922 painting *De Stijl 1* has strong echoes of Van Doesburg's *Composition XVIII in Three Parts* (1920). So, too, does Albers' second, lower window. Both men are experimenting with De Stijl at the same time. Unlike Keler, Albers' name does not appear on the

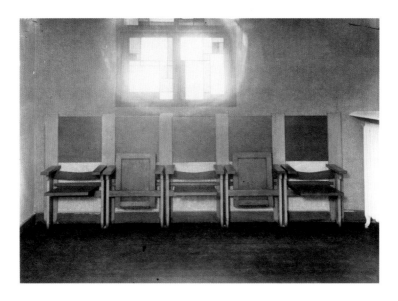

3.12 Lucia Moholy/Atelier Eckner, Vestibule of the director's office, Bauhaus Weimar: folding chairs and glass window, *ca.* 1924.

list of Van Doesburg's lecture-goers. For all that, he not only knew the De Stijl master's work but was excited by it. Typically, he would later deny this. More, he insisted that Van Doesburg had played no part in the transformation of the Bauhaus from a vaguely Expressionist *Kunstgewerbeschule* to the rationalist, industrial-led school it was to become. Van Doesburg, he said, had 'opened a shop across the street. Wanted to set himself up as the anti-Christ. We had right away a clash....That cruel insistence on just straight lines and right angles. For me it was just mechanical decoration. So we came apart – no, better – we never joined.'

In another interview, he would put it differently:

> I knew Van Doesburg personally. But I do not consider him very important. He thought he had invented everything when in fact he had invented very little. He taught in Weimar; I never went to his studio, but I knew his work. Yes, he was doing glass paintings at the same time as I was.

This version of history is matched by that of only one other major figure at the Bauhaus, and that is its director. Gropius, too, was later to downplay the threat De Stijl had posed. 'We were all interested in Van Doesburg's philosophy,' he would later concede, 'but his influence was temporary and has been exaggerated.' This is not borne out by the Bauhaus's sudden *volte-face* in the months after Van Doesburg's arrival, announced by Gropius in words that echo the Dutchman's verbatim. 'It was necessary to revive sound handwork...to give young people an understanding of the entire process of creative activity,' the director wrote to his masters. 'But a rejection of the machine and industry is by no means involved in this.'

A year earlier, Josef Albers had written to Franz Perdekamp from Weimar. He has been to Pirna, Hannover, Bamberg, Regensburg and Zwiesel, where he found the glass for the Weimar window. He stayed en route with Gunta Stölzl, summering at her parents' country house, eating cheese and apples and drinking cream and wine. He 'had a wonderful time with a good peasant woman'. He had also been entrusted with a budget of 20,000 marks for buying glass. German hyperinflation began in August 1921; a year later, the mark's value had fallen 8,000 per cent. Banknotes designed by another Bauhaus student, Herbert Bayer, would soon be printed in denominations of millions of marks. Albers' letter must date from the summer of 1921, when 20,000 marks was still a handy sum. That Gropius should have entrusted him with this when *Bauhäusler* were fetching their own coal and sleeping on straw palliasses says much for his early recognition of Albers' abilities. In 1923, with Itten gone, the schoolteacher from Bottrop would briefly become Gropius's right-hand man.

In part, the Weimar anteroom window explains why. By 1922, the school was split between those who loved Van Doesburg and those who hated him. The threat of the first group was clear. But to reject De Stijl was to embrace Itten, as a number of the masters, notably Lyonel Feininger, privately did. And Gropius himself had lost his way. His Fagus factory had been a masterpiece – a glass-walled structure which Pevsner claimed as the first in Germany to have 'feeling for the pure cube'. But this had been finished in 1913. Post-war, Gropius's style had gone into reverse. Both of the commissions on which he employed *Bauhäusler* – the Sommerfeld (1920–1) and Otte (1921–2) Houses – were in an old-fashioned, Itten-ish expressionist style; likewise the windows Albers made for them (figs 3.13, 3.14). Although he was later to deny it, Gropius knew that Van Doesburg was right: the Bauhaus had to rid itself of Expressionism. His Dutch nemesis, perversely, was his saving. 'The [school's] change of direction was a change in the founder, a recovery

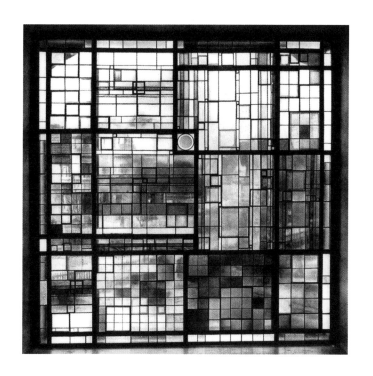

3.13 Window at the Otte House, Berlin, 1922 (lost).
3.14 Windows at the Sommerfeld House, Berlin, 1920–1.

by him of his senses,' one *Bauhäusler* noted. 'In 1922, Gropius found his old, straight road again.' Yet employing the Dutchman would have been fatal to him. What Gropius needed were allies who were both anti-Itten and anti-Van Doesburg, who could replace them both. As the two halves of the anteroom window showed, one of those men was Josef Albers.

That Albers would later deny Van Doesburg's influence is both typical and odd. It is also understandable. Although there was little warmth between him and Gropius, the two men would back each other professionally until the director's death in 1969. In 1922, Gropius was under attack from all sides. Itten, ordered to hand over a number of workshops on 1 February, had continued in private to dominate them. Meanwhile, Carl Schlemmer and Josef Zachmann, masters of craft in the glass-painting and cabinetmaking workshops, had started a whispering campaign against Gropius. This ended in a case being brought before the *Meisterrat*. Among charges levelled at the director were that he had slept with a Fräulein Dörte Helm – a student – and a typist whose name his accusers had forgotten. 'Even apprentices and journeymen, such as Albers, are said to have spoken negatively about Mr Gropius' morality,' Zachmann blustered, citing a remark he had heard Albers make at a party – 'That damned, etc.' Itten, always loath to pass up a chance to undermine Gropius, mourned the Bauhaus's lack of moral leadership. It was left to Albers to come to the director's rescue.

Cited as a witness for the prosecution, he furiously denied the comments Zachmann claimed to have heard him making: Zachmann, he said, was 'sick'. So, too, the remarks alleged by Carl Schlemmer. The minutes of the inquiry record the exchange:

> As to Schlemmer's question, whether [Albers] had not made a similar remark to him more than a year ago about Fräulein Hirschfeld, [Albers] denies it. He can no longer remember what he said word for word. But he considers it impossible, considering his kindly feelings towards Fräulein Hirschfeld at the time.

Albers, apprenticed in both enemy workshops, showed himself the friend of neither. Loyalty to his father was now transferred to Walter Gropius; Gropius was not long in repaying it. When, thanks to Albers' testimony, the inquiry found in the director's favour at Christmas 1922, Zachmann and Carl Schlemmer were instantly dismissed. Albers was given the latter's job in the

Glasmalereiwerkstatt, with Paul Klee as his master of form. Klee, he later said, left him to work on his own. Six months afterwards, Albers would receive the most important cabinetmaking commission then given to a Bauhaus student. The furniture that came from the commission would prove two things: that Itten's day at the Bauhaus was over, and that the school could out-Doesburg Van Doesburg.

On 18 May 1923, Albers received a brisk note from Walter Gropius's new secretary: 'Since Mr Itten cannot return to Weimar in time, the exhibition commission for the antechamber passes to you. Weidler.' Outmanoeuvred by Gropius, Itten had finally left the school six weeks earlier. The situation, nonetheless, remained urgent. The problem of Van Doesburg aside, the government of Thuringia was agitating to have the Bauhaus closed down. Among other complaints were that its students were overwhelmingly 'cosmopolitan' – code for Jewish – and had been seen swimming naked in the Ilm, both sexes together. Aware that a lack of funds had prevented *Bauhäusler* from making work, the government demanded an exhibition of it as soon as possible. There was nothing else for it. In April 1922, Albers and others – Marcel Breuer, Ludwig Hirschfeld-Mack, Kurt Schmidt – had written to Gropius, objecting to the idea of a show. 'The number of works that can claim to be "Bauhaus" is far too small,' they complained. 'A premature exhibition would blur our image.' Now, their objections were overruled. The *Meisterrat* scheduled a show for the following summer. The survival of the Bauhaus would depend on it.

For Gropius, this threat was also an opportunity: having got rid of Itten, he could now rid himself of Van Doesburg. Gropius's work had assimilated much of the Dutchman's style: with Adolf Meyer, his collaborator on the Fagus factory, he now submitted a competition entry for a new Tribune Building in Chicago. The insistent verticality of this is strongly suggestive of the models which Doesburg, in 1922, was making in Weimar with Cornelis van Eesteren, a fellow-Dutchman. From these would come the drawings known as *Space-Time Constructions*. Albers was later vaguely to recall that 'Van Doesburg [had been] doing architectural designs with Van Eesteren.' That he was fully aware of these designs is clear from the furniture he made for Itten's reading room. Two years later, in Dessau, Gerhard Richter was apprenticed in the carpentry workshop. 'I had in mind to study with [Marcel]

Breuer [but] I was not so lucky,' he recalled. 'Breuer went from wood to bent metal. That was my first day, so I had another teacher. He was good too, but he didn't know much about woodworking. What was his name? Josef Albers.' Richter was a qualified cabinetmaker, a *Gesellentischler*. He had no animus against Albers. If anything, his recollections of the *Vorkurs* teacher are obsequious. That Albers was no carpenter makes his work for the new *Vorraum* all the more extraordinary.

The Bauhaus exhibition was to begin on 15 August. Albers had less than three months to reform what was intended to be one of the most visible spaces in the show, to de-Ittenise it and make it his own. The reading room was now reinvented as an anteroom to Gropius's office. Everything that could be prised from it was removed. Only Konrad's door and Slutzky's door handle were left where they were: there was no time to remake them. The whole school was caught up in preparations for the exhibition. It was every man for himself. For the *Vorraum*, Albers would make a conference table, a bookcase, a display cabinet and the folding stools, *Kirchenstühle*, that appear in the photograph which includes his lost window (fig 3.12).

The influence of De Stijl on these objects is clear. Van Doesburg's *Space-Time Constructions* had played off the vertical against the cantilevered horizontal: Albers' furniture makes these drawings concrete. The lack of sides to his bookcase leaves its shelves appearing to hang in space (fig. 3.17). So, too, the glass show case which, fixed to the wall behind, seems to stand unsupported. The cabinet's use of three kinds of glass – clear, mirrored and opaque – makes it visually ambiguous. As one critic put it, Albers' glass is 'noticeable, but not quite visible'. In the same way, the counterpoised light and dark oak of his table's vertical and horizontal planes give the latter the appearance of floating. And yet Albers' handling of materials is the opposite of complex. Cutting and planing apart, his planks are left untouched. Boards are insistently boards: this is woodwork about wood, not work. Although it was Marcel Breuer's furniture for the Haus am Horn that would grab the headlines at the Bauhaus Exhibition, Albers' work for the *Vorraum* was the more radical.

While the original *Formmeister*, painters to a man, railed against Gropius's new turn against *Handwerk*, Albers had shown himself its adept. There was a problem, though. In the many reviews of the 1923 exhibition, his glass was mentioned just once, and then under someone else's name. *Das Werk* in Zurich noted, in passing, 'the luminosity of the stained-glass

3.15 Row of five folding chairs, 1923 (facsimile by Justus Binroth, 2009), 48²⁄₅ × 135⁴⁄₅ × 23³⁄₅ in.
3.16 Bookshelf/magazine stand, 1923 (facsimile by Rubert Deese, 1999). Baltic birch, 57¹⁄₈ × 68¹⁄₄ × 11²⁄₅ in.

windows', adding that 'Klee [was] the master responsible.' Klee, Kandinsky, Feininger, Itten (who had already left the Bauhaus) and Schlemmer were all singled out for praise, as were students such as Marcel Breuer and Ludwig Hirschfeld-Mack. Albers was not mentioned at all. The problem was clear. Gropius had used the exhibition to declare a new dispensation at the Bauhaus. Under the slogan 'Art and Technology – a New Unity!', he had called for an end to craft. From now on, the school's focus would be on what might broadly be called industrial design. Actually, there was, and would always be, a confusion at the Bauhaus between an industrial aesthetic and industrial production. Wagenfeld's famous lamps might be described as '*industrialisiert*' – industrialized – but the metal workshop had turned out each of them, slowly and expensively, by hand. For all that they looked machine-made, they were *kunstgewerblich* – arts and crafts – and priced accordingly. Nonetheless, critics understood Gropius's embracing of industrial production and approved of it. They were not going to waste time on a hand-made thing like the *Vorraum* window.

By the early 1920s, glass was the modernist material *par excellence*. Paul Scheerbart, an apostle of the Glass Pavilion architect, Bruno Taut, was not alone in prophesying that it would 'shed new light over the entire world'. As Albers recognized, it was his window's technique, not its medium, that had been wrong. 'Stained glass was the old method,' he said. 'I wanted to make something in one piece.' To be modern would mean using machinery. After the arrival of László Moholy-Nagy at the Bauhaus, it would also entail delegating the actual making of works to someone else. Moholy's ideology was the opposite of Itten's. That, for Gropius, was his point. Itten was subjective, Moholy ostentatiously not so. His *Telefonbilder* (Telephone Pictures) were shown at Herwarth's Sturm (Storm) gallery in 1922. Their enamel panels had been manufactured by a commercial sign-making factory: Moholy claimed to have placed the order for them by telephone, giving instructions with a piece of graph paper in one hand and an industrial colour chart in the other. Individual *Telephone Paintings* were titled not with words but with letters and numbers, like a factory production code. They were the very opposite of *Handwerk*. Albers would find his own *unhandwerklich* aesthetic in the sand-blasting of glass, in works that had an industrial look even if they had been designed, and mostly made, by hand. It is possible that he began experimenting with the process in Weimar, although his great sand-blasted works would be made by Puhl & Wagner in Berlin, while he was in Dessau.

For the months the Bauhaus had left in the small town by the Ilm, though, he would have little time for art-making.

The threat of Van Doesburg aside, Gropius's shift to industrial production had been meant to get *Bauhäusler* earning. At a *Meisterrat* meeting in May 1923, he had asked for suggestions for saleable objects that *Vorkurs* students might usefully make. Kandinsky hazarded 'geometric shapes in clay and wood', Christian Dell 'ashtrays, napkin rings, cigarette cases'. Albers, pragmatically, proffered 'building blocks'. The minutes list him as a journeyman; that his suggestions were canvassed at all is noteworthy. So, too, Gropius's response to them. 'Albers will be in charge,' the director pronounced. 'Albers will have overall supervision, [since] he possesses the technical and pedagogical abilities.' A year earlier, still just an apprentice, Albers had been appointed – with Klee, Lothar Schreyer and other masters – to the board of the Bauhaus *Siedlung* (settlement), set up with the aim of getting students to build. The Haus am Horn was to be its principal flowering. Shortly afterwards, he was told to devise what was in effect an extra *Vorkurs*, dubbed 'Studies in Materials', in anticipation of Itten's departure. Albers recalled his director's order to do this: 'Gropius called the students present and me, and said me that I was going to teach a work class in the *Reithaus* in the park.' He protested that he wanted to put teaching behind him, that he wanted to get on with his art; Gropius put his arm on Albers' shoulder, said, 'You're the man to do it,' and walked away. Gropius, for his part, recalled merely that 'Albers took charge of the studies in materials,' adding that he 'continued this work even when László Moholy-Nagy was called to the Bauhaus.'

Although written fifteen years after the event, Gropius's recollections retain something of his tone. It was natural that Moholy-Nagy should come to the Bauhaus – he had international connections, links to the Constructivists. Gropius had seen his work in Berlin and been impressed by it. And Moholy-Nagy, like him, had been to a *gymnasium* and a university. He was from the officer class: when he came to the Bauhaus, it was as an officer. Moholy was straightaway made a full master and given charge of the *Vorkurs*. As Herbert Bayer recalled, 'Moholy came in this way and sort of pushed Albers aside. And Albers was just a person to whom you couldn't do that.' Albers, who had reinvented the course, was now to be Moholy's assistant on it. That he had been allowed to go on teaching 'even' after the Hungarian's arrival clearly struck Gropius as admirably democratic; actually, Albers had taught the *Vorkurs* alone from March to October 1923. For all that, it was not until 1925 that he would be asked to join the *Meisterrat*, and then as a *Jungmeister*, a Young Master. He was thirty-seven years old. Moholy-Nagy, in his third year as a full master, was then just turning thirty.

It would have taken a saint not to be stung by this, and Albers was not saintly. He would resent Moholy-Nagy for the rest of his life. Thirty years later and a professor at Yale, he would confide to a student that he had never been taken seriously at the Bauhaus because Gropius could not get beyond thinking of him as a student. Ungrammatical with rage, he would snap at an interviewer who made the mistake of comparing his work to his hated ex-colleague's:

> When you relate me to Moholy, that is impossible! – I hate that man so much, I never tried to do anything that he has done....I would hang myself before to imitate something what Moholy did.

The tape picks up the sound of him banging the table. In old age, Albers would accuse Moholy-Nagy of having stolen his ideas – indeed, of having stolen the Bauhaus. We will come back to this later. As to Gropius, he had pilfered his phrase 'Search versus research' for the title of a book. Asked whether it was Gropius who had described him as a frustrated architect, Albers sniffed, 'Gropius was not so witty.'

In mitigation, it must be remembered that Albers was officially still a schoolmaster, and drawing a schoolmaster's salary. He had presented his request for leave from Bottrop as a temporary measure, although with no thought of returning. In January 1924, the authorities smelled a rat. He was ordered home, to teach a semester in his old school, the Josefschule, or lose his salary. Pleading letters from Gropius cut no ice; only when he wrote, in September 1924, that Albers was 'irreplaceable to our institution and its development' did the school board finally relent. Albers was to be away from Weimar for nine vital months, the last time he would live in Bottrop. Opportunities for creativity there were few. In July, he designed the programme for a festival of *Sport und Spiel* held to inaugurate Bottrop's new stadium. If the city fathers could swallow Bauhaus style on the cover of a brochure, though, Albers' proposal for a new town seal (fig. 3.17) was more than *bürgerlich* flesh and blood could stand. The design was turned down flat.

From the outset, Gropius had planned for his ally's return. A *Meisterrat* meeting on 24 April decreed, 'From 1 October [the date of Albers' arrival], the preliminary course will last two semesters instead of one, with work in the workshops beginning at the end of the first semester...so that the apprentices do not lose their practical skills.' Gropius clearly imagined Albers' teaching would be craft-based, although, as it turned out, the opposite was true. As Albers would later gleefully recall, 'In return for the surprise Gropius gave me with his appointment to teach craft, I surprised him, after the first semester, by changing the subject of my course from "Principles of Craft" to "Principles of Design".' It was a change in more than just name. Before October 1924, materials at the Bauhaus, as at any other art school, had been secondary to their intended use – wood as a constituent of carpentry, glass of stained glass. Now they would be the starting point. One *Bauhäusler* remembered being 'swept away' by the radicalism of this new approach. Albers began his *Vorkurs*, she said, by asking students to bring to class anything that caught their eye – 'a bit of wire or soil, a piece of cardboard, whatever.' The rules were few. One was that there should be no waste. This new direction might have marked the end of Lorenz Albers' way of life, but Josef Albers was still his son. Another *Vorkurs* requirement was that materials should be used on their own, paper standing up because it had been folded or pleated, not glued.

Materials were now central to Albers' lessons, and the notion of the student went through a parallel transformation. The *neue Pädagogik* had stressed learning *vom Kinde aus*, from the child outwards. The problem with

3.17 Coat of Arms for the City of Bottrop, 1924. Gouache on cardboard.

this, when applied to adults, was that it might lead to what Gropius called 'vanity'. The only alternative was for the teacher to be vain. This was Albers' overriding complaint about Itten. 'We had nothing in common,' he said. 'I opposed that sentimental self-expression business – [Itten] himself was the only measure saying good or not good. Therefore there are many Ittens later. There are no Albers.' Self-expression – 'vomit with the elbows' – had been key to Expressionism. Now students would learn the opposite. This did not mean that Albers' lessons were restrictive. As one *Bauhäusler* recalled, 'It was only in [his] *Vorkurs* that [students] were free to express themselves.' As the semester progressed, so did the range of materials used. A Dutch student solemnly listed the types of paper with which Albers had had him experiment: blotting paper, cardboard, *Steinpapier*, cigarette papers, writing paper, banknote paper, tracing paper, parchment, blueprint paper, embossed cardboard, wrapping paper, photographic paper, white chocolate wrappers, *papier maché*. The archive of exercises starts sedately enough with the cut-out word *Zwangsversteigerung* (foreclosure) glued repeatedly across a page of newspaper small ads – a process Albers called 're-ordering'. They end with the collage of a baby making a speech from a podium.

If this last suggests the zaniness of Dada, Albers himself was no more a Dadaist than he was an Expressionist. Nor, for all his focus on what he called 'constructional thinking', was he ever a Constructivist. As with his art, he would maintain that his pedagogy owed nothing to any person or movement. In fact, his *matière* lessons were not entirely unlike Itten's: both men had been *neue Pädagogik* schoolteachers. The emphasis in Albers' lessons on building upwards – folded-paper skyscrapers, pleated domes (see p. 174) – owed something both to Doesburg and to Moholy's studies in equilibrium. But his exploration of the 'inner energies' of materials went far further than Moholy's, and was shaped to a different end. Where constructivism aimed at art with an industrial appearance, Albers' interest lay in something far deeper.

He was insistent that teachers, like their students, should learn. As he moved on to Dessau, Berlin, Black Mountain and Yale, so his own pedagogy built on itself. At the Bauhaus, he taught more than anyone else – twenty hours a week to Moholy's eight, Klee's five and Kandinsky's three. Even so, it was Moholy who grabbed the headlines. As a student of both men recalled, 'Albers never communicated the results of his *Vorkurs* to the public. Moholy was a dazzling personality, hungry for publicity. His *Vorkurs* consisted primarily of brilliant lectures followed by discussion periods. Practice of course also played a role, but it was relegated to the background.' It would take two decades and a move to America for Albers' genius as a teacher to be recognized. 'What has made the Bauhaus famous is the teaching method of enveloping the youngsters to free them,' he was to say. 'This is what has made the Bauhaus famous. Not its lamps or its furniture.' That method was almost entirely his own. As another of his Weimar students put it, what made the school extraordinary was its role as a 'creative vacuum'.

The student was Annelise Fleischmann. She had come to Weimar in 1922 to join the Bauhaus, and had been turned down. Quietly tenacious, Fleischmann, known as Anni, sought help from a friendly *Bauhäusler* – 'a lean, half-starved Westphalian with irresistible blond bangs,' she would later say. He led her through exercises in paper-folding; his name was Josef Albers. Fleischmann re-applied to the school in October, and this time was admitted. That December, she went to her first Bauhaus Christmas party. Naturally reserved, she hung back as Gropius, dressed as Father Christmas, handed out presents. To her surprise, one was for her: wrapped in gold ribbon was a print of Giotto's *Flight into Egypt*, with a card from Josef Albers attached. Three years later, they would marry. Anni Albers was by then on her way to becoming the preeminent textile artist of the 20th century. Theirs was to be the only marriage of artistic equals among the Bauhaus teachers. '[Albers] married a Bauhaus girl, he had a Bauhaus family,' one German historian noted. 'He incorporated the Bauhaus idea on all levels of his life. He was a Bauhaus man with his whole being.' A decade later, his gift to his future wife would turn out to have been curiously prescient.

For all that, the Albers were not an obvious match. Josef Albers was thirty-four, a house painter's son from a Ruhr mining town. Anni Fleischmann was twenty-two, the daughter of assimilated Berlin Jews who had had their children baptized as Lutheran. Her mother, Toni, was an Ullstein, from a dynasty of eminent publishers: Ullstein Verlag owned the *Berliner Zeitung* and other respected newspapers, as well as publishing books by authors such as Erich Maria Remarque. Annelise had been raised with an Irish governess, in a house full of servants; her mother was a champion tennis player. The Fleischmanns and the Albers could not have been more unalike. Even so, Anni's parents quickly took to their putative in-law. The same cannot be said of Josef's family.

It is clear from his letters to Franz Perdekamp that Albers counted himself a sexual adventurer. Besides the peasant woman, there had been a Bulgarian communist named Mara with whom he spent 'three shining days of Sunday' on the North Sea island of Sylt. There had even, perhaps, been the future Mrs Perdekamp: in the letter about Mara, he goes on to say that Friedl has been to stay with him again, and sends Franz her greetings. 'Be like me, happy and whole and easy-going,' Albers eggs on his shyer friend; then, in a rueful *volte-face*, he describes himself as 'amoral'. As a widow in the 1980s, Anni Albers would recall the many affairs her husband had had in their half-century of marriage. One may have produced a child. His infidelity may not have been one-sided. Sexual freedom was the norm at the Bauhaus, for women as well as for men; perhaps also for Annelise Fleischmann. In a postcard to Perdekamp, also from Sylt, undated but apparently written in late 1924, Josef Albers mourns that 'Anke' is being difficult. 'She wants to see someone else,' he says. Theirs, like most marriages, was to be complex.

In his last months in Weimar, Albers burst into print. First, there was an essay called '*Historisch oder Jetzig?*' – 'Historical or Modern?' – in a special Bauhaus edition of the magazine *Junge Menschen* (Young People). In this, Albers acted as Gropius's mouthpiece. 'We cannot bring the dead back to life,' he wrote of the crafts. 'What has been chewed cannot be eaten again.' The school's future direction lay not just in a 'technical-industrial working method' but in 'levelling out', unification through uniformity. In right-wing Weimar, these were dangerous ideas. In February 1924, the government of Thuringia had become the first in Germany to include Nationalist Socialists in its ranks. It sounded the death knell of the Bauhaus. The following month, the school's frugal budget was cut in half and its director put on notice. Gropius, though, had been busy. There had already been several offers of refuge for the Bauhaus, the most attractive from a small town near Leipzig. Before the school could be closed by the Thuringian government, its council of masters beat them to it. On 26 December 1924, Gropius announced that the Bauhaus would shut on 31 March 1925. It was to re-open the next day, its sixth anniversary, in the Anhalt city of Dessau.

It is the middle and end that shed light on a dark beginning.

Goethe, Unbounded

That Albers would follow the school to Dessau had been by no means a foregone conclusion. In December 1924, in a letter to Franz Perdekamp, he wrote that he, Anni and Marcel Breuer were thinking of setting up on their own. 'No one believed in the Bauhaus ideals as much as I did,' Josef mourned, but those ideals had been sacrificed to 'polishing the facade' while an 'inner tuberculosis' was left to rage unchecked. His main complaint was of independence lost to 'destructive centralization'; he had also discovered that he was being paid less than any other Bauhaus teacher. Where Gropius was concerned, he confided to Perdekamp, it was 'time to bring on the big guns'.

They worked: whatever it was that Albers threatened, Gropius agreed that he would go to Dessau as a *Jungmeister*, with a new glass workshop. He would also continue his work on the *Vorkurs*. Later, Gropius was to recall that 'Albers had the very rare quality of a teacher who treated every student in a different way.' Students, like paper or wood, were materials; the point of educating them was to unlock their innate potential. But the other side of Albers' talent for engaging with individuals was a refusal – perhaps an inability – to join groups. Despite the talk of uniformity in his article 'Historical or Modern?', his social model was one in which the will of each expressed the will of all; a Nietzschean super-democracy. For Gropius, this made him doubly useful. Besides being competent, Albers was safe. Represented graphically, the Weimar Bauhaus had been a mass of feverishly intersecting circles. Only Albers had stood outside them all.

His decision to go to Dessau reflected an upturn in the school's finances. In Weimar, the Bauhaus had suffered from being a state institution wished on a resentful small town. In Dessau, it would be funded by a grateful municipality.

The school's main attraction had been its focus on building, even if, as of 1925, it still had no department of architecture. Dessau was home to the factories of the Junkers aircraft company and the chemical giant, IG Farben, among many others. Business was booming; the town's population would grow by more than half in the three years after the Bauhaus's arrival. The Haus am Horn was to be replicated, in a more affordable form, to solve the problem of workers' housing – a tract of land in the suburb of Törten had been set aside for this purpose. More generous funding allowed the appointment of five additional *Jungmeister* after Albers. At least as attractive was Gropius's design for a central Bauhaus building of workshops and classrooms, to be clad predominantly in glass – 'Glass, glass and more glass', as one astonished visitor was to put it. This new structure would include a student accommodation block, the *Prellerhaus* (figs 4.1, 4.2).

These new buildings would not be habitable until October 1926, however. By then, Josef Albers and Anni Fleischmann had married. Their wedding, a Roman Catholic nuptial Mass, took place on 9 May 1925 at the Ludwigskirche in the elegant Berlin district of Wilmersdorf, with lunch afterwards at the Hotel Adlon. These luxuries were paid for by the bride's parents. None of the Albers family attended; whether they had been invited is unclear. That Josef had married into a Jewish family clearly horrified them, doubly so for the Fleischmanns having had their children baptized as Protestants. In a letter to Franz Perdekamp written from a late honeymoon in the Italian Dolomites, Albers remarks that 'at home, they do not like to talk about my bad match'. He will not be bringing his new wife to Bottrop any time soon, he says: 'Our interracial marriage is still too new for me to show my face.'

Still, there was much to be done. The couple had rented a flat at 33 Mariannenstrasse, a street of villas running west from the city park towards the site of the new Bauhaus. The roster of their fellow tenants – an army major, an industrial chemist and two retired ladies, *die Frauen* Marcus and Schwabe – speaks of *Mittelstand* (middle class) respectability. In the eighteen months that the Bauhaus buildings took to finish, Josef's *Vorkurs* would be taught in the Dessau *Kunstgewerbeschule*, or arts and crafts school, handily around the corner from the flat. Anni, after completing her own preliminary course in Weimar, had signed up as an apprentice in the weaving workshop. Initially dismissing textiles as 'sissy', she had found in the orderliness of the

4.1 Annotated image of Bauhaus at Dessau, pasted onto paperboard.

4.2 Photographer unknown, L–R : Josef Albers, Hinnerk Scheper, Georg Muche, László Moholy-Nagy, Herbert Bayer, Joost Schmidt, Walter Gropius, Marcel Breuer, Wassily Kandinsky, Paul Klee, Lyonel Feininger, Gunta Stölzl and Oskar Schlemmer on the roof of the Bauhaus in Weimar, *ca.* 1920.

loom an antidote to the Bauhaus's esoteric mess – 'a railing', as she put it. Her husband-to-be's discovery of the grid in glass had come at much the same time.

The move to Dessau had not changed the Bauhaus entirely, however. The factory aesthetic of Gropius's new building may have signalled a shift towards functionalism, but along with its design had gone another for a row of houses on Burgkühnauerallee, a few hundred metres away. There were to be four of these, one free-standing and three pairs of semi-detached, set in a clump of pines. The biggest, detached house was for Gropius. The six other *Meisterhäuser* were for Bauhaus professors and their families – one pair for Kandinsky and Klee, one for Georg Muche and Oskar Schlemmer, and a final pair for Lyonel Feininger and László Moholy-Nagy. Albers, like other junior masters, was relegated to the new *Prellerhaus*, meant as a 'student welfare wing'. This contained twenty-eight studio flats of twenty square metres each, with shared kitchens on each storey and communal lavatories and showers in the basement. Floors being segregated by gender, the Albers, newly married (fig. 4.3), were given rooms on different levels.

The disparity between the Masters' houses and the *Prellerhaus* spelled out all too clearly the relative status of professors and young masters at the new Bauhaus. If Gropius's designs for the *Meisterhäuser* had 'evolved from the lives within them', then he clearly imagined those lives to be led on a grand scale. The buildings were imposing, particularly in a town short on housing. They were also expensive: anger at the overrunning of their budget would in part precipitate Gropius's resignation. That the *Meisterhäuser* were part-prefabricated also enraged Dessau's building guilds. Schlemmer professed himself worried by the stares directed at his house by resentful workers; Kandinsky, alarmed that these might presage actual attack, had his roadside windows painted over. Albers and the other *Jungmeister* shared the workers' resentment. As Ise Gropius noted in her diary:

> The young masters make very arrogant demands....They expect the same reverence that is given voluntarily and without hesitation to Kandinsky and Klee and are deeply hurt that they didn't get their own houses yet....I hear from Irmgard that they are all 'embittered'.

They were. In the weeks after the official opening of the new Bauhaus on 4 December 1926, Albers' co-junior master Marcel Breuer proposed a colony of more modest *Kleinhäuser*, called 'Bambos', to be sited across the road from the Bauhaus and occupied by the men whose acronymized initials made up their name: Bayer, Albers, Meyer, Breuer, Ottens and Schmidt. The prefabricated structures, Breuer pointed out, would take less than three weeks to build, and would be cheap. The plan came to nothing. Although Gropius would design sixty rather similar houses for the estate at Törten, the Bauhaus's own junior masters were never housed.

4.3 Marianne Brandt, Anni and Josef Albers
on the balcony, Bauhaus Dessau, 1928–9.

What made this particularly bitter was that the *Jungmeister* were the new Bauhaus's most compelling innovation. The Weimar school had been intrinsically archaic: however enlightened, old masters could only teach old ways. Not until a generation of *Bauhäusler* themselves became Bauhaus teachers could the school claim to be genuinely new. For all Gropius's inveighing against salon art, the Dessau professors – Klee, Kandinsky et al. – were all salon artists. All had been *Formmeister*. Now the distinction between masters of form and craft was abolished: *Jungmeister* would be both. The hour, if not the housing, belonged to men like Josef Albers.

But he, like the Bauhaus, had a problem. If Gropius's 'new unity' did not quite do away with fine art, it did deny the distinction between it and other forms of making. Art had now to be functional, industrial; or at least, it had to look that way. Yet another fault line opened at the Bauhaus, this time between old and new masters. Georg Muche, one of the former, railed publicly against Gropius's new technocracy. 'Art cannot be bound by utility,' Muche raged. 'Art and technology are *not* a new unity.' He was quickly disposed of; other masters held their peace. This left Moholy-Nagy, 'the champion of youth', as the only professor whose art openly toed Gropius's line. Albers' art would have to do so as well, but in an identifiably non-Moholian way. For this, he would turn, as before, to glass.

What made the problem more acute was that he had no intention of giving up on painting – indeed, that he still saw himself first and foremost as a painter. As Nina Kandinsky recalled, the move to Dessau saw a further devaluing at the Bauhaus of the *beaux arts*. Her husband had challenged Gropius on this: 'Why did you ask so many painters here if you are hostile to them?', Kandinsky snapped. 'Gropius', said his wife, 'had no answer.' The director himself had now acquired the nickname *WohnFord*, 'Housing-Ford', for his application to German house building of the American car maker's production-line methods. Gropius's any-colour-as-long-as-it's-white orthodoxy riled many at the Bauhaus, not least the odd but brilliant architect Siegfried Ebeling. In his book *Der Raum als Membran* ('Space as Membrane'), Ebeling threw down the gauntlet. 'All architecture that has naked functionality as its basis and sole intellectual aspiration will expire along with the life-form that appears to be supporting it today,' he said. Painting, the fine arts, would not cease to exist, but they would be subsumed under architecture in a *Gesamtkunstwerk* house whose walls would be 'porous', 'transitional'.

Despite this attack, Ebeling, who left the Bauhaus in 1926, remained highly influential there. A copy of *Der Raum als Membran* sits on Gropius's desk in a famous portrait photo of him. Mies van der Rohe, the school's third and last director, owned a heavily annotated copy of the book, and praised it. Ebeling's essay 'Cosmological Space-cells: Thoughts towards an Ethics of Constructive Thinking' had appeared alongside Albers' 'Historical or Modern?' in the special Bauhaus issue of *Junge Menschen*. When he wrote it, Ebeling had just completed Albers' *Vorkurs*. His fascination with un-wall-like walls echoed his teacher's for building in non-building materials. Samples of *Vorkurs* coursework show an endless requirement for students to construct – in cut paper, folded card, almost anything that appeared unbuildable-with. 'We do construction experiments with straw, matchboxes, paper wire,' Albers writes cheerily to Perdekamp. Like Ebeling's, these constructions elided physics and metaphysics. Influence between master and student went both ways (fig. 4.4).

Key to the Bauhaus's new art-and-technology credo was a drive to commercial production. Thus the school's partnership with Junkers: the prototypes of both Breuer's B3 tubular steel chair and Muche's Törten Steel House were made in the company's workshops. Hajo Rose, a student on Albers' preliminary course, recalled being taken on trips to the aircraft factory. But for Albers himself, working in glass, Junkers held little promise. This was troublesome. Other than the windows for Gropius's private architectural

4.4 Otto Umbehr (Umbo), Josef Albers and students
in a group critique at the Bauhaus Dessau, 1928–9.

projects, the Weimar glass workshop had had no commissions at all. As a result, it was decided that the promised *Glasmalereiwerkstatt* would be merged, in Dessau, with the sculpture and stagecraft shops as a *Versuchsplatz* (testbed). Ominously, this was not to be thought of as 'purely productive'. There remained little prospect of Albers' glass paintings going into industrial production. They might, though, be made using industrial methods; and glass could, like Ebeling's walls, be conceptually porous. The distinction between glass paintings and such eminently manufacturable objects as glass fruit bowls, glass coffee cups and glass tabletops might be blurred. If Albers' varied output in glass at the Bauhaus cannot be seen, in its totality, as a *Gesamtkunstwerk*, glass is at least his *Gesamtmaterial*.

This need to appear functional is behind the architectural plan Albers published in a special Bauhaus edition of *Offset*, a manual for the advertising and typography trades. With its cover by Joost Schmidt and articles by, *inter alia* and predictably, László Moholy-Nagy, *Offset* was both about advertising and itself an advertisement for Gropius's new, commercially-minded school. Artworks by Klee, Kandinsky and the other Dessau professors (including Moholy-Nagy) were reproduced, although, typically, none by Albers. Instead, his contribution was a blueprint for a small shop on the corner of Friedrichstrasse and Leipzigerstrasse in Berlin. This shop would sell *Schnittmuster*, sewing patterns: that these were two-dimensional renderings of three-dimensional objects may have added to the appeal. The project's unnamed client was Hermann Ullstein, the youngest of Anni Albers' maternal uncles.

In that year, 1926, Ullstein had launched a magazine called *Blatt der Hausfrau* – Housewife's Journal – to alert the younger woman to the company's lucrative line of sewing patterns. The company already had a chain of shops selling these; Albers' design, like Hermann Ullstein's new magazine, was intended to update their image. It would also offer Albers a chance to explore in architecture the questions he had been asking in his glass paintings. Indeed, the blueprint for the shop – a worm's-eye-view plan oblique – might easily *be* a glass painting. Two decades before the *Structural Constellation* series, it plays a similar game with flatness and recession (fig. 4.5).

In 1924, Herbert Bayer had produced a set of designs for trade stands. The best-known of these, for a toothpaste called Regina, shows the influence of Moholy-Nagy: its use of photography, broadcast sound and, challengingly, smoke signals follows Moholy's thoughts on *Gesamtkunstwerk* advertising. In spite of their subsequent fame, Bayer's axonometric plans are neither

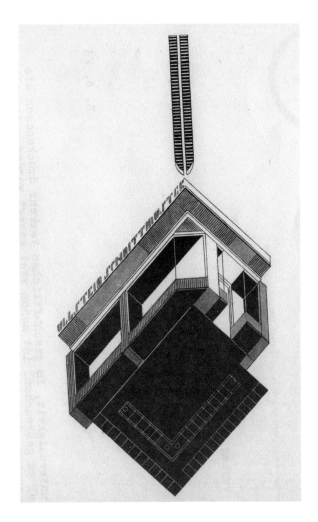

4.5 Design for the Ullstein sewing-pattern shop, 1926, in *Offset* 7.

particularly original – they draw heavily on both Van Doesburg and the agitprop kiosks of Gustav Klutsis – nor practical. Albers could turn out architectural *Denkspiele* (puzzles) when he wanted to – his drawing in Nina Kandinsky's visitors' book is an example (fig. 4.6) – but the shop design in *Offset* is different from these. His projection is not merely more complex and spatially ambiguous than Bayer's. It is thought through to the last detail, and eminently buildable.

Forty years later, in America, Albers would praise art's ability to reach 'from the church to the plaza'. Just as Ullstein Verlag could print both sewing patterns and the *Berliner Zeitung*, so art could encompass both glass paintings and glass-walled shops. The unifying feature, for Albers, was glass. His *Vorkurs* was dominated by transfigurations, the alchemizing of flimsy things into structures that could stand up for themselves. Like Ebeling's porous walls, the point of these was their contradiction. For the Catholic Albers, the oxymoronic nature of glass, solid but transparent, sacred and profane, made it not just modern, but miraculous.

The problem, as with most miracles, would be getting the public to believe it. Albers' shop design is all about legibility. The brief text that accompanies his blueprint agonizes over the precise angling of plate glass to allow exhibits to be seen from all sides. The shop's more literal reading lies on its roofline. Along this would run the words 'Ullstein Schnittmuster', picked out in a new typeface of Albers' inventing. The letters would, of course, be made in glass. Of the type, called *Schablonenschrift* (stencil script), Albers wrote:

> Time is money: events are determined by economics. We live at a fast pace and move accordingly. We use shorthand and the telegram and code. They are not the exception, but the rule....Because we must increasingly think in economic terms, we will become more and more Americanised. A new world is coming.

4.6 Page 18 of a guestbook belonging to Nina Kandinsky,
with 43 sheets of work by 18 different artists.

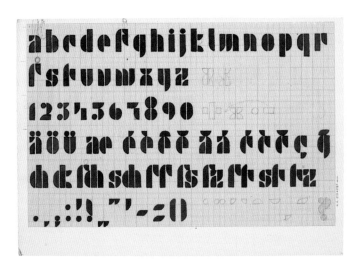

4.7 Design for a universal typeface, *ca.* 1925. Ink and pencil on paper, 8³⁄₁₀ × 11¼ in.

These are among his more easily understood thoughts; for a writer whose subject is clarity, Albers' style is peculiarly opaque. Broadly, *Schablonenschrift* (fig. 4.7) – made up of just three forms (the triangle, quarter-circle and square) and composed on an unvarying ratio of 1:3 – would be legible, replicable and cheaper to make than conventional type. The letters' lack of concave surfaces made them rainproof and easy to clean. The *Schnittmuster* sign also advertised the adaptability of glass as a material. It was opaque enough to be read in silhouette by day, but sufficiently transparent to be through-lit at night. These were the same ambiguities that Albers was exploring in his glass paintings.

Critics, predictably, affected not to be able to tell these from his shop signs. In 1932, the last full year of the Bauhaus, he would exhibit a selection of his recent glass paintings in the Thuringian capital, Erfurt. These were paired with canvases by a minor Weimar artist called Karl Pietschmann. Given that Pietschmann showed nudes, landscapes and flower-paintings in Erfurt, it seems likely that Albers was being set up. Predictably, reviews in the local press contrasted his 'lack of deep content' and 'radical one-sidedness' with Pietschmann's 'gossamer textures', 'vigorous colours' and 'inner affinity with nature'. This was not the critics' lowest blow, though. To a man, they noted similarities between glass paintings such as *K-Trio* and *Treble Clef* (see p. 300) and his use of glass in advertising. 'Beyond the ornamental qualities [of Albers' work] are those of a compelling advertisement,' purred one critic. Another, sweetly hypocritical, wrote, 'It is easy to imagine these pictures as extraordinarily effective advertisements.'

That Albers cut out and kept the reviews begs the question of his response to them: given his plaza-to-church beliefs, their comparison of his art to advertising may possibly have pleased him. Certainly, he was happy to have made his mark in the new printing and advertising workshop in Dessau, led first by Herbert Bayer and then by Joost Schmidt. In the Bauhaus section of the exhibition 'New Advertising' at the Jena Art Association in 1927, Albers is listed firmly as 'an advertising artist'. The following year, he boasts to Gottfried Heinersdorff of a display window he has made for a gramophone needle company, on show at the Leipzig trade fair (fig. 4.8).

Alongside all this, he was experimenting with more workaday uses for glass. In 1925/6, he designed a glass teacup and stirrer (fig. 4.9) – a functional readymade, built entirely of pre-manufactured or easily replicable parts. The cup is a standard laboratory beaker from the scientific glass-makers Schott; the saucer is Meissen; the chrome-plated steel ring is manufactured by Krupp. Only the ebony button handles seem to have been specially made for the cup, perhaps in the Bauhaus woodworking shop. One handle is set vertically and the other horizontally, to make the cup easier to pass from pourer to drinker.

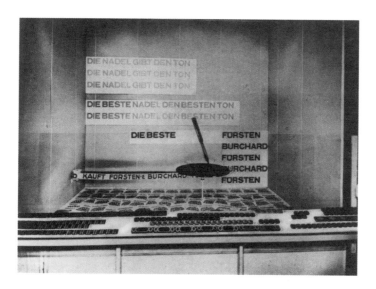

4.8 Design for a window display for 'Drei-S-Werke' exhibited in 'Shop Window' at the Grassi Museum, Leipzig, October 1928. Image in *Gebrauchsgraphik* International Advertising Art Magazine, November 1928 (Druck und Verlag Phönix, Berlin).

4.9 Tea glass with saucer and stirrer, 1925. Heat resistant glass,
chrome-plated steel, ebony, porcelain, 2¼ × 3½ in.

Also in 1926 came the Nesting Tables – a set of four occasional tables
stacked one under the other (fig. 4.10). These were made soon after Marcel
Breuer's Stacking Tables (1925–6), and are similar in size, number, purpose
and in having tops of different colours. The most obvious difference between
the Nesting and Stacking Tables is in their materials. The frames of Breuer's
are of tubular steel, of Albers', ash veneer. The second are clearly a response to
the first, but of what kind? To design in wood when the head of the Bauhaus
carpentry workshop had just abandoned it for steel seems perverse. The
Nesting Tables inevitably look more traditional than the Stacking Tables,
which is to say less modern and – importantly at the new Bauhaus – less
manufacturable. Where they score over Breuer's tables is in their coloured
tops. The Stacking Tables are of painted plywood, and feel utilitarian. Albers'
tabletops are rich, refulgent and made of glass.

These blocks of pure colour reflect a new understanding on his part
of what glass could be. Although his earlier shard paintings had rejected
the traditions of church glass-making, they were still, like church windows,
made up of small parts. Now, in Dessau, Albers discovered the monolithic
pane. 'Stained glass was the old method,' he would say. 'I wanted to make
something in one piece.' For this he returned to a material he had used in
his Weimar window. In 1922, it had been the rarity of flashed glass that had
appealed to him. Now it was its industrial ruggedness. To this workaday
material, he would bring an equally everyday treatment: sandblasting.

Earlier, in Weimar, Albers had experimented with the acid etching of glass. This he found insufficiently modern:

> So I learned to sandblast that glass. Covered it airtight and cut it this way, and this way, this way, this way, and this way. And where I want to remove that red, I just took the paper out and exposed it to sandblasting. It's eaten away. And at the same time makes frosted glass. So that was of great interest to me. And I made all this nonsense independent of anyone's style, you see?

Although he hinted to the contrary, Albers did not do his own sandblasting. By 1925, the year of *Factory* (fig. 4.11), such hands-on making would have been viewed at the Bauhaus with suspicion.

Designs were done in the studio – 'I have to cover that glass in an airtight cover, a specially prepared paper. And I have to cut out with a knife what is to be sand-blasted, either white or red. The black was later painted on it and baked in a kiln' – but the making of them was farmed out, *à la* Moholy, to technicians. 'I took [the glass] to Leipzig to be executed under my supervision by a man who could handle [it], or even when we moved from Dessau to Berlin,' Albers said. 'And then it is always straight lines cutting, which was simple.' As he wryly explained, the technique had originally been invented for cutting letters on gravestones.

4.10 Stacking table, set of four, *ca.* 1927 (facsimile, 2001).
Ash veneer, black lacquer, and painted glass, 24⅗ × 23⅗ × 15⅞ in.

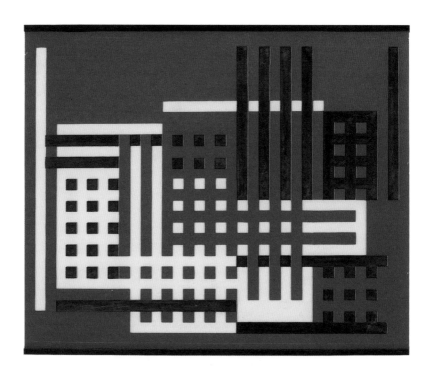

4.11 *Fabrik (Factory)*, 1925. Sandblasted flashed glass, black paint, 11 × 14 in.

A quick look at *Factory* shows how far his art had come, and how fast. Gone is the traditional stained-glass palette of *Park*, made a year before (see p. 124). Gone, too, is the leading together of small pieces. The red sheet-glass Albers now uses would have been made for shop fittings or signage. Parts of it have been abraded through to a core of white milk glass, black elements being painted on later and annealed in a kiln. Although the work is abstract, its title is not: in *Factory*, facade, window and chimney stack unfold into their basic forms. It is like flat-packing in reverse. Albers' process isn't entirely one of simplification, though. The resultant forms register differently according to the relationship of their colours to the colours around them – black stronger than white when the two are set against each other, but weaker than white when both are set against red. As a result, similar elements – black rectangles, say – may read as foreground, mid-ground or background, according to their context. Of another work, *City* (1928), Albers would write,

> Despite this rectangular, frontal and, therefore, distinctly flat subdivision, there is a feeling of many-sided spaciousness. This spaciousness is created above all through the constant change between separating and joining, within divided and undivided surfaces, of red, white and black.

That particular phenomenon – flatness read as depth – had fascinated him since, as a boy, he had stood with his mother on the marble floor of a Bottrop bank. It would intrigue him until his death.

With a couple of exceptions, Albers' glass works for the next five years would explore these same questions in broadly the same way. 'I called it the Thermometer style,' he said. 'That's my name for it. I have invented the Thermometer style.' As their name implied, Thermometer works such as *Frontal* (fig. 4.12) set out to look self-calibrating. Seen as a group, they suggest (and set out to suggest) scientific experiment, the empirical jigging and re-jigging of a formula.

Albers had begun working in series in 1915, with his iterations of Bottrop miners' houses. Now repetition would come to rule his art. It would do so for the rest of his life, most pronouncedly so at its end. 'That is the stubbornness of working in variants,' he would say. 'Of working in series. It is studies.'

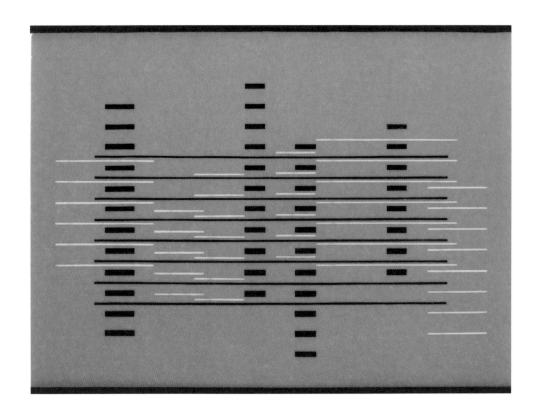

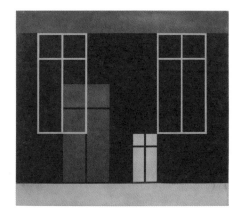

4.12 *Frontal, ca.* 1927. Sandblasted opaque flashed glass with black paint, 13⁷⁄₁₀ × 18⁷⁄₈ in.
4.13 *Windows, ca.* 1935. Sandblasted black anodized aluminum mounted on plywood. 5 × 5½ in.

In 1929 came a group of monochrome glass paintings, the first four called *Interior*. As with *Factory*, the title implies a narrative: window-like forms are rotated against three 'storeys' of white, black and grey, scaled up vertically. The formula is prefabricated, which is fair enough since it is inspired by architectural prefabrication.

These are technically very much more sophisticated works than the earlier flashed glass paintings, combining areas of white, fully sandblasted glass with others of grey where the glass has been only partially eroded. Their compositions are correspondingly more complex, their spatial ambiguities drawing on Albers' experience as a printmaker (fig. 4.13).

In February 1928, Walter Gropius had suddenly announced his resignation as director. The school's move to Dessau had not brought an end to his woes. Animosity from an increasingly right-wing town council was met by internal pressure from an ever more left-wing student body. The tension finally proved too much. When Gropius left Dessau in March, his lieutenant, Moholy-Nagy, went with him. So, in short order, did Herbert Bayer and Marcel Breuer. Albers took over as head of the carpentry workshop, and of both parts of the *Vorkurs*. This now began with a month spent working only in glass, followed by another month with paper, a third with combinations of materials, and finally a month where students could work with whatever materials they chose. Despite all this, Albers was still not made a professor. Only in March 1930, after a decade at the Bauhaus, would he finally be put on the same academic footing as Klee and Kandinsky. Still, he and Anni were at least now given Moholy's vacant *Meisterhaus*, No. 2, with the Feiningers next door at No. 3. If Anni scoffed at the house's roof garden – 'It was under trees anyway,' she sniffed – she was pleased by its clean lines. Josef was less so. As he wrote to Franz Perdekamp,

> Furnishing an apartment is always a cause for concern....My rooms are still very empty. I would like to leave them that way, but you have to be a bachelor for that. I long for my [*Prellerhaus*] apartment. Without washtub and stepladder. No closet and no worries about windows, stairs and toilets. Well, you get older and there is nothing you can do about it.

For all that, life with his colleagues could now be lived on terms of equality. On Kandinsky's birthday, 4 December, Josef and Anni would drop round for 'a cup of birthday tea, orange tea and so many bright, sweet things, and Klee, and new gramophone records'. The Albers were now invited to the Kandinskys' New Year's Eve parties, at which even the notoriously wallflowerish Klee took to the floor. 'Our standard dance,' Nina Kandinsky recalled, 'was always Strauss's *Blue Danube Waltz*.' (fig. 4.14)

Living with Gropius's bare volumes proved inspiring in other ways. The worm's-eye view of Hermann Ullstein's shop had looked like a glass painting; now Albers' glass painting, *Interior A*, looked like a modernist house. It was linear, architectural, seemingly industrial; very Dessau. And yet a comparison of the piece with (say) a Mondrian *Composition* of the same year shows Albers still rooted in representation. The aesthetic of *Interior A* wasn't just derived from a house, it was derived from *his* house: its story was both public and personal. Together with tensions between flatness and depth and colour and volume in the painting is another of modernity and tradition. Fifty years later, Albers' *Homages* – thousands upon thousands of squares made serially on hardboard – would retain a stubborn air of painterliness: an interest in finish, edges that looked scumbled.

4.14 Photographer unknown, Oranienbaum, Bauhausfest,
Josef Albers dancing with Nina Kandinsky, 1928.

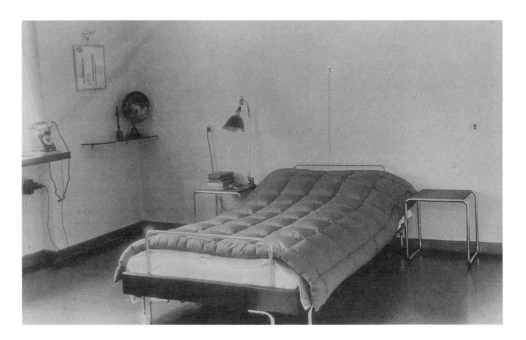

4.15 Josef Albers, Anni's bedroom in Dessau, *ca.* 1928.

The Albers now had a house of their own. Josef's photographs of its interior suggest a very un-German austerity. Featherdown quilt and an Egyptian bronze figure apart, Anni's bedroom is an advertisement for Bauhaus restraint – a lamp by Curt Fischer, Breuer tables, one of Josef's Thermometer paintings on the wall (fig. 4.15). So, too, the drawing room with its Breuer chairs, Brandt ceiling lamp and ti244 armchair.

Nor was the life led in Meisterhaus No. 2 one of traditional domesticity. Whether polyamory had been written into the contract of the Albers' marriage, it seems soon to have become a part of it, on Josef's side at least. With his new salary, he and Anni could travel – to Biarritz, Barcelona, the Swiss lakes. Moholy's house had come with a darkroom; in 1928, Albers bought himself a Leica and asked T. Lux Feininger, son of his new neighbours, for lessons in its use. A favourite holiday subject was sunbathing women, often nude (fig. 4.17). Whether Anni knew of these photographs or cared is impossible to say. Something of the tenor of the Albers' relationship is captured in a poem by Hubert Hoffmann, an architecture student in Dessau:

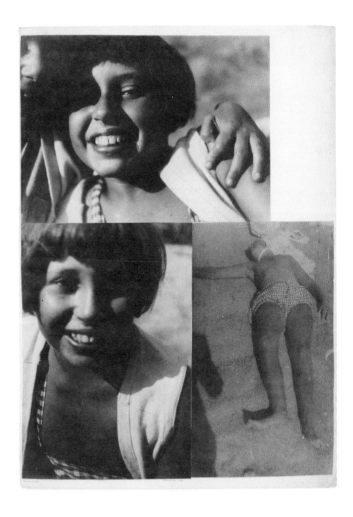

4.16 Photographer unknown, Josef and Anni Albers, Oberstdorf, Germany, 1927–8.
4.17 *Susanne, Biarritz*, 1929. Photocollage: gelatin silver prints mounted on cardboard, 16⅛ × 11⅗ in.

Albers foolishly fooled around
In the atrium
With ambitious, attractive apprentices.
When Anni, askance, assumed that other
Things were going on,
Albers argued artfully:
'Abstraction, adaption, assumption
And amour have,
Since Adam and Aristotle,
Been the alpha and omega
Of true aesthetics.'
'Ah,' answered Anni, alluringly:
'In America, all is outrage, unlike here.'
'Art', she said, 'is free to choose,
And architecture tells us nothing of amour.'

Although Hoffmann's tone is comic, it is clear that Josef's flirtations were notorious. Depictions of him as deceiving, and Anni as wronged, are drawn from life. Among Albers' dalliances was one with Otti Berger, among the most talented weavers at the Bauhaus. This was not her only similarity to his wife. Like Anni, Berger was *haute bourgeoisie*, Jewish, and disabled: Anni walked with a limp, Otti was partially deaf. As with Anni Fleischmann, Albers' relationship with Otti Berger seems to have begun while she was still a student. In March 1930, he wrote to her: 'I am alone. Anni is in Berlin. She was in bed here for two weeks. The 'flu had her looking like hell.' Discussing his wife with his lovers would remain characteristic of Albers' affairs; one can only guess at the psychology behind it. The letter ends, 'Keep yourself trim, in that shape I love....Old love, Juppi.' In July, Berger is, 'My sweet angel, flown so far away.' 'You cannot imagine how true I am,' Albers says, adding that he and Anni are going to take 'the girl' – 'a charming creature' – with them on holiday to Berlin. The girl was their maid, Charlotte Hesse; correspondence between her and Albers make it clear that she, too, was his lover. Both the Albers would continue to write to 'Lottchen' until Josef's death in 1976. He signs his 1930 letter to Berger, 'with warm love from us both'.

In that same year, Albers made two glass paintings which he called *Dom* (Cathedral). The one that survives, *Dom auf Schwarz*, is an extraordinary work (fig. 4.18).

Snagged in the verbal thickets of *Werklicher Formunterrich* – 'Teaching Form Through Practice' – his 1928 essay on education, had been this: 'the activation of negatives (residual, intermediate and minus values) is perhaps the only entirely new, perhaps the most important element in contemporary formal innovation'. *Dom* untangles these literary knots. Anticipating fractals, Albers uses an alphabet of similar but evolving geometric forms to beat out a rhythm of architectural volumes and voids. If *Dom* is among the greatest of his glass paintings, it is also a statement of intent. A decade had passed since Lyonel Feininger's Expressionist *Cathedral* announced the birth of the Bauhaus. Now, in post-Gropius Dessau, it was to be Albers' cathedral – depersonalized, abstract, industrially made – that was the school's new emblem.

If that was the thinking behind *Dom*, then Albers was in for a shock. In a letter to Otti Berger of March 1930, he wrote:

> What is sickening here is the intrigue, the war of cliques that dresses itself up itself as objective argument. The 1st motto is: broader education (we recently heard the opposite). Then, 2, get rid of the painters....Not that A[lbers] is rejected because he is 'also' a painter. But the atmosphere here is such, that no one can help but feel embarrassed about making work.

Three years before, Gropius had finally found funding for an architecture department at the Bauhaus, appointing a Swiss architect, Hannes Meyer, to run it. For Albers, it would prove a fateful choice. Meyer's clear-eyed boyishness belied his radicalism. He was a devout functionalist, a man for whom aesthetics could play no part in design (fig. 4.19).

Meyer numbered the uses of a house from one to twelve, beginning with sex, pets and gardening and ending with car maintenance, cooking and heating. 'These', he wrote, 'are the only questions to be considered in building.' Not surprisingly, his dislike of salon art ran deep. If Gropius had viewed painting as annoyingly old-fashioned, the man he appointed his successor at the Bauhaus found it morally repugnant. So far, Albers' glass paintings had managed to fly under the wire by appearing industrial. After Meyer took over on 1 April 1928, that cover would no longer suffice.

4.18 *Dom auf Schwarz, ca.* 1930. Sandblasted opaque flashed glass, 13½ × 19 in.

4.19. Otto Umbehr (Umbo), Portrait of Hannes Meyer against a drawing board of 'Ideas – Competition' (for a new building at the Basel Kunstmuseum), 1922-3.

The motto for Gropius's new Bauhaus had married art to industry. Meyer's – *Volksbedarf, statt Luxusbedarf* (roughly 'Necessities, not Luxuries') – took the school in a baldly political direction. This brought into sharp focus the question of Albers' place there. If, like Lorenz before him, Josef could turn his hand to anything, he nonetheless saw himself first as an artist. How his glass paintings would fare under a regime that set its face against luxuries was a matter for concern. This proved justified when, in May 1928, Meyer hired the Hungarian art theorist Ernst Kállai to edit the school's magazine. Gropius had understood the need to bring the public to the Bauhaus; Meyer would take the Bauhaus to the public. A Marxist fellow-traveller, he knew the value of propaganda. With Kállai, he waged war on what he called 'Bauhaus style'. Albers would be among their first targets.

This quickly became clear. In 1927, Meyer had written that 'painting and sculpture [were] dead as images of the real world; in the age of photography, both are a waste of energy'. Josef's discovery of photography was lent a new urgency. One of his favourite subjects was shop-window mannequins (fig. 4.20). Meyer may have championed photography over painting, but this was not the kind of photograph he had had in mind. His own illustration, in the next *Bauhaus*, of a careworn proletarian woman viewed from inside a shop window, was clearly meant as a rebuke. Albers, it seemed, could do nothing

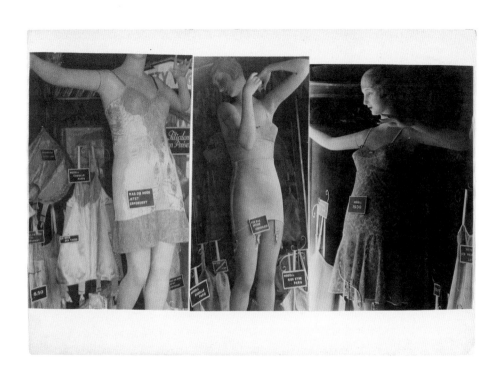

4.20 *Mannequins, ca.* 1930. Photocollage: gelatin silver prints mounted on cardboard, 11⅗ × 16⅛ in.

right. In October, *Bauhaus 4* carried a broadside against formalism, 'fashionably flat surface decoration, horizontal-vertical division and neoplastic self-indulgence' being singled out for particular contempt. Meyer's words might have been written with the Thermometer paintings in mind. Perhaps they were. Now Albers' *Vorkurs*, too, came under attack.

Hajo Rose recalled the ensuing battle:

> After a time, there were increasingly heated debates with Marxist students about the usefulness of the Vorkurs – there were machines that could test materials much more thoroughly and accurately than we could with our sense of touch, etc. Albers: And I can't box with Schmeling.

'On this point', ends Rose, sadly, 'he lacked the words to speak to us.' If students now dismissed Albers' teaching as paternalistic, they were egged on eagerly by Kállai. Early in 1930, Meyer's sidekick drew a pair of caricatures of the *Vorkurs* master, widely circulated among students. Kállai had also made cartoons of other Bauhaus figures, including Meyer himself. The ones of Albers, though, were of a different order (fig. 4.21).

In the first, Albers is lampooned as a be-ruffed school matron, dosing the hapless *Vorkursbaby* with a spoonful of Bauhaus Aesthetics. The formula for

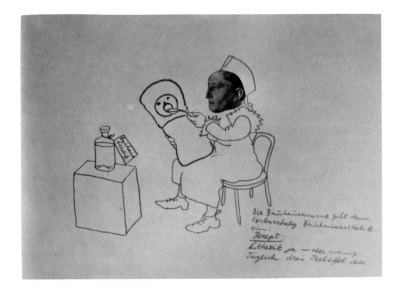

4.21 Ernst Kállai, Caricature of Josef Albers, 'The Bauhaus nurse gives the *Vorkurs* baby one (dose of) Bauhaus Aesthetic. Formula: Aesthetics, yes – but just a little. Three teaspoons full daily', 1930.

this is 'Milk of high-mindedness: artistic/creative learning for the Bauhaus's gifted offspring'. In the second, the *Vorkursmeister* appears as a pince-nez'd *Anstandsdame* (chaperone), showing a passionate young art student the door. If ostensibly light-hearted, Kállai's humour is barbed: 'milk of high-mindedness' is a quotation from Schiller's *Wilhelm Tell*, suggesting that Albers, imagining himself a legendary hero, was actually a spinsterly old fusspot. An anonymous letter to Otti Berger recalls the *Vorkurs* master's response to the rebellion:

> [Albers] talks about the Vorkurs.
> 12 men work
> 12 men do nothing but sit and gape.
> He suggests harsher selection!
> He suggests extending the Vorkurs!
> More work with tools!
> Albers thinks that Vorkurs students are being told that work in the Vorkurs isn't that important – by former Bauhaus members! He rants! They are denying the importance of working with Albers! The student ends:
> H[annes] M[eyer] wonders whether the Bauhaus can allow itself to go on turning out specialists, when hardly any proper architects are to be found among them.
> He was right.

As early as 1923, the critic Walter Passarge had found art at the Bauhaus reduced to the status of an architectural accessory. Now, five years later, Passarge's words took root. Architects were to be at the top of Meyer's Bauhaus tree, followed by the heads of the new building (*Bau*) and interior design (*Ausbau*) departments, the latter of these Alfred Arndt. Below Arndt came the heads of the wall-painting, metal and furniture workshops, newly subsumed under interior design. Once again, Albers found a younger man promoted over him. Painters, insofar as they had status at all, were to be at the bottom of Meyer's tree. Albers' *Interior* paintings of 1929 reflect his move into a *Meisterhaus*, but they also respond to a new and urgent need to look architectural – to find a way of being abstract while avoiding the accusation of formalism.

For all this, Albers' experience of Meyer was contradictory. Under Gropius, he had lived in the *Prellerhaus* and been a Young Master: under Meyer, he was given a *Meisterhaus* and a professorship. Something of the new director's view on luxury also appealed. As a designer, Albers' two years under Meyer were to be his most ingenious. The Model ti244 armchair (1929) (see p. 294) was made for the Bauhaus *Volkswohnung* (People's Apartment), an affordable model flat that marked the populist high point of Meyer's directorship.

Like the chair for the Berlin apartment of Dr Hans-Ludwig Oeser (1928) (fig. 4.22), the ti244 was groundbreaking in being flat-packed. Either chair could have gone into commercial production, although, typically, neither did. In this, they resembled almost every Bauhaus design. The only product that was to become genuinely popular was the school's least probable: its wallpaper.

Maria Rasch had joined the Bauhaus just before Albers, in 1919. Rasch's family owned a large wallpaper firm, with a factory near Osnabrück and offices in Paris, London and Sydney. Her brother, Emil, sensing the commercial threat of bare Bauhaus walls, took action. In March 1929, he persuaded Hannes Meyer to allow Rasch & Co. to produce a line of Bauhaus wallpapers. As a nod to the school's tastes, these would be textured rather than patterned; the clincher for Meyer was that this would make them less prone to waste. *Bauhaus-Tapeten* would be designed in a student competition run by the head of the wall-painting workshop, Hinnerk Scheper, with winning designs to be chosen by a panel of teachers, one of whom was Josef Albers. When, in the summer of 1929, Scheper left for a two-year sabbatical in Moscow, Albers took over the wallpaper studio. It was he who oversaw the launch of the first collection that September. Although little is known of them, Albers seems also to have produced designs of his own. Attached to a set of samples given by him to Harvard is a note in his hand: *1 set of Bauhaus Wallpaper/designed by J. Albers/ca. 1929/manufacturer:/Rasch & Co. Bramsche near Osnabrück*.

Writing to Scheper in Moscow, Meyer mentions that Albers is running what he calls the second 'wallpaper campaign'. The letter is dated 19 March 1930, eight days before the forty-two-year-old *Jungmeister* was finally made a professor. The commercial success of the *Tapeten*, the first of any Bauhaus product, may well have played its part in his promotion. Certainly, Mies van der Rohe, third and last director of the Bauhaus, could not have moved the school to Berlin without the income guaranteed by its wallpaper. From 1933 to 1945, the *Tapete* was to be the only product in Germany permitted to be

4.22 Armchair for Dr Oeser, 1928 (facsimile, 1928). Walnut and maplewood veneer, upholstered in Anni Albers' Maharam fabric, 29⅛ × 24¼ × 26½ in.

sold under the Bauhaus brand. Among other buildings to be papered with it was the Osnabrück 'Brown House', the city's Nazi headquarters.

All this makes Albers' subsequent behaviour towards Meyer vexing. On 20 June 1930, he wrote to Ludwig Grote, Chief Conservator of Anhalt and the man responsible for bringing the Bauhaus to Dessau:

> How would it be if we asked...the City to demand written statements from each Master, saying whether they want the leadership to explain if it means [the Bauhaus] to go Marxist?....Yesterday Engemann...spoke harshly to me of the current course....Only Kuhr and Heiberg (and perhaps Hilberseimer) are for it. Gunda, although anti-'bourgeois', is for a raise and a professorship. Kuhr is leader of a Marxist work group. There are 3 of them. The second is led by Borowski who was turned down after the First Semester but stayed on, believing that the KPD38 would authorise a Bauhaus State (!)....There is also protest in the building department against Heiberg, [who] is all for a Marxist working collective. His appointment clearly marked a shift....Why hire him without probation?...Why starting at the highest salary?

It was not his first such letter. If Albers' resentful tone is familiar, his aim is not personal gain: it is to oust Hannes Meyer as director. To Franz Perdekamp, a day later, he wrote: 'Here, the atmosphere is very tense. The [Bauhaus] is completely politicized. It cannot go on like this much longer. [The *Meisterhaus*] is great, but work is being poisoned.' Dessau's mayor, Fritz Hesse, was struggling with a new National Socialist bloc on the city's council; Meyer's supposed communism was already under attack in the pro-Nazi local paper, the *Anhalter Anzeiger*. That Albers, with Kandinsky, acted as an informer against him was to prove fatal. On 29 July 1930, Hesse summoned Meyer to his office and sacked him on the spot.

This incident raises a number of questions, among them of how Albers saw himself at Dessau. His status as both a designer and teacher had improved significantly under Hannes Meyer. Despite the director's attacks on art, it was Meyer who had arranged the first Bauhaus *Wanderschau* (travelling exhibition): twenty of Albers' glass paintings toured Switzerland, their first international exposure. Later, Albers would recall the cause of the rupture as political: 'Meyer was very supportive of me at the beginning, until he found out I wasn't of his political conviction, you see. And then there came that other thing out....When that came out that I was not a Party member.' Certainly, Albers remained doggedly anti-communist: a childhood in strike-torn Bottrop had seen to that. Later, in America, his staunch apoliticism would at times seem political. In 1930, though, it was art more than politics that troubled him. Under Meyer, experiments in colour and materials, the twin planks of his work and teaching, were denounced as formalist. With Kandinsky, Albers fretted that the new Bauhaus would do away with art altogether, not to mention their means of teaching it. In informing on Meyer's politics, their behaviour was Machiavellian. It made the pair unpopular at the Bauhaus, and beyond it. In August 1930, a letter for the school's student representatives arrived from Moscow:

> Every Bauhäusler...will know, that [Meyer's dismissal] was less a matter of [his] political opinions...than of the unfair and underhanded behaviour...[of] two reactionary Bauhaus masters, who did not have the courage to say openly what they wanted, but were so cowardly as to use political events...to mask their subversive activities, and cover up the truth to avoid compromising themselves.

But, like Kandinsky, Albers was willing to sacrifice popularity for art.

Although Gropius had left the Bauhaus in 1928, he remained the school's *eminence grise*. It was to him that Hesse now turned in finding Meyer's successor. Gropius's advice was unhesitating: Mies van der Rohe. Mies, a cigar-smoking showman, was Meyer's opposite. One of his first actions on taking over in Dessau was to hire a butler for the *Meisterhaus*, with instructions that he wear livery. The Bauhaus's third (and, as it turned out, last) director was Germany's preeminent modernist architect. He was also ruthless. Arriving in Dessau in August 1930, he ordered the school to close while its statutes were redrafted. Existing students would have to apply for readmission, acceptance being conditional on their forswearing politics. Communists were purged, student representation on the *Meisterrat* ended. Mies, wrote Albers to Perdekamp, 'is a great guy'.

The new director had taken the job on condition that he live in Berlin and commute to Dessau three days a week. The record of subsequent masters' meetings show day-to-day decision-making increasingly delegated to Albers. After 1930, his signature is on more Bauhaus minutes than anyone else's, his tasks ranging from soliciting free magazines to turning down tubercular applicants. On 19 March 1931, plans for a dance party called *Aufruhr am Bauhaus* (Riot at the Bauhaus) are 'attacked by Herr Albers'. Five days later, in anticipation of a town council visit, 'Herr Albers takes charge of the removal of inappropriate works' from a student show. At the same meeting, he is elected the school's deputy director.

But problems loomed. Like Meyer, Mies was intent on reshaping the Bauhaus in his own image. Not everyone liked this: Gunta Stölzl and Paul Klee soon resigned. Mies may have seen off the Marxists, but in doing so he turned the Bauhaus into an architecture school with vestigial workshops attached. Compulsory apprenticeships in these were ended: students could opt to take classes in the principles of construction instead. Most seriously for Albers, the *Vorkurs*, necessary for all students since 1919, now became optional – students with architectural experience could skip it altogether. The course, in effect, was reduced to lessons in drawing. The American *Bauhäusler* Howard Dearstyne recalled Albers' reaction:

> Mies felt that Albers's basic course was too little directed toward... architecture....On becoming director, he reviewed the subjects being taught....[W]hatever it was that Mies told Albers,...he greatly wounded the latter's feelings. He went out of the way to mollify the injury by a show of camaraderie. 'Josefchen,' said he, throwing his arm over Albers's shoulder as they walked together towards the masters' houses, 'come and have a drink with me.'

The rift was soon healed. By 1932, Albers could write to Perdekamp that his 'nightly walks with Mies [were] nice'. Nonetheless, his role at the Bauhaus had shifted, and not in the direction he had hoped.

These internal problems would soon be eclipsed by external ones. In a council election held four days after the Bauhaus reopened, Dessau's government went National Socialist. The Nazis had been elected on a ticket promising not just to shut down the school but to demolish its flat-roofed, non-Aryan buildings. A few weeks later, Hitler arrived in Dessau to address

4.23 Howard Dearstyne, Ludwig Mies van der Rohe's Bauhaus Berlin (Building previously a telephone factory) being renovated by students, 1932–3.

a victory rally ten thousand strong. The end was nearing. On 22 August, government funding of the Bauhaus was withdrawn; on 30 September, the school closed. By now, Mies had found it a new home in a disused telephone factory in Berlin (fig. 4.23). What was left of the Bauhaus – Feininger, Arndt and Joost Schmidt now departed – reopened the next month.

Assaulted on so many fronts, Albers might have been expected to stop making art. In fact, the opposite was true. In the thirty troubled months of Mies's directorship, Albers' glass painting entered a new phase, one whose ambiguities would follow him to America. Where the Thermometer paintings had been studiedly impersonal and non-representational, works such as *Stufen* (*Steps*) are characterful and teasingly illusionistic (figs 4.24, 4.25). It was as if, having perfected the sonnet form, Albers now chose to write poems in free verse. There is something playful, even humorous, about *Stufen*. The titular steps (if they are steps) have a cartoonish jauntiness; the smaller figure to the upper left feels like an artist's doodle. *Falsch gewickelt* (*Rolled Wrongly*) (fig. 4.26) calls to mind Wittgenstein's meditations on the duckrabbit, his distinction between 'seeing that' and 'seeing as'. As with Wittgenstein, Albers' paper rolls (if they are paper rolls) – a working-out, perhaps, of his own *Vorkurs* thinking – use an apparently light-hearted idea to ask serious questions about seeing and knowing; questions that would dominate his art for the next four decades.

4.24 *Steps, ca.* 1931/1935. Sandblasted opaque flashed glass, 16 × 21 in.

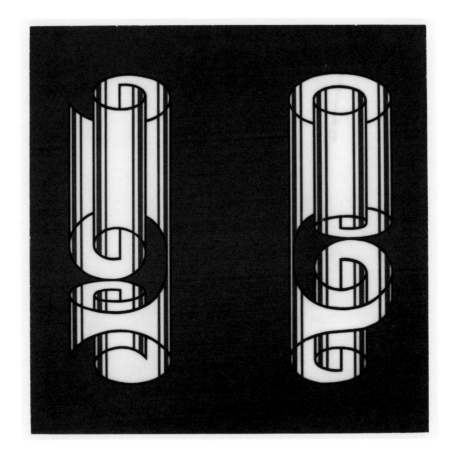

4.25 *Steps*, *ca.* 1935. Sandblasted black anodized aluminum mounted on plywood, 6²⁄₅ × 7²⁄₅ in.

4.26 *Falschegewickelt (Rolled Wrongly)*, 1931. Sandblasted opaque flashed glass, 16³⁄₅ × 16³⁄₅ in.

Soon a letter arrived from the Dessau Magistrate's Office saying that Meisterhaus No. 2 had been let to a Dr Hagemann at Junkers: the Albers were to vacate it at once. Two years after they had moved in, they left the house for a small flat in Sensburger Allee, a nondescript street in Berlin's Westend. This they set about painting white; drinks were served from laboratory beakers. Money was tight. Dessau had grudgingly agreed to carry on paying masters to avoid breach of contract. In June 1933, the agreement was rescinded: a letter accused Albers of having acted as a mouthpiece for the Bauhaus – 'a Bolshevik cell' – thus forfeiting his right to a salary. The accusation of Bolshevism horrified him. So, as he wrote to Franz Perdekamp, did the fact that teachers were now required to 'show a family tree' proving pure Aryan ancestry. 'I can't pay the rent,' he says. 'We are waiting for the end. Everything we worked for was in vain. No prospects. We make few plans.'

Five years before, two young Americans had visited the Bauhaus in Dessau: Alfred Barr, shortly to be director of the new Museum of Modern Art in New York, and an architect named Philip Johnson. Barr would later recall 'the three days which I spent [there] in 1928 as one of the most important incidents in my own education'. Albers' teaching impressed them especially. In early 1929, Barr wrote to him in erratic German, asking for photographs of material studies from the *Vorkurs* to illustrate a book he proposed to write on it. 'How do you like Hannes Meyer?', Barr goes on, innocently, followed by 'How much teaching are you doing these days...?' It took four years for Albers to reply.

When he did, in June 1933, it was in a tone of desperation. 'You know how attached I am to teaching and how few opportunities [for this] there are here now,' he says. In Berlin, the *Vorkurs* had been downgraded to an *Erste Stufe* (First Step), attended by just twenty students. Now, even these were gone. On 11 April, Mies stepped from the Steglitz tram to find the Bauhaus surrounded by Gestapo. A search of the school found communist propaganda, almost certainly planted; the Bauhaus was locked and sealed. At the time of the letter to Barr, it remained in a state of suspended animation. Three weeks later, Albers was one of seven masters to attend the final meeting of the *Meisterrat*. Minutes record that 'Herr Mies van der Rohe proposed a motion to dissolve the Bauhaus.' It was passed unanimously. 'I would be grateful', Albers wrote to Barr, 'for a suitable recommendation.'

At this point, America was not the Albers' only possible destination, nor even their most desired. In 1928, Josef had represented the Bauhaus at a conference in Prague. There he had met the art teacher Frantisek Mokry, to whom he wrote for help:

> The Bauhaus is no more and prospects for work look bleak. So I have turned to Mr Alois Pizl (department head) at your Ministry of Education to ask about possible uses for me in the art and vocational schools there. And considering my nationality and language, only for courses offered to German students.

He solicits Mokry's help in showing his new work – not glass paintings this time, but woodcuts. The last prints Albers had made had been in Essen in 1917. Since 1920, almost his entire oeuvre had been in glass.

Now, in the final days of his German life, his art went into reverse. The experiments he had begun in *Stufen* were carried on in works such as *Weisser Kreis* (White Circle) (fig. 4.27), a print that explores the dualities of glass, but this time on paper. As he wrote to the ex-*Bauhäusler* Paul Citroën in Holland,

> I haven't made any glass pictures since last summer, because they are too expensive. So I've been looking for cheaper paths. With woodcuts. A series are already printed and now I need exhibitions. Do you know any dealers in Amsterdam who are interested in abstract art?

Although some Bauhaus glassworks would be remade in America, *Stufen* would be one of the last original glass paintings Albers was to make.

Deliverance, when it came, was from America rather than Europe. In August, a letter arrived from Philip Johnson with the offer of a job at a new liberal arts college in North Carolina. The Albers had never heard of such a place: Anni wondered whether it might be in the Philippines. Josef telegraphed, 'I do not speak one word English'; by return came the reply, 'Come anyway.' On 30 August, they sent a cautious acceptance, conditional on Josef being paid $150 a month and Anni employed to teach weaving. A fortnight later, Albers wrote to Ludwig Grote in Dessau complaining that he had been refused a job with a German wallpaper company, and of teething problems with his new woodcuts. He mentions that he and Anni have given up their flat, and that he is taking English lessons, although not why. The

4.27 *Weisser Kreis (White Circle)*, 1933. Woodcut print, 14 × 19¾ in.

times called for caution. The couple's first application for a US visa had been turned down: it took an appeal by Philip Johnson to Abby Aldrich Rockefeller for the decision to be reversed. Finally, in mid-October, the visa was granted. Albers invited friends to a last show of his work, at Sensburger Allee. As was customary, the invitation listed the nearest U-Bahn station. Formerly Reichskanzlerplatz, it had recently been renamed Adolf Hitlerplatz (fig. 4.28).

It would be twenty years before Josef Albers returned to Germany, seven more before Anni Albers went with him. Between 1933 and 1938, when *Kristallnacht* made history crystal clear, Mies and Gropius would both tender for Nazi building contracts. Herbert Bayer, whose wife, like Anni, was Jewish, designed Party propaganda. The Albers themselves were excused this moral uncertainty, although not its effects. Heinrich van Bömmel, husband of

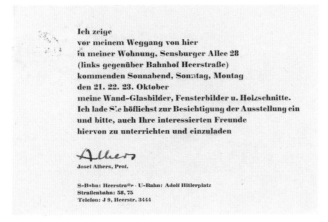

4.28 Invitation from Josef Albers to Oskar Schlemmer
(front and back), postmarked 19 October 1933.

Josef's sister Magdalena, would be an active Nazi. In 1939, he was made *Zellenleiter* – cell leader – for Coesfeld North, where the couple had moved. After the war, a court found him *minderbelastet* – criminally culpable – and banned him from teaching. He died in 1950. In 1938, Ullstein Verlag, like all Jewish-owned firms, was 'aryanized'. Anni Albers' immediate family escaped the ensuing storm, although not so her much-loved cousin, Robert Mayer-Mahr, son of her Aunt Mathilde. Mayer-Mahr was deported from Paris to Auschwitz in 1942, and is assumed to have died there. So, too, in 1944, did Otti Berger. The chief architect of the camp, Fritz Ertl, a *Bauhäusler*, had been a student on Josef's *Vorkurs*.

5   *Amerika:* Black Mountain College

Utopias always end as stories.... In that strange clearing amid the Great Smoky Mountains, everyone's character and history were magnified.
Alfred Kazin, New York Jew

If I had to sum up Albers' philosophy, that would be it. He taught you to see.
Jacob Lawrence, art teacher, Summer Session 1945

Art is performance.
Josef Albers

In the photograph on the front page of the *Asheville Citizen* of 5 December 1933, Anni, in a seal-skin jacket and veil, eyes the camera with upper-class *hauteur*. Josef, as often in photos, looks shifty. The picture had been taken aboard the *SS Europa* in New York harbour the week before; the *Citizen* ran it under the doubtful headline, 'GERMANS TO TEACH ART NEAR HERE' (fig. 5.1). Faced with a small bevy of reporters, Anni, who had had an Irish governess, did the talking. Although she claimed only to have been taught the words 'guinea pig', she dealt easily with the press. '[Josef] says that art must have freedom...and that is no longer possible in Germany,' she said. After celebrating their first Thanksgiving in Brooklyn with the parents of Theodore Dreier, a colleague-to-be, the Albers set off by train for the rural North Carolina town of Black Mountain.

They would spend the next sixteen years there. Black Mountain College had been founded earlier in 1933 by a group of disaffected academics and students from Rollins College, a like-minded place in Florida. Like Rollins, Black Mountain was a liberal arts school, teaching the humanities to undergraduates; Ted Dreier, meanwhile, would train the new school's thirty-odd students in mathematics and physics. He was also the nephew of Katherine Dreier, patron of the arts and sometime visitor to the Bauhaus. 'We didn't know about Albers when we started, but we heard about him through people at the Museum of Modern Art,' Dreier later said. 'Mr Rice and I interviewed Philip Johnson and [Alfred] Barr....and they suggested Josef Albers....And that's what happened.' For their part, the Albers had been taken by the word *bahnbrechend* – pioneering – in the long letter in German they had had from Dreier in Berlin. 'When we came across this word, we both said, "This is our place,"' Anni Albers recalled.

Final approval, though, lay with John Andrew Rice. It was the charismatic classicist's sacking from Rollins that had led to the resignation *en bloc* of Dreier and others, and to their leasing of the Blue Ridge Assembly, a YMCA campus near Asheville. As soon as he saw photographs of work from Albers' *Vorkurs*, Rice said, 'This is just the kind of thing we want.' There was a problem, though. 'Johnson said, "He has one defect,"' Rice recalled. 'I thought, my God, there's a cleft palate coming up, because I knew a linguistic expert who had a cleft palate. Or he's blind.' Johnson went on, 'He doesn't speak a word of English.' Relieved, Rice answered, 'What's the matter with that?' Four months later, the Albers were in the Dreiers' Model A Ford, on their way up from Black Mountain station.

5.1 Photographer unknown, Professor Josef Albers and his wife Anni
aboard the S.S. Europa in New York City, 25 November 1933.

They were astonished at what they saw. The new college stood in the
foothills of the Blue Ridge Mountains, along a drive that wound through 1,600
acres of dogwoods and wild rhododendrons. At the end lay Robert E. Lee
Hall, a white, Doric-porticoed wooden building in the style of an antebellum
Southern mansion. In New York, they had been warned that Black Mountain
was a nudist colony. When the school's secretary – 'a very healthy, luscious
girl' – met them in the porch, they looked down to see 'fat, little pink toes'
showing through her sandals. 'I thought, "Maybe this is a true story,"' Anni
recalled. The place's oddity was confirmed when she spotted a photograph
pinned with a tack to one of the porch's apparently stone columns.

The Albers fell for Black Mountain mutually, heavily and at once. The
day after their arrival, they sent a carbon-copy letter to friends in Europe.
One went to Wassily Kandinsky, by now in exile outside Paris:

black mountain is wonderful, deep in the mountains, the same
height as the harz i think, but everything lush.
the woods are full of wild rhododendrons, as big as trees.
we go out without coats and sat in spring sunshine this morning.
accommodation and food very good, we 2 have 2 bathrooms of our
own adjoining our bedrooms.
the atmosphere is youthful and very pleasant.
a lot of the feel of the bauhaus and even bauhaus faces.
and our work is received with open arms.

Josef added a handwritten postscript. In New York, they had been introduced
to 'Duchamps' [*sic*], who had recently curated a show of 'Brancousi' [*sic*].
Albers' pictures – the glass paintings he had shipped from Berlin – were
held up in customs, but '[Philip] Johnson got them out the next day.' Both
Albers had studios in Lee Hall, Anni's on the ground floor next to her weaving
workshop, Josef's in the portico, overlooking the porch. The only cloud was
the other German on the faculty, Emmy Zastrow, who left pro-Nazi articles
on the hall table. Anni, furious, had to stop herself from throwing them on
the fire. It was Josef who came up with a solution. He hid the cuttings in
the small ads section of the *New York Times*, which was customarily thrown
away. All was well.

All was well, too, with John Andrew Rice. Four decades later, he recalled
meeting Albers. 'He was a charmer!' Rice said. 'Gracious – every now and
then you meet a gracious German, and by God it's wonderful. And he was it.
We took to each other at once.' Rice speaking little German, they set off to
look at wildflowers. Unexpectedly for a man with no interest in art, he had
insisted that it be at the centre of Black Mountain's teaching. Three years
later, in an article that would mark the end of his friendship with Albers,
he said, 'We at Black Mountain begin with art. The artist thinks about
what he himself is going to do, does it himself, and then reflects upon the
thing that he himself has done.' Here was Albers' education *von Kinder aus*,
Americanized by the philosopher John Dewey. Drawing on German theory,
Dewey had made art the starting point for democracy: 'Works of art', he said,
'are the most intimate and energetic means of aiding individuals to share
in the arts of living.' Rice modelled Black Mountain on this thinking. The
college was to be 'a living example of democracy in action...the very "grass
roots" of a democratic way of life'.

In another regard, too, Rice had understood Albers. Although Anni's letter drew happy parallels with Dessau, he quickly saw that 'the Bauhaus had evidently not been paradise and [Josef] Albers showed no inclination to building another'. Black Mountain, it was said, 'was an outhouse of the Bauhaus'. Nothing could have been further from the truth. Albers' courses there may have drawn on his Bauhaus *Vorkurs*, but they were shaped to a very different end. In an interview in the 1960s, Anni reminded him of this:

> MRS ALBERS: Also, Juppi, you didn't bring up the one thing you always stressed so much, and that was different from [the] Bauhaus, and different from Yale, and that is – art in general education.
> ALBERS: I should speak on that?
> MRS ALBERS: Yes, because that was one of your main points at Black Mountain, that you felt art became a means of general education. And at the Bauhaus, art was a professional school....Isn't that true? And that is something that came to you mainly in Black Mountain I think.
> ALBERS: Yes, probably yes.
> MRS ALBERS: That you can build the general character through art, that you can incite interest in science, in knowledge of any kind through art.
> ALBERS: This is really what I was asking.

Thirty years earlier, in a faculty meeting at Black Mountain, Albers had noted that German divides the word 'education' in two: *Unterricht*, the imparting of information, and *Erziehung*, 'the development of will'. Joe Martin, an English professor, drawled that dentists needed to learn dentistry, not 'personal development'. 'I would like a dentist also to learn about decency,' Albers snapped back. Ethics and aesthetics had fused. If his *Vorkurs* had turned out better designers, his course at Black Mountain would produce better people. It was a distinction lost on other teachers, including Xanti Schawinsky, who Albers managed to get over from Europe in 1936. Although Schawinsky's interdisciplinary dramas would remain influential at Black Mountain until its closure, he himself was too dogmatic to do well there. In March 1938, Albers turned fifty: Xanti and his wife Irene made him a card of nine paper circles, one typewritten in English and the others in German. Soon after, they left to work for Moholy-Nagy in Chicago.

A few months after he arrived in America, Albers received a letter from Bennington, a liberal arts college in Vermont, where Philip Johnson had proposed him for a job. Regretfully, the letter said, 'Our department already has one member with [a] German background.' Albers took this casual chauvinism in his stride. Bennington would have wanted him to teach his old *Vorkurs*, and that was not now what he had in mind. In 1937, Walter Gropius would write to him that Marcel Breuer – both men had arrived at Harvard that year – lamented the lack of culture in America. Albers testily wrote back, 'more important than having a culture...is that people here are very hungry to have [one]'. Thirty years later, he would say, 'I've been asked often...which students I preferred, Europeans or Americans. You see? And I have always said I prefer the Americans because they are very curious.' This would certainly be so of his students at Black Mountain College.

Before he could start teaching them, though, he had to master a new language. As recalled by Ted Dreier, who witnessed Albers' arrival at Lee Hall,

> One peppy student said, 'What do you think you're going to do here, Mr Albers?' And his answer was very good. He didn't say he was coming to teach art. He said he was coming 'to make open the eyes'.

A woman in the welcoming party – Frau Zastrow? – asked his age. When told, she sniffed, 'You will never learn English.' Rice, Albers recalled, was furious.

> ALBERS: [He] told this lady all week long that she had spoiled my interest in English. No, but the lady was right, it was too late to start another tongue. You know? Another flexibility of the mouth. Anyway, then I had two students who started with me Mary in Wonderland – to read Mary in Wonderland.
> MRS ALBERS: Alice.

The Harlem painter Jacob Lawrence was to recall Albers' English as 'limited'. The two men met in 1946; Lawrence was under the impression that the older man had recently arrived. But he did get one thing right. As a result of Albers' inability with words, Lawrence said, 'his demonstrations were very visual'. Ted Dreier's wife, Bobbie, put it more poetically. Albers, she said, 'had a wonderful inability with English'.

To his curious young Americans, this was a source of awe. At first, Josef tried to teach through translators, the first being Emmy Zastrow. Anni quickly put a stop to that. 'My English was good enough to know that her translations were incorrect,' she said darkly. '[Zastrow] put a very Prussian tone of command into his translations.' The German-speaking poet John Evarts also proved unsatisfactory. Finally, the students took charge. 'At the end of about three weeks, I got a delegation from the class,' John Rice recalled. 'And you know what they said? Cut the translation.' Bobbie Dreier remembered Albers being asked not to speak. 'Eventually we said, "Please don't say anything,"' Dreier laughed 'We got it, you know.'

She was not the only non-student to sit in on his classes. Communalism and a lack of hierarchy were key to Rice's thinking. Students and childless staff, the Albers among them, lived in the same building. Both groups served food in the communal dining hall. In the 1940s, Josef Albers would in turn sit in on the lessons of the mathematician Max Dehn, a fellow exile from Nazism; in 1933, his own lessons were attended by John Andrew Rice. Rice's experience never left him. 'He gave you a pair of eyes,' he recalled in old age. 'You saw things. I've never forgotten him. Hardly a day passes but my eyes say "Albers". It was wonderful.'

Five months after he had arrived at Black Mountain, Albers wrote to Kandinsky: 'I am doing a lot of work for myself, and have already finished 8 new woodcuts. I am painting in oils! and even making wooden sculptures. When I feel like it, I take time off from teaching and do my own work. The only difficulty is getting materials.' He had not painted since 1920. At the Bauhaus, for thirteen years, art had meant glass; but there was no *gold rosa* in Asheville, never mind a Puhl & Wagner. In any case, his glass paintings had suffered a disaster. Ten had arrived in America broken, six beyond repair, and an eleventh badly cracked. His ex-student Howard Dearstyne believed that the shock of this turned Albers against the medium. He himself took a more sanguine view: 'At that time, I said, well, let me just have it in painting. I did some of it on paper, some on canvas.' Nonetheless, he was proud enough of the glassworks to want them shown, on both sides of the Atlantic. From Budapest, Marcel Breuer wrote: 'In spring, there will be a so-called craft-guild exhibition here. I am on the committee and would certainly place your glass pictures if we could import them. Then we could say, despite your name, that they were made in Hungary….You would only have to send exact designs. I would arrange the rest.' Nine of the surviving Bauhaus glassworks were the focus of an exhibition at J.B. Neumann's New Art Circle in Manhattan in 1936. As in Germany, they were poorly received. Dismissing them as 'glassware', the *New York Times* called the paintings 'little decorative panels'. 'Mr Albers's abstractions never transcend a certain simple elegance,' the reviewer gibed.

The new woodcuts fared little better, their first American showing, in 1935, eliciting no reviews at all. 'Most of the people who come to our exhibitions are not yet used to abstraction,' an abashed curator had written. The curator of another show was 'accused of corrupting the young'. Things didn't improve. Typical of the press Albers received is the front page of a Midwestern newspaper showing a young woman staring blankly at one of his woodcuts over the word 'Perplexed'. To add insult to injury, his work was not included in MoMA's groundbreaking 'Cubism and Abstract Art' show in 1936, the catalogue to it mentioning only his 'elaborate…pedagogical system'. 'Poor Barr, who believes only in the works he sees reproduced most often,' Albers fumed to Kandinsky. MoMA's 1938 'Decade of the Bauhaus' showed one of his chairs, not his glass paintings. Albers' argument that the Bauhaus was an idea rather than a school and that the exhibition should thus include work made at Black Mountain fell on deaf ears. He did at least get to see Frank Lloyd Wright, who swept into the museum late one evening in a 'Wagnerian velvet cape', thundered 'You are all *wrong!*', and swept out again. 'He is always frank,' Alexander Calder had quipped, 'but he is not always right.' A mild consolation was that the writer Thornton Wilder, who visited Black Mountain in 1934, had bought a print, *Umschlungen*, for $10 – '*Ein fabelhafter Kerl!*' – 'a great guy!', Josef declared his first American buyer. Another was that a Bauhaus glass piece had been included in an exhibition shut down by the Nazis – Albers would always be hurt that his work was not blacklisted as *Entartete Kunst*. By the 1940s, the glass paintings were hanging on the walls of Black Mountain's dining hall, or in its student studies.

If glass was now impossible as a material, it left the daunting question of what to replace it with. Anni described the Bauhaus as 'a creative vacuum'; Black Mountain took this to extremes. As Josef ruefully wrote to Kandinsky, 'Life is so funny. Years ago, when I had great opportunities to have shows, I did not take advantage of them. Now it is so difficult to arrange from here, I long to.' In art as in politics, the United States spent the 1930s in isolation. The American avant-garde, such as it was, was amorphous, besieged, and a long way from Asheville. Albers was among the founding members of the American Abstract Artists group, showing with them from the mid-thirties on. Even so, the AAA was not Europe. Isolated, Albers reached out to friends. 'We are very far away here, and so long to be near to the work of others,' he wrote to Jean Arp. To Georges Vantongerloo, also in Paris, he complained of not having received the magazine *Abstraction-Création*, despite sending a five-dollar cheque. By return came discouraging news. Having discussed Josef's problems in recruiting American contributors to a new journal, *Plastique*, Arp added the gloomy postscript, 'conditions for artists in this revolting dungheap called Europe are becoming more impossible by the day'. Confirmation came from Paul Guermonprez, a photography student at the Berlin Bauhaus. Writing from Amsterdam, Guermonprez apologized for a lack of Dutch interest in Albers' new woodcuts. 'I have read through the printed letter you sent me,' the ex-*Bauhäusler* ends, wistfully. 'I almost envy you; things are so beautiful for you there.'

It was not what his ex-teacher wanted to hear. Albers' woodcuts had been shown in Milan, in an exhibition arranged by Xanti Schawinsky. But this European market was drying up; there were, as yet, few signs of a local replacement. Although he would have more than forty American shows in his years at Black Mountain, these were largely at provincial museums and universities, or in galleries such as Neumann's. An attempt to get his work into the new Guggenheim Museum was met with a brutal rebuff from its director, Hilla von Rebay. 'To her mine [*sic*] she finds the titles very "irreleitend" [misguided] and dangerous,' Rebay's secretary wrote. 'But as you are only making small accords and have no sonatas or symphonies with invention or motives and rhythmic life it does not really matter.' Nonetheless, there was no going back. As ever, Albers had sent his new woodcuts to Franz Perdekamp for comment. Perdekamp's reply bothered him. 'As to your censoring of me, I can say nothing,' Josef wrote bitterly. 'It is just that my statement "abstract is Nordic", taken out of context, is not unambiguous. So it would be better to say "to render something abstract is Nordic".' Language in Germany had turned treacherous.

The Albers were under no illusion as to what was happening back home. Later, Josef would tell his students at Yale of the first time he had seen a swastika, on the arm of a young stormtrooper crossing the street – how 'he had noticed the crossed arms were black, and set into a red field on the diagonal. That it was Faustian. Endless movement, out of balance and at rest nowhere. It filled him with great dread.' Asked why he had stayed so long at a small and ill-paid Southern college, Josef replied, 'My gratitude to Black Mountain, [that] they had saved us from the Nazis.' Anni added, quietly, 'In fact, we had to leave because of my background.' In 1939, the couple were naturalized as US citizens. In June, they had met Anni's parents and uncle off a boat in Mexico. 'To get them was a job of the hell,' Josef wrote. 'But we got them after 4 days and almost without bribe, whereas others had to pay 1000 pesos, 100–200 dollars... *"Gott sei Dank" das ist vorbei.'* (Thank God it's over.) In all, fifty-two refugees from Hitler would come to Black Mountain, including Anni's niece, Renate Benfey, and the parents of Paul Guermonprez's wife, Trude Jalowetz. Not so the photographer himself, however. On his letter to Albers is a note, handwritten in German: 'Paul Guermonprez, my student in Berlin, from Belgium, was murdered by the Nazis.'

The most inventive part of Albers' career was now about to begin. John Andrew Rice had a Rhodes Scholar's reverence for Oxford: Black Mountain, like an Oxford college, was to be wholly self-governing. There were as few rules as possible, to encourage what the poet M. C. Richards called 'the chaos out of which creativity constellates'. This applied equally to faculty. Until the war, Albers would be the only painter at Black Mountain – there was no Klee or Kandinsky to measure himself against, no Gropius to tell him what to teach. Just as his ethics and aesthetics had fused, so what he preached and practised now drew closer. One senses a pleasure in his new woodcuts at the easy movement of the hand, a freedom quite missing in glass. The early Black Mountain prints, pulled on the ancient letter press in Lee Hall, break out in biomorphic loops and whorls, surrealist in feel if not fact (fig. 5.2). There is a new link between eye and hand, art and the action of making it. 'Art is not an object,' Albers would say. 'Art is an experience.' Small and sometimes clumsy, his early American woodcuts hold the seeds of that interdisciplinary practice for which Black Mountain College would later become famous.

There were signs of this in his teaching, too. Jane Slater Marquis, known as 'Slats', recalled Albers in the classroom. 'He put on a real performance,' Marquis said. 'He always came in after we [had] assembled – it was like an entrance, a theatrical entrance.' A fellow student agreed: 'It was like a drama!' she said. 'Like going to the theatre!' The painter Elaine de Kooning,

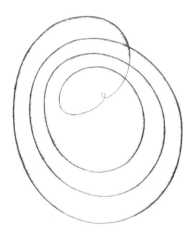

5.2 *Alpha*, 1939. Lithograph, 25½ × 19¾ in.

accompanying her husband to Black Mountain, also found Albers' teaching dramatic, although less happily so. 'I don't think I've ever seen an instructor more involved with teaching as a military performance,' de Kooning said. Here, as at the Bauhaus, design and drawing were taught separately. The first, *Werklehre* – de-Germanized to 'basic design' after 1941 – included *matière* exercises in which students worked with the textural appearance of materials. To this duo was now added a third course, in colour. As Albers was keen to point out, colour had not been taught at the Bauhaus. Kandinsky, he said, had preached his 'dogma' – 'a circle is red, a square is blue' – but got little further than the French chemist Chevreul.

A comparison of classroom photographs from the Bauhaus and Black Mountain suggests an obvious change (see p. 174; figs 5.3, 5.4). In Dessau, the emphasis was on words: students stand respectfully around while Albers, professorial, discusses their work. In America, deprived of language, he is thrown back on gesture – expansive movements that take in his entire body. Work is done on the floor, teacher and students bent double over coloured paper or *matières*. Art is no longer just of the eye and hand. Albers, holding a cigarette, is invariably dressed in white. (So, to the awe of the students, was Anni. 'They were male and female of the same species,' one said.) Lessons spilled out of Josef's classroom into the lobby – in warm weather, from there to the porch. In a photo of one Albers class from *Life* magazine (fig. 5.5), it is not clear what is being taught, or by whom. The choreographed gestures of teacher and students could be a lesson in musical composition by John Cage or of dance by Merce Cunningham. Both men would visit Black Mountain in 1948, when interdisciplinary practice was already well established there. 'I found my ideas were absolutely like two peas in a pod with Albers',' Cage would later recall.

Alongside this blurring of disciplinary boundaries went that of other rules. North Carolina was a segregated state. Some knew first-hand what this meant. Robert Wunsch, a Southerner, drama teacher and future rector of the college, remembered, as a child, his uncle throwing the thumb of a lynched black man onto the kitchen table. Clark Foreman, who taught history, had seen a man burned alive: 'Every time the fire would spring up, catch his clothes....they'd beat the flames down so [that he would die] slowly,' Foreman said. Black Mountain's students – with few exceptions, from liberal northern states – had been pro-integration from the start. Unsurprisingly, their teachers were more wary.

5.3 Genevieve Naylor, Art class meets on a deck at Black Mountain College, North Carolina.
5.4 Photographer unknown, Josef Albers teaching at Black Mountain College, *ca.* 1948.

5.5 Barbara Morgan, Josef among the cabbages outsideLE studies building, Black Mountain College.
5.6 Photographer unknown, Josef Albers teaching drawing on the porch of
Lee Hall, Black Mountain College, *ca.* 1935–6.

Their caution should be seen in context. African Americans may have been the most obvious target of prejudice in the South, but they were by no means the only one. A year before Black Mountain, another college had opened in Asheville. Called Galahad, this preached the mystical anti-Semitism of its founder, William Dudley Pelley. The day after Hitler became German chancellor, Pelley announced his new Silver Legion, an 'American Aryan Militia' which agitated for Jews to be resettled in ghetto-cities called Beth-Havens. The Albers also faced the intractable problem of being German. As far as locals were concerned, Black Mountain was a nest of libertines who practised free love and went about unclothed. A preponderance of foreign faculty hardly helped.

From the beginning, Rice tried to involve locals in college affairs – Josef's design for the school's logo is notable in including the names of both the town of Black Mountain and its educational twin. Described as 'a simple ring', the emblem is anything but. A typical piece of Albersian doublethink – black–white, field–ground, solid–void – it suggests a unity that was mostly wishful thinking: 'coming together, standing together, working together...colour and white, light and shadow, in balance'. Rice also recruited the Albers to show that foreigners were just like Americans, really. To the Asheville Lions' Club and Junior Women's Club of Lenoir, Anni spoke on

5.7 Logo design for Black Mountain College, 1934.

'Design' and 'Handweaving Today', Josef on 'Education and Art Education' and 'Abstract Art (with slides)'. They gamely showed their work anywhere that would have it, including the 1946 North Carolina Artists competition. Josef's painting *Lozenge Horizontal* came joint third, after one of a hen and her chicks. Rice's charm offensive was only partly successful. When, in the war, a Black Mountain student applied to the army, his application was turned down on the grounds of his referees' German names: Wunsch, Dreier and Kocher. Even Rice was not immune from anti-Teutonism. Later, explaining why he and Josef Albers had fallen out, he said, 'You can't talk to a German about liberty. You just waste your breath. They don't know what the hell you mean.'

For Albers, the debate over race carried unpleasant echoes. Just as Hannes Meyer's Marxism had threatened the Bauhaus, so desegregation might now threaten Black Mountain. The Ku Klux Klan's antipathy to integration was well known, as were their methods of showing it. Even Clark Foreman, a keen desegregationist, allowed that *emigré* faculty had reason to be scared. 'They had been through very hard times in Germany,' Foreman said. 'We were going to antagonize the community.' Nonetheless, the idea that Black Mountain could (and should) have integrated in the 1930s has stuck. So, too, the belief that the failure was Josef Albers'.

Typical, if inaccurate, is the idea that 'the most shocking aspect of [Black Mountain] during the Albers years is the studied obliviousness to contemporary events'. It is only in the mid-1940s, when Albers' views begin to carry weight, that the topic of desegregation finally appears in faculty minutes. Albers himself takes little part in the debate. In January 1944, Bob Wunsch, by now rector, suggests a visit to Black Mountain by 'coloured students', although in secrecy, 'lest our relations with people in Asheville...be endangered'. The German phenomenologist, Erwin Straus, predicts disaster: 'if we are going to do things which might destroy the college, we should...be prepared for the consequences'. Albers, by contrast, is mild: 'Perhaps our Social Survey group might find out from local people what they think?' In May 1944, he mordantly points out that arguments over admitting one black student or two rest on the assumption that they will get on because they are black. Only in September, when Black Mountain has had its first black student, does he enter the fray. As the minutes record, 'J. Albers suggested that the question be broadened and that we try to get members of the yellow or other races' (specifically Japanese). At a time when anti-Japanese feeling in America was at its highest, it was a courageous thought.

By now, Black Mountain was a very different place from the one the Albers had come to. In 1938, John Andrew Rice was forced to resign. If their relationship started well, Albers had come to resent Rice's dominance. 'Rice says all the time that the artist is important in education,' he growled. 'Why not let the artist say it?' In 1936, the Yugoslav writer Louis Adamic wrote about the college in *Harper's* magazine. Mildly hagiographic, his piece portrayed Rice as, if not Black Mountain's Christ, then its John the Baptist. That Adamic would later describe Albers' role as 'equal, and in many respects superior, to Rice's' came too late. With the rest of the faculty keeping their heads down, Albers stepped up as the rector's challenger. When Rice began an affair with a woman student, he saw his chance. In January 1938, he wrote to Rice, demanding he consider his position. Unmoved by the congenial reply – 'I welcome your letter. I hope that it means the reestablishment of communication between us' – Albers wrote again: 'The situation in the College has developed to the point where we feel that it is absolutely essential...that you take a leave of absence.'

Then, too, Black Mountain had moved. A recurring problem at Lee Hall had been the Blue Ridge Assembly YMCA's return each summer. Black Mountain's chattels were consigned to the basement, its faculty ejected. In 1937, the college took out a mortgage on a nearby property called Lake Eden. That autumn, Albers wrote to Lawrence Kocher, editor of the *Architectural Record*, asking him to recommend a teacher – not, tellingly, for architecture, but for 'modern painting'. The following summer, Kocher was invited to

5.8 Josef Albers, Roadside Cottage.

propose an architect for Lake Eden. His suggestion was a Bauhaus quartet of Walter Gropius, Marcel Breuer, Xanti Schawinsky and Josef Albers. When Gropius's plan proved too expensive, Kocher himself got the job. By then, 1940, Albers had made his own contribution to Lake Eden's design. In February 1939, the college scraped together $800 for the construction of a small house: Albers drew the layout. Known as New Cottage, it was meant as a prototype for faculty accommodation. It would play home to several families, including Max Dehn's. Albers, who had intended the cottage for himself, never lived there. From 1941, he and Anni would share a double house with Ted and Bobbie Dreier, the Dreiers and their children on side and the Albers the other, with a communal living room in between. This was furnished with wood-and-leather chairs designed by Josef in a Mexican vernacular and made by a local carpenter, Edward DuPuy. The painting he nicknamed 'fried eggs' hung on one wall and the remake of a lost glasswork, *Flying* (1935), on another. Visiting students thought of the room as archetypically Bauhaus: many copied its decor in their own studies. Later, German gardening would also captivate them. 'There are cabbages and onions as well....Lettuce, radishes and (bewilderingly enough) cactus and lilies too, are in the Albers' garden,' the College Bulletin marvelled. The Dreiers' and Albers' shared house was called Roadside Cottage (fig. 5.8).

5.9 Ted Dreier, Josef Albers at Black Mountain College, *ca.* 1940–9.

When the writer William McCleery spent a semester at Blue Ridge in 1939, he had found Black Mountain irksomely naive. When he went to Lake Eden five years later, he mourned the college's lost innocence. Built around the eponymous lake – really a large pond – the new campus looked up at mountains. One busty pair was dubbed 'Mae West'; the hill behind Kocher's new study building was 'the Garden of Eden'. It was suitably snake-ridden. For Albers, the move was marked by a growing fascination with deception. As one student noted, 'He trained you to be so skilled [as] to be able to deceive the eye, even the knowing eye.' Walter Gropius's daughter Ati, who had known him from birth, saw this new interest biographically. 'I don't think there was one single comment [Albers] made that pertained to the visual world that he didn't also intend to pertain to the human world,' she wrote. Both art and life were now predicated on doubt.

This became clear in *matière* lessons, held in the open undercroft of Kocher's study building (fig. 5.10). Melding the visual with the haptic, *matière* asked students to consider not how things felt but how they looked like they felt. As with Albers' own early glass paintings, materials might be found anywhere – in the woods, on walls, filched from the college rubbish tip. The aim was to fool the eye into seeing texturally unalike things as similar: chicken wire and moss, cement and driftwood, cardboard and lightbulbs.

5.10 Gabriel Benzur, Study building at Black Mountain College.

A student recalled the lessons. '[Albers] would come in…and he'd say, "Ah, *ja, ja, ja* – this looks really shiny." Or, "This looks soft, this looks really gooey." He would poke or tap the study to see what it was, hoping that he himself would be surprised by what it turned out to be.' As the years passed, this interest in *Schwindel*, the deceiving of the eye – including, or primarily, his own – grew.

In faculty meetings, he now sang the virtues of 'mental unrest'. Habit and certainty were the enemies of invention: its friends were discomfort and doubt. An action as familiar as signing one's name could be made troubling when done backwards. Certainties were relentlessly picked at. Elaine de Kooning was astonished to see, at Albers' prompting, that Coca-Cola bottles were not a single green but four. The Japanese American artist Ruth Asawa – a beneficiary of Albers' move to admit 'the yellow races' – recalled deconstructing Lucky Strike packets. Along with disorientation went repetition – the reward for doing something well was a laconic, 'That's fine. Make another.' Students took courses in one semester and repeated them the next, sometimes for years. As ever, Albers applied this repetition to himself. A surprisingly perceptive record of him at Black Mountain comes from the magazine *Arts and Decoration*. 'I am tempted to call Josef Albers' own workroom in the school a laboratory rather than a studio,' the article says. 'He studies like a scientist, bent on discovering forms, values and colour relationships that are sure, and eliminating by trial and error the uncertain and false.' The piece ends, 'I exclaimed at his patience in making over the same subject again and again. He said, "Life is always changing – no object is ever for two minutes exactly the same. A shift in light, a change in temperature, a slight turn of your eyes in looking make it something else."'

Among the earliest paintings Albers made at Black Mountain was *Black Frame* (1934) (fig. 5.11). Painted on masonite, it is, and sets out to be, an oddity. What reads as its background is built up of flat rhomboids of colour, on which is superimposed the black frame of the title, painted illusionistically. The effect is disconcerting, if a little clumsy. The work is abstract in one plane, representational in another. Its trickiness calls to mind surrealism, although *Black Frame*'s equivocations have nothing to do with Freud and everything to do with perception. Within a year, Albers was painting *Etude: Red-Violet* (1935), an even odder work (fig. 5.12). It is tempting to see the picture's looseness as anticipating abstract expressionism, although this came two decades later

5.11 *Black Frame (Picture Frame)*, 1934. Oil on masonite, 15½ × 23⅞ in.
5.12 *Etude: Red-Violet (Christmas Shopping)*, 1934. Oil on wood composition board, 15 × 14 in.

and Albers would reserve a particular loathing for it. To a later generation of students, at Yale, he would say of Jackson Pollock, 'You may as well rub *shit* on the canvas.'

For Thanksgiving 1938, two faculty members composed a song called 'There Ought to Be a Law at Black Mountain'. Its lyrics summed up the college's paradox nicely:

> Oh you cannot be a lib'ral at these dam' progressive schools,
> For a lib'ral gets no exercise except by fighting rules.

Albers, too, was plagued by an excess of freedom. Both *Black Frame* and *Etude: Red-Violet* are individualistic works, one-offs. Experiment meant repetition: what was needed was a template for sameness. He would find it not in America, but Mexico. In December 1935, he and Anni made a trip to the Mesoamerican sites at Teotihuacán and Monte Albán. They would visit the country five more times before 1941, more than a dozen times in all. Mexico was cheap: although, after tireless badgering, Josef had won himself a small German pension, its $40 a month barely topped up his meagre salary. Mexico was also accessible by the couple's new car, Josef being frightened of flying. Above all, though, it was Mexican art that drew them back. To Kandinsky he wrote, 'Mexico is truly the promised land of abstract art. For here it is already 1000s of years old. And still very much alive.'

What the Albers saw in Mayan art was a heady combination of continuity, anonymity and utility. The pottery they bought from roadside vendors – Josef habitually overbid – made no distinction between the spiritual and everyday. Works were anonymous, patterns unvarying: the very opposite of the hated individualism. Here was a template for experiment, an antidote to the endless possibility of America. It was above all Mexican architecture that fascinated, its formulaic simplicity, interaction of geometry and colour; its earthiness. If New Cottage was built in wood, that had not been the plan. From Black Mountain, Albers wrote to Franz Perdekamp:

> We checked [Lake Eden] for a site for our house, which I will
> make in adobe....Here, wood construction is typical....But it has
> disadvantages that I hope to overcome by building with clay. Almost
> all of Mexico has buildings of this kind and even the largest pyramid
> in the world there was built with clay stones. Well, we will see.

In a letter to Lawrence Kocher a month later, he discusses the feasibility of building New Cottage in adobe. It was Kocher's questioning of the quality of Black Mountain clay that changed his mind.

In 1937, the Albers put on a Mexican exhibition at Lee Hall. While the future abstract expressionists were discovering Native American art, Black Mountain soaked up Mesoamerica. The discovery was particularly urgent for the Albers themselves. Josef's painting *Mexican* (1936) ponders the tension between colour and form, a strong graphic line trying, but failing, to encircle white-on-blue rectangles. Later, at Yale, he would describe the difference between the Greek and Mayan use of line: 'The Greeks enslaved their neighbours, and their black line enslaves...but Pre-Columbian Indians shared their culture with their neighbours, so...their black line says, "Neighbour, you go first."' This back-and-forth between line and colour continues for a decade – the former in the nine *Graphic Tectonic* prints (1942), where Albers flattens Mayan pyramids into a graphic rebus that advances and recedes equally and at once. *Equal and Unequal* (1939) has the look of a lithograph or axonometric drawing, although it is an oil painting: its double forms both imply and deny three-dimensional space. By *Layered* (1940), Albers had begun what would be a lifetime practice of writing his 'recipes' on the backs of his paintings. But it took a year-long Mexican sabbatical to unite form and colour in a single form and template. Writing to Perdekamp from Mexico in September 1947, Albers says:

> Since January [I've been painting] only one theme in about 70 studies. What interests me now is how colours change one another according to [their] proportion and quantity....I'm especially proud when [I can get] colours to lose their identity and become unrecognisable. Greens become blue, neutral greys become red-violet and so on....And what is amazing is that I use colours exactly as they come out of the tube.

He had begun these new works in New Mexico, although the lion's share would be made south of the border. All were drawn on the grid, their colours strictly apportioned by mathematical formula. It was a method more typical of the laboratory than the studio. The new works were called *Variants*, or, alternatively, *Adobes*.

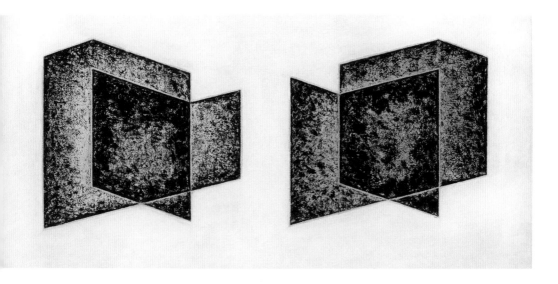

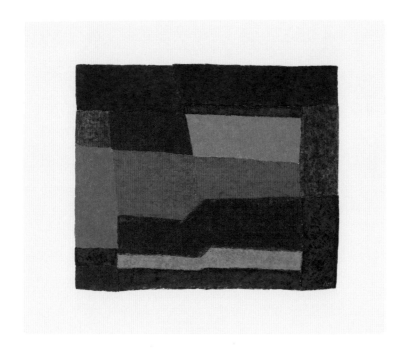

5.13 *Equal and Unequal*, 1939. Oil on masonite, 19 × 40 in.
5.14 *Layered*, 1940. Oil on masonite, 23½ × 28 in.

Monument to Quetzalcoatl (Calixtlahuaca)

5.15 *Monument to Quetzalcoatl, Calixtlahuaca, Mexico*. Photocollage: gelatin silver prints, found postcards, and printed matter on cardboard, 10⅛ × 8⅛ in.

Twenty years later, he would claim that the name 'Homages to the Square' was a misnomer, that the series was all to do with colour and nothing with form. So, too, with the *Adobes*. At the Bauhaus, architecture had been the end point of all: now, Albers' new paintings would be built architecturally. There was no mistaking what the *Adobes* were – graph paper schemata marked their various parts as 'windows' or 'walls'. If Albers' alchemy with colour perplexed the eye, it was now taxed by images that were at once narrative and abstract. So, too, with the Mexican collages, made from photographs taken with Josef's trusty Leica. Found after his death, these are an enigma. On the one hand, their constituent parts are just snapshots – one, *Monument to Quetzcoatl, Calixtlahuaca*, shows Anni, sun-hatted and in white. Yet Albers' placing of individual photographs is clearly intended, a response to the abstract rhythm of solid and void in the architecture they depict. To read the collages, the viewer is called upon to see and, at the same time, not to see.

By the time the Albers and Dreiers moved into Roadside Cottage, Josef and Bobbie Dreier were lovers. Their affair had begun early. Letters between them are mostly undated: an exception is one sent by Josef from a hotel in Virginia in 1934. Bobbie is 'Böbbschen'; Josef is sleepless, cannot feel the air about him (fig. 5.16). Often, there is a private code – he is Firestone, she is Mrs Goodyear; there is talk of the end of a 'rivalry of five years', perhaps his own with Ted Dreier. There is mention of 'nices times' [*sic*] had in a car. Josef photographed Bobbie incessantly, often in the nude and sometimes in rumpled sheets, presumably developing the images himself (fig. 5.17). Some were pasted up in the style of the Mexican collages. Who took the picture of the couple together is unknown. Josef was godfather to the Dreiers' son Eddie, born in 1937. After this, he took to signing his letters to Bobbie 'DoE'. Can this have stood for 'Daddy of Eddie'? Albers' encrypting of the boy's name in the title of the print *Eh-De* (1940) lends weight to the idea (fig. 5.21). In April 1941, Bobbie is '*Süsses, süsses Böbbel mein*' – 'my sweetest, sweetest Böbbel'. In October, Eddie's elder brother Mark was killed falling from a truck at Lake Eden. Josef delivered his eulogy to a stunned gathering:

> we remember his admiration
> for ability to work
> how he loved hard working people
> above all his daddy

Warren Green Hotel
WARRENTON
VIRGINIA
4. VII. 34   RALPH McKEE, PROPRIETOR

Best Böbbchen,

Because of the shaking I must write it once more :

> IN THE CAR:
> THE WORLD IS WUNDERFULL
> AGAIN. BUT WITH MY
> CLOSED EYES. BECAUSE I CAN
> IMAGEN SO MUCH ABOUT SOMBODY.[1]
>
> I LEAN AGAINST THE WALL
> AND SLEEP. BUT I DON'T BELIEVE
> THAT IT IS THE WALL.
>
> FRESH AIR IS TUCHING ME,
> MY HEAD AND FACE. BUT I DON'T
> FEEL AIR.[2]
>
> IT SEEMS THIS IS'N DIFFERENT
> CAR. I THINK ABOUT AN
> OTHER CAR. AND OTHER
> NICES[3] PLACES.

[1] or: Some Body?
[2] or: I am feeling never Air
[3] Plural because of Rythmo, Balance, Proportion.

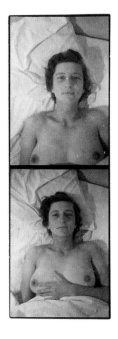

5.16 Josef Albers, letter to Bobbie Dreier, 4 July 1934.
5.17 Josef Albers, Bobbie Dreier.

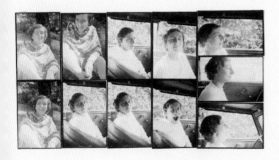

5.18 *Untitled (Bobbie Dreier)*, 1936–7. Photocollage:
gelatin silver prints mounted on cardboard.

5.19 Photographer unknown (possibly Anni Albers), Josef Albers
and Bobbie Dreier near Black Mountain, NC, 1938.
5.20 Claude Stoller, Juppi and Eddie (Josef and Eddie Dreier), *ca.* 1940.

5.21 *Eh–De*, 1940. Drypoint print, 9 × 11 in.

After that, letters between Josef and Bobbie cease. There would be another affair with Betty Seymour, who housed the Albers in New Mexico for the start of their 1946 sabbatical. To her, Josef was 'Crazus' – he wrote, 'I can't lie down/without calling/again and again/a name/and over and over again'. Another letter is doodled with musical notes. It ends 'Benedicamus Domino!/ Because because because/that you are coming home so-o-on'. It is signed 'Anni's husband'.

All marriages are complex, the Albers' no less than most. John Andrew Rice recalled overhearing them argue: 'Albers and his wife were quarrelling about something and he said, "Well, it was *your* notion we should get married."' It is not known why they were childless. To Ruth Asawa, Josef said, "Your paintings are your children": "He was very opposed to [her] having children," Asawa's husband recalled. "And Ruth said, 'I'm not going to forego that. I'm not going to forego having children.'" Josef's affair with Bobbie Dreier seems to have been discreet: in none of the extant (and gossipy) Black Mountain literature is it mentioned. His behaviour towards female students, by contrast, was infamous. Elaine Schmitt recalled him jiggling her breasts, Nancy Smith being groped by him in her study. Letters to 'Slats' were signed 'your squeezer'. This was the culture of Black Mountain College: Ilya Bolotowsky was 'a butt-pincher', and a visiting Fernand Léger sketched women bathing naked until, at a pre-agreed signal, they turned their showers on him. John Andrew Rice had an affair with a woman student; the sculptor Richard Lippold with a man, Ray Johnson. It is telling of the times that none of the students seem to have lodged an official complaint about their treatment. As to Anni, her response to her husband's philandering, in public at least, was a weary, 'Have you finished pinching all the girls yet, Josef?'

He freed the eye, yet had no notion of freedom: Rice's description of Albers is paradoxical, but typical. To one student, Leonard Billing, Josef was 'withdrawn', while he hugged another, José Yglesias, for showing 'real feelings' in class. Elaine de Kooning found Albers' teaching 'autocratic', Josephine Levine 'organized, structured, [but] not authoritarian'. 'Albers was the schoolmaster, and even if he did dream, he wouldn't admit it' (Charles Burchard). 'Josef Albers taught me to draw in the same way that my father taught me to ride a bicycle' (Alexander Eliot). And so on. Some, like Ruth

Asawa, found his discipline liberating. 'I liked the rigid and the things that I learned from [Albers],' Asawa said. 'I had come from a culture that didn't think very much of one's feelings.' Other fans were less expected.

Robert Rauschenberg had read about Albers in *Time* magazine. 'I was willing to submerge any desires I had into [Albers'] discipline, but he never believed that,' Rauschenberg was later to say. 'I don't think he ever realized it was his discipline I came for.' The two did not get on. 'I was Albers' dunce, the outstanding example of what he was *not* talking about,' Rauschenberg would say. 'He'd pick up something of mine and say, "This is the most stupid thing I have ever seen, I dun't even vant to know who did it."' And yet Rauschenberg's work, like Albers', is relativist, preoccupied with the way position and juxtaposition change perception. It is hard to see one of Rauschenbeg's combines – the famous *Monogram* (1955–9), say – without hearing Albers' dictum, 'There is no extraordinary without the ordinary, and the root of both is order.' Albers remained, for Rauschenberg, 'the most important teacher I've ever had'. 'Years later,' he said, 'I'm still learning what [Albers] taught me, because what he taught had to do with the entire visual world.'

A problem in writing about Black Mountain is the college's propensity to myth. If all students are equal, then their memories are, and the histories written from those memories. Stories about Josef Albers abound. His bad relationship with Rauschenberg is one, with Kenneth Noland another. Repeated, among other places, in his obituary, the Noland story has him 'gravitat[ing] toward...[Ilya] Bolotowsky' at Black Mountain because Bolotowsky was 'less *doctrinaire*' than Albers. The more prosaic truth is that Albers was on sabbatical when Noland arrived in 1947, Bolotowsky being his stand-in. Of the semester he spent as Albers' student in 1948, Noland was to say, 'Actually, I studied with him just for half a year. But I was very affected by the climate that he created there.' Albers' teaching, he said, was of 'immense value'. Although Noland was not alone in painting concentric circles in the 1950s – Jasper Johns beat him to it – works such as *This* (1958–9) are unusual in their sculptural feel for solid and void. This may call to mind Albers' Black Mountain logo; or, of course, not.

If Dreier's use of the word 'pioneering' had seduced the Albers in 1933, by 1943 Black Mountain's *laissez-faire* had begun to pall. To Leonard Billing, who was a student at both campuses, Josef 'became more autocratic' with the move to Lake Eden. With any thought of grades or progress deemed illiberal, there was an annual return to academic zero – 'every year, the same thing', as Richard Lippold wearily recalled. By 1944, he found Josef Albers 'exhausted'. 'Black Mountain wore him out,' Ati Gropius agreed. 'It wore everybody out.' Anni simply said, 'Finally, after sixteen years, when we grew older also, it got too much.'

Calls on faculty time were endless. The least thing had to be discussed with students – 'over-democratic nonsense', Josef snapped. Others concurred. Alfred Kazin, writer-in-residence in 1943, found 'the demands of students for total enlightenment, information, moral sustenance, and total friendship...frightening'. Things got worse when, in 1948, the Albers returned from sabbatical to find that the rectorship had been taken over by Bill Levi, a left-wing philosopher. Faculty rank had been abolished, farmers and librarians made equal with teachers. Economics was now taught by Karl Niebyl, a Marxist whose students sang the Comintern in the shower. Josef was appalled: it was Hannes Meyer all over again. In his eighties, he would splutter, 'That was like the Bauhaus! – If you were not....I was asked – If you were not for us, on...you – you see?' Anni quietly interjected: 'I can't remember that it was political.' In October, Josef managed to force Levi's resignation; the only possible replacement as rector was himself. By November, as he wrote to the college treasurer, he was planning to kill two birds with one stone by turning the school into the Black Mountain College of the Arts, at a stroke professionalizing it and ridding it of its leftists. But there was a problem: student numbers had halved. As Albers admitted, 'we have now only 55...and several may leave as they do not find enough social science'.

There was trouble, too, with the few who remained. The mood at Black Mountain had changed. Student ditties were a staple of college life. One was the 'Matière Song':

> Let your slip show under your DRESS
> It's Ma-ti-ere.
> Let your ROOM stay in a MESS
> It's Ma-ti-ere.
> If your GIRDLE looks like a TIRE
> It's Mat-iere

When you sit in a cane seated CHAIR
It's Mat-iere!
[CHORUS]
For [Albers] has really opened our eyes
And now we will see for the rest of our lives.

This was written in 1935; a decade later, its lyrics might have been less genial. Albers had always been a man of fixed views – on how beer should be drunk ('hitting the back of the throat'), wood cut ('the polite saw goes *sie-sie-sie*, the rude saw goes *du-du-du*'), grapefruit tins stacked (brick-style), hot dogs roasted on a stick (his promptly fell into the fire). Until 1945, these things were indulged as eccentricities. But male students who arrived after the war were largely ex-servicemen, paid for by the GI Bill. They were in no mood to be disciplined. This became clear in *matière* lessons. Where once these had prompted general excitement, in the lost innocence of Lake Eden they might provoke ridicule. Two students writing under the pseudonym 'Gerard Legro' lampooned the exercises in a poem called 'Father Albers's Notebook (*Series du matière*)'. It was tacked to the college noticeboard until Albers tore it down. Egged on by this, three more students took to class a *matière* that looked like a cowpat. Albers, delighted at the *Schwindel*, prodded it with his stick: the dung was real. Furious, he banned the boys from his class. All this weighed on him, and on his art. The painter Leo Lionni arrived at Black Mountain in 1946. Bumping into him in the corridor, Albers said, 'You have a good time painting, don't you?' When Lionni laughed that he did, Albers blurted out, 'This morning I hate it. It's hard work.' 'I was shocked,' Lionni recalled. 'Albers clearly meant what he said.' Things couldn't go on.

And yet. Many of the things for which Black Mountain is now most famous happened not during its semesters but in the three months between them. From 1944 on, this long vacation was taken up with so-called Summer Sessions. John Cage and Merce Cunningham (1948), the architect Buckminster Fuller (1948), artists Robert Motherwell (1945), Willem de Kooning (1948) and many others taught at these, all of them at the invitation of Albers (figs 5.22, 5.23). Most were little known at the time: Motherwell and de Kooning had each had one small show apiece, from which they had sold little or nothing. As a

5.22 Photographer unknown, Josef Albers and Robert Motherwell at Black Mountain College, 1945.
5.23 Clemens Kalischer, Merce Cunningham teaching dance, Black Mountain College Summer Session, 1948.

future colleague at Yale was to put it, 'Bucky Fuller wasn't Bucky Fuller when Albers invited him. And that was also true of most of the people he invited. They were absolutely unknown.'

From the start, the Sessions were Albers' baby. First mention of them comes in January 1944: 'J. Albers reported on plans for the Art Institute, [this] summer.' By April, he was fretting about funding. To the Quaker American Friends Service Committee, he wrote: 'Black Mountain is trying to do an important step forward in behalf of the negro problem....I am looking for help to make such attendance of several races possible.' The FSC referred him to the Rosenwald Fund. In 1946, Albers wrote to its director: 'It might interest you that in the meantime I got a very good Negro painter as teacher for the Summer Art Institute here.' The teacher was Jacob Lawrence: the Fund underwrote the whole cost of hiring him and his wife, the artist Gwendolyn Knight.

Lawrence's case is interesting. In 1943, as part of Black Mountain's Black History Week, Albers had lectured on 'Negro art'. On a piece of paper headed with those words, he jots random notes – 'Compare with Egypt, Mesopotamia', then, more surprising and underlined, 'Ruskin, Maillol'. 'If we are disappointed not to find Greek qualities, then we should consider...' – here, as often, Albers' handwriting fades into illegibility. He wrote to the Museum of Modern Art for slides of 'Negro plastic'. It may have been then that he discovered Lawrence's work – the *Migration* series would be shown at MoMA the following year. Like all teachers at the summer Institute, the young Harlem painter was given a show in Lake Eden's dining hall. His art was figurative and narrative, qualities that Albers disliked. Yet, in Lawrence's memory, 'When my show was up, every day [Albers] had lunch, he would [go] and sit in a different place and look at a different work.' 'I have never forgotten this experience,' Lawrence said, fifty years later. 'It was a wonderful experience for me.'

Keen not to turn out artistic copies of himself, Albers was at pains to recruit to the Art Institute teachers whose work was not like his. 'Any form [of art] is acceptable if it is true,' he would say. 'And if it is true, it's ethical and aesthetic.' As to summer students, they were encouraged to relax: holidays were not for working in. So, too, the teachers – 'I hope that they will consider their time here...as vacation,' Albers wrote to one. Freed from the strain of college politics, he relaxed, too. The Josef of the Summer Sessions was very different from the Josef of the two semesters. That term-time Albers only became more beleaguered: a 1947 photograph shows him, not yet sixty, looking twenty years older. As M. C. Richards remembered it, he and Anni 'were no longer at their ease, or loved'. Their early infatuation with Black Mountain was gone. Ted Dreier had briefly taken over as rector. On 24 January 1949, he in his turn was forced to resign. It was the last straw. A week later, in solidarity with their friend, the Albers quit as well.

5.24 Photographer unknown, Josef Albers eating at Black Mountain College, 1948.

6   Ends and Beginnings: Yale

It would not be an exaggeration to see Albers as the father of the last generation of American Modernists.

Michael Craig-Martin, 'On Albers' Influence on American Art'

He had a lot of sons and daughters out there, although he had no children.

Robert Slutzky, student, Yale Department of Design, 1951–4

In the dying days of December 1950, Josef Albers wrote to his friend Franz Perdekamp. It had been snowing all day. Albers apologizes for the lateness of his Christmas greetings, blaming them on 'the school, the house...obligations and our own work'. Teaching, especially, had been 'a big problem – It is not easy to translate "tradition" into up-to-date thinking.' Still, he says, 'the students are beginning to come around, [so] I have hope and patience'. He wrote from the house that he and Anni had bought three months before, the first they had owned – a clapboard, Cape Cod two-up, two-down, built in 1946; one of a dozen just like it on North Forest Circle, West Haven, Connecticut. The Albers would live there for twenty years.

It had been an eventful eighteen months. In May 1949, 'in the middle of packing', Albers had written a final letter to Perdekamp from Black Mountain College. He and Anni are off to Mexico until mid-August, after which they have been lent a flat belonging to the aunt of a student, Alex Reed – a favourite who had taught for Josef, made jewelry with Anni and built the Quiet House at Black Mountain College in Mark Dreier's memory. Reed's aunt lived at 199 East 76th Street, New York 21 – 'write the 1s like this: I', Josef frets, lest American postmen mistake German ones for sevens. After Mexico, he will teach in Cincinnati for six weeks. 'That', he ends, 'is all we know for sure about our future.' After Cincinnati, he would teach for a semester at the night school of the Pratt Institute in New York, camping out in the flat of the German-American abstract painter Carl Holty. It was a tenuous life. Although he tells Perdekamp that he will be taking part 'in twenty exhibitions again this year...financial success is by no means in proportion'. The bright spots are that he had 'attended a conference in Yale University', and would teach a summer school at Harvard. At the latter, he was to paint the first of the series of pictures that would occupy him for the rest of his life. The former would bring the recognition that had eluded him for six decades.

Diverse paths led Albers to Yale, the first commencing with Charles Sawyer. It was Sawyer who had given Albers his earliest American show, and written to apologize for its pallid reception. After wartime service with the US Army's 'Monuments Men', he was made dean of the Yale School of Fine Arts. Mired in the Beaux Arts tradition, the school was noted for its devotion to egg tempera painting. Things needed shaking up, and Sawyer was the man to do it. During the 1950 summer vacation, Yale art students received a letter warning of a change when they returned. That change, as yet unnamed, was Josef Albers. His arrival, Sawyer drily recalled, precipitated 'a pretty rugged year or two' at Yale. George Heard Hamilton, professor of art history there, put it more pithily: 'Albers came,' he said. 'Blood was spilt and feathers flew.'

His appointment reflected a divide in post-war American thinking about art. Yale was pulled in opposing directions – towards the solipsisms of abstract expressionism on the one hand, and a new sense that art should be functional on the other. An apologist for the second view was Henry-Russell Hitchcock. It was Hitchcock, an architectural historian, who curated 'Painting Toward Architecture' – an exhibition that toured twenty-eight US cities between 1947 and 1952, branding art as socially relevant and bringing modernism to Middle America. The art historian Robert Rosenblum, then a Yale student, remembered the show as suffused with a 'pre-war belief that the heroic innovations of modern art [might allow] the cleanest and purest of slates'. Its roots lay firmly in the Bauhaus.

Work in the exhibition came from the collection of the Miller Company of Meriden, Connecticut, a lighting firm that had bought Albers' *Flying* for $300. Albers wrote to thank them: 'It might interest you that [*Flying*] represents a repetition in oil of a broken glass painting, one of my earlier ones in which I used sandblasting as a new means for wall paintings in glass.' The work's graphic potential was clear: *Flying* was used on the cover of Miller's 'Ceilings Unlimited' catalogue later that year. In May 1945, the company invited Albers to make 'a trade-mark along modern lines' for $500 – a flattering offer, given that Philip Johnson had recently been hired to do Miller's corporate design. It proved a poisoned chalice. Albers' proposals were batted back and forth for three years, after which, to his fury, he was paid $50 to go away. The logo the Miller Company adopted soon afterwards was virtually indistinguishable from his own. Still, there were compensations. Having work in the Miller collection put him in the company of Mondrian, Picasso and Klee; the drawing he doodled on a letter from the company remains among his earliest known nested squares (fig. 6.2). Then, too, the Miller Company's views on art matched his own. As Emily Tremaine, wife of the owner, told *Newsweek*: 'Our scheme is directed toward a small industrial audience – engineers and designers who have open minds.' It had been twenty years since Albers could act on his belief that art reached from the church to the plaza. Now, he had a second chance.

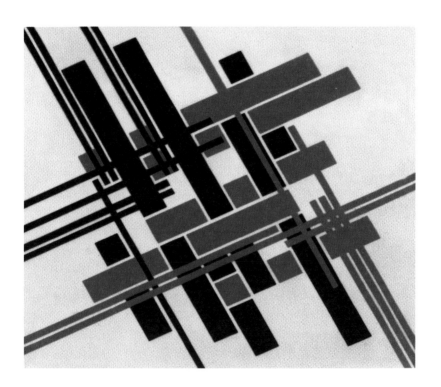

6.1 *Flying*, 1931. Sandblasted opaque flashed glass mounted on cardboard, 11⁹⁄₁₀ × 13¾ in.

6.2 S.R. Naysmith, letter to Josef Albers, 23 January 1946.

The call for change at Yale had come not from artists but architects – men like Louis Kahn, whom Charles Sawyer described as 'more aggressive' than their fine arts colleagues. Kahn's belief in the unity of art and architecture was of one with Albers'. 'Any design connected with an architectural structure should be related to that structure, whether to...emphasize or to complete, to change or to correct [it],' Albers was later to write. As Sawyer recalled, when, in 1947, he had asked Alfred Barr to recommend someone to help reform art at Yale, Barr had suggested the painter Ben Shahn. It was Kahn and George Howe, the latter appointed chair of the Department of Architecture in August 1949, who were to press for Albers in early 1950. All three men went to see him in New York, 'somewhere', as Sawyer vaguely recalled, 'up around 94th Street'.

Albers' and Kahn's paths had crossed before. Both had written for a book called *New Architecture and City Planning*. Albers' insistence, in his chapter, that buildings must be true not just to their materials but to the means of their construction struck a chord with Kahn; so, contrariwise, did Kahn's assertion that 'the finest material…need [not] enter a work of monumental character….The finest ink was not required to draw up the Magna Carta.' The two men had also shown together, in a print exhibition in 1947. And Kahn's Estonian father, like Lorenz Albers, was a craftsman. More, he was a worker in coloured glass.

In February 1948, Albers had had a letter from Charles Sawyer, inviting him to join 'a small Advisory Committee…for Painting and Sculpture' at Yale; other members would include the Finnish architect Eero Saarinen. The committee's brief was to modernize design teaching at Yale. Its first meeting, that April, went well: the 'Possible Basic Curriculum' it proposed was so like the Bauhaus *Vorkurs* as to suggest Albers as its principal author. In October 1949, a second letter from Sawyer appointed him Visiting Critic in Advanced Painting for 1949–50, with a fee of $1,000 – half his year's Black Mountain salary for five weeks' work. Albers' brief was to advise on 'the Collaborative Problem' under Louis Kahn. When he arrived at Yale, he found Kahn running a studio of sixteen architecture, painting and sculpture students who had been set the problem of designing a National Center for UNESCO. Albers joined them.

It was not his only involvement with the United Nations that year. In his Christmas letter to Perdekamp, Albers describes what would have been his largest and most notable work:

> You will be interested to hear that I am doing sketches for windows in the General Assembly building of the United Nations. 25 windows, each more than 4 ft wide and about 70 ft tall. All in the front, just outside the public entrance hall. My proposal is a large circle covering about ¾ of the height and 1/3 of the width. Everything in white-grey. In a new kind of glass, where shades of grey are created 'almost' photographically: with ultraviolet rays. I was asked to submit a sketch because, it seems, no one 'can be simpler' than I. In any case, it is an interesting task. Some weeks ago I was in the glass works to have samples made of possible greys. – So far, the United Nations buildings look – 'great'; i.e., overwhelming.

Nine months later, he frets that 'the architects are particular, peculiar – finicky and undecided. When the plans are finished (probably soon), the glass work will start.' It never did. In March 1952, Franz writes that he has heard from Albers' sister that the project is cancelled. 'It is sad,' he says. 'I would have been so proud if your path had led from the attic of Horster Strasse to the buildings of the UN, the great hope of our time.' It was to be Franz's last letter to Juppi. In December, at sixty-two, Perdekamp died. The following November, Albers arrived in a Germany he had not seen for twenty years.

His United Nations project remains a mystery. Wallace K. Harrison, the UN's chief architect, had met Albers through Howard Dearstyne in New York in 1938, Albers instructing Harrison to reach him via 'Mrs Dreier on Main 4-3763'. In 1950, Harrison commissioned a floor from Albers for the new US Steel building in Pittsburgh; the design – the literal reproduction of a diagram of a cementite molecule – coincided with the shift in Albers' etched laminate work from *Transformations* to *Structural Constellations*. In 1950, Harrison himself designed a museum for the Corning Glass Works. The photosensitive glass Albers describes to Perdekamp was a recent Corning invention – presumably it was Harrison who alerted him to it. But despite the scale of Albers' General Assembly project, there is no record of it in either the UN or Corning archives. The Harrison papers contain a sole reference, typed on a box index card: 'Spring 1951 – [Albers] Preparing design for north wall of General Assembly. Design not used. U.N. paid Albers $500 for his studies; Corning Glass agreed to pay another $500.' All that survives otherwise is a handful of Albers' own sketches, recently rediscovered. The General Assembly Building would open in October 1952 with Fernand Léger murals on its walls and photosensitive glass in its north facade windows – its 'debut as a structural material', as the Corning Glass Works' in-house magazine boasted. '[The panels] are adaptable in almost any design and can be employed to great advantage in artistic decorating,' wrote Wallace Harrison. The General Assembly glass, though, was left undecorated.

Albers' description of his unmade project is intriguing. In 1949, the circle-in-rectangle motif had appeared three-dimensionally in the columnar bathroom of Philip Johnson's Glass House in New Canaan, Connecticut. Johnson started as visiting critic at Yale the following year. In 1951, the circle-rectangle motif would recur in the cylindrical staircase of Louis Kahn's Yale University Art Gallery. That gallery's stepped-back facade relates to the series of drawings Kahn had begun in 1949, and which in turn show signs of Albers' influence. Later, Kahn would describe his design process as 'always starting with the square'. George Howe's successor at the architecture school,

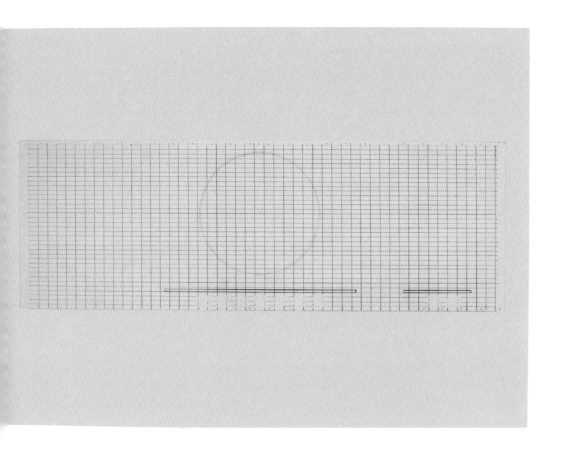

6.3 Headquarters of the United Nations, New York, 1951. Pencil and ink on paper, 14¼ × 19½ in.

Paul Schweikher, also turned to Albers for advice, crediting him with the 'interrupted pattern' of his own Chicago Hall building at Vassar College (1959). Although Albers' plans for the General Assembly were to be scotched, he had been involved in the making of a building seen in its day as 'the new "World Capitol"'. For the first time since the Bauhaus, he was at the heart of a dialogue between art and architecture.

Meanwhile, George Heard Hamilton's feathers had been flying. The dual appointment of Albers as Professor of Art and chairman of Yale's new Department of Design was big news. The *New York Times* noted that painting, sculpture and the graphic arts would all be subsumed under this new department, in 'a revised professional curriculum...closely affiliated' with the Department of Architecture. Albers' headquarters were to be Street Hall, an American imagining of Oxbridge Gothic. A view long held within its walls was that Cézanne was a charlatan: news of a chairman who painted squares was not met with joy. Some of the old guard jumped before they could be pushed, among them Lewis York, head of the Department of Painting, spluttering that Sawyer's changes were 'stupid, narrow and intellectually dishonest'. Eugene Savage, five years Albers' senior, tactfully retired, as did the muralist Rudolph Zallinger. Those that chose to remain – notably the painter Deane Keller – set about waging quiet war. Bernard Chaet, an Albers appointee, recalled silence falling whenever he entered Kaye's art supply shop on Park Street, a bastion of 'the egg tempera people'. These would bide their time.

In Charles Sawyer's telling, part of the point of hiring Albers had been to steal him away from Harvard. Offered a post, he had appeared to weigh up his options before casually answering, 'Yes, I'd rather come to Yale.' In fact, there had been no Harvard offer. Albers' connections there ran deep. He had first taught Basic Design for Gropius in the spring of 1940; it was while working at a Harvard summer school in 1950 that he had made his first *Homage to the Square*. In that year, too, had come his first architectural commission in the United States – a brick fireplace for the new Harvard Graduate Centre. 'To me, the composition presents growth,' Albers said. 'I gave it the name *America*'. For all that, Albers was never offered tenure at Harvard. The Dean of the School of Design, Joseph Hudnut, seems to have feared a Bauhaus clique, and to have found Albers' basic design course too basic. In any case, the reputation of the so-called 'Harvard Bauhaus' had

6.4 *America*, 1950. Brick, 7½ × 8 ft.

begun to fade with the resignation of Marcel Breuer in 1946. Strife between
Gropius and Hudnut did not help. By 1950, Yale was the coming place.

There, Albers was faced with reforming a department with little appetite
for reform. Dealing with faculty was easy enough: he sidestepped dissent by
abolishing staff meetings. Lest malcontents ambush him, he ran to his car
each evening and drove off 'at monstrous speed, straight out of the parking
lot, into the traffic'. Harder to elude were students from the old regime. Some
he simply expelled, glaring at the work in their carrells and saying, 'You I don't
want. You can stay on as a sophomore. You I don't want. You can come back
as a junior.' To survivors, he was merciless. When, in answer to the question,
'Vere, *vere* is your colour?,' one unwisely replied that colour was 'the icing on
the cake', Albers ordered him straight to the bursar to get his money back.
Replacements came from New York's Cooper Union. Among the more radical
US art schools, Cooper was a three-year college, awarding certificates: Albers
gleefully exploited the cachet of an Ivy League degree to poach its students.
Troublesomely, these were almost uniformly abstract expressionist – 'Tenth
Street people', as one of them, Robert Birmelin, says. Birmelin recalls his

interview at Street Hall, the result of an Albers impressment. As ever, Albers wore a grey flannel suit: it was rumoured that he dressed by texture, reaching into his wardrobe each morning with his eyes closed. 'He said, "Vell, who vill show their vork first?", Birmelin recalls. 'I said, "I will". I got about thirty seconds into my spiel and he blitzes New York, blitzes the *shit* out of abstract expressionism. Then he went on to the other people and blitzed the shit out of them. Finally, he said, "Right, I take you, you and you."'

This was something more than perversity. In the early fifties, abstract expressionism was the *dernier cri*: it was natural that the best students should have embraced it. So, too, the most talented teachers. A pillar of Albers' pedagogic faith was that seeing, not art, could be taught. As at Black Mountain, he set about recruiting faculty whose work he personally disliked but whose eye he had grudgingly to acknowledge. These included Willem de Kooning and the abstract expressionist painters Ad Reinhardt and James Brooks. Invitations were sent through gritted teeth. One student whose work began to show the influence of de Kooning received the barked Albers critique, '*Chicken guts*'. Another recalls James Brooks being introduced by his professor as '"Brooks James".... We all felt Albers did it on purpose, because he was very good with names.'

The brutality of his critiques, or 'crits', soon became legend. Irwin Rubin, poached from Cooper Union in 1952, remembered Albers 'tearing student work off the wall...and stomping on it'; Rubin himself nearly left when he was cuffed on the ear. People would know you'd had a rough crit, said a friend, 'because your ears would stay red. You would walk down Chapel Street and strangers would smile.' One Second World War veteran 'went home [from a crit] and cried'. Albers' harshest treatment, though, was reserved for work like his own. 'If [a student painting] even remotely began to approach his *Homage to the Square*, that was a no-no,' Rubin recalled. 'He would become enraged and yell, "This is mine. You go find your own."' It was, Rubin concluded, 'very, very difficult studying with him. I would not have missed a day of it.'

For all his harshness, few questioned their new professor's dedication. As the years went by, lessons were delegated to trusted apostles – colour to Sewell ('Si') Sillman, who had followed Albers from Black Mountain; drawing to Bernard Chaet; basic design to Neil Welliver (fig. 6.5). Albers' contact with his students came increasingly through crits, officially delivered on Thursday mornings in the ten-by-ten-foot carrels that lined the walls of Street Hall's

6.5 John Cohen, Josef Albers and Si Sillman, 1955–6.

painting studio. Irwin Rubin joked that unfortunates given a drubbing at these could 'receive absolution' in the afternoon, beginning with the formula, 'Forgive me, Albers, for I have sinned.' Wags circulated a Yale *Ten Commandments*, the first being, 'Thou shalt have no other authorities before Mr Albers.' The consensus was that he, like a wise God, allowed suffering. To a particularly vicious attack, Albers would softly add, 'If you can't take it here, you won't survive outside.' To Neil Welliver, he once confided, 'I took to my father some of my drawings and the things that I had done at the Bauhaus, and he built a fire in the years and burned everything I had done.' 'I said, "That must have broken your heart,"' a horrified Welliver responded. Albers said, '"No, I was on my own then."'

He knew, too, the sting of public criticism. Alfred Barr and Hilla Rebay were not his only antagonists. The year before coming to Yale, he had had a pair of shows in New York, both visited by Clement Greenberg. Greenberg's reviews recognized a disjunction in Albers' work between 'sensuous, even original' colour and the 'dogma of the straight line', even if they did not see that this was their point. More in sorrow than anger, he mourned 'that

Albers has so rarely allowed the warmth and true plastic feeling we see in his colour to dissolve the ruled rectangles in which all those potential virtues are imprisoned'. Then Greenberg delivered the killer blow. 'Alas,' he said, 'Albers must be accounted another victim of Bauhaus modernism, with its doctrinairism, its inability to rise above merely decorative motifs.'

If harsh crits were meant to inure the young to this kind of attack, Albers' love was not always tough. 'He knew everything that you had done, every day of the week,' recalled Steven Barbash, later an art teacher himself. 'He knew every piece of paper, every scrap, every picture, every study.' Others recalled Albers haunting Street Hall late at night. 'You'd never know when he'd be there,' said Allan Denenberg. 'And it was quite wonderful, because he'd tell you about parts of your painting that you didn't realize he'd seen.' This devotion was repaid in kind. 'We went to school seven days and six nights a week,' Denenberg went on. 'Sunday the school was closed, and we had a way of jimmying a window in the basement and getting in, so we didn't miss a day's work.' 'Such extraordinary attention,' Barbash ended. 'You know, he really loved us all. In his own difficult way.'

It was a return to Germany that brought this home to Albers himself. In August 1953, a design school opened in Ulm, in Upper Swabia. Called the Hochschule für Gestaltung (HfG), it was the brainchild of the *Bauhäusler* Max Bill and Inge Aicher-Scholl, sister of the murdered anti-Nazi activists Hans and Sophie Scholl. The foundation named in their honour aimed to rebuild German culture on humanistic lines: the HfG was to be its centrepiece. If the Bauhaus had preached design's social relevance, the remit of Ulm was more broadly idealistic. In 1953, though, the HfG's prospectus heralded it as a Bauhaus for the new world. In March, Albers had a letter from the US State Department inviting him to teach there; this was followed by others from Aicher-Scholl and Bill. Finally, in September, he telegrammed his acceptance. This was followed by an anguished letter begging passage by sea rather than air, flying being 'a great nervous strain for me'. Early on the morning of 24 November, Albers landed at Bremerhaven.

He hadn't been home for twenty years. In that time, Germany had been laid waste and cut in two. Weimar and Dessau now lay in the communist East; Albers' windows in Bottrop and Leipzig, at the Sommerfeld and Otte Houses and Ullstein Verlag in Berlin, had all been destroyed. His sister

Lisbet and her husband Rudolf came to meet him off the ship – both looked well, Josef wrote to Anni, although he had to control himself so as not to be 'washed away' by emotion. Despite heavy bombing, Ulm is 'wonderfully real and lovely'. Josef's descriptions of paintings often invoked old cheese, warm chocolate, ham sandwiches; the stew – 'schtinky schtuff' – served at a café in New Haven. Talk with Anni now turns, inevitably, to food – his favourite Roter Ochsen beer and Swabian red wine. On 24 November, Anni thanks him for the package of *Würste* that has just arrived; later, there are others of chocolate. They write to each other almost every day, Josef in German, Anni in English. She is *Änki Änk Änkeksen*, he is *Mein Juwe*; Anni's letters are signed *Love and love and love*, Josef's, *love and love and love von deinem weit weg-en aber doch nahen alten Alten* (from your far-off but still near old Old Man).

If Albers was rediscovering Germany, Germany was rediscovering Albers. Claims made for him there were wide-ranging. In 1950, he had been invited to take part in the Ruhr Festival as one of a 'small, select band' of native artists. The following year, Franz Perdekamp had shifted the focus: now, Albers was Westphalian – 'an enemy of playful formalism, like all Westphalians...steeped in the daemonic instincts of the Westphalian spirit'. Choosing his words with care, Josef wrote to thank Franz for his 'very poetic little book'. The next month, in what was to be his last letter to Perdekamp, he gently turned down the offer of a group show in Recklinghausen. Soon Bottrop, too, was clamouring for him. 'Shouldn't the people in charge of our cultural organizations talk to his publisher and dealer so as to organize an exhibition of [Albers'] works here?' protested the local paper. 'One of his sisters still lives in our town. She will be able to tell him that the spirit of our Fatherland has changed.'

Ulm offered an antidote to this parochialism. For Clement Greenberg, the word 'Bauhaus' might signify narrowness, but in Germany it meant the opposite. If student numbers at the HfG were limited, student backgrounds were not. As Albers wrote in his report to the Office of the High Commissioner for Germany, 'They were twenty in number and came from six different countries. It was interesting and stimulating...to have people from such different [cultures] as Great Britain and Brezil [*sic*] among the group.' German students are not mentioned. At Yale, contact with his charges had increasingly come through critiques; these were predominantly of painting. At Ulm, as at Black Mountain, Albers could get back to basics – 'the development of vision and acquiring of articulation', taught as colour, drawing and basic design for three hours each weekday morning. Twenty years earlier, it had been the word 'pioneering' that had won him over to Black Mountain. Now, he used the same word for Ulm.

But Ulm turned out to be not so much pioneering as radical. Although he would teach there again in the summer of 1955, it would be for the last time. The next year, Max Bill resigned as rector over the growingly theoretical stance of the HfG's younger faculty. Bill's successor was to reinvent the school as 'a [place] where you are taught not just a particular subject... [but] a community whose members share one aim: bestowing structure and stability on the world'. It was a creed unlikely to appeal to Albers. 'At Ulm, they think they can solve it scientifically,' he snapped. 'The captain of a ship should start with a sailboat...not out of books.' Worse still, Ulm students now viewed the Bauhaus as expressionistic and old hat, qualities they found embodied in Johannes Itten, who, to Albers' rage, Max Bill had also recruited. Irwin Rubin recalled Albers' return to Yale in January 1954. His departure in November had come at the height of bad feeling with the Cooper Union intake, twenty of whom had threatened to quit Yale *en bloc*. When, on consideration, they changed their minds, Albers told them they were no longer welcome. Then he, too, changed his mind. Once he was in

6.6 Margit Staber, Max Bill and Josef Albers, Ulm, July 27, 1955.

6.7 Margit Staber, L–R: Inge Aicher-Scholl, Josef Albers and Otl Aicher, Ulm, 1955.

Germany, the mutinous students had missed him. They made twenty tiny leaf studies, put them in hand-made envelopes in a box and sent it to him for Christmas. 'From somebody who was there when he received it,' Rubin said, 'he virtually burst into tears.'

The day he got back, Albers called the school together. 'He said going to Germany had completely revised his feelings – that he found us imaginative where he did not find German students imaginative, and so on,' one student recalled. 'And he actually apologized to us, which was quite unusual.' To another, he said, 'Ach, in America, you're so free, so free of Europe.' After this, students marked a softening in his attitude. They noted something else as well. Like their counterparts at Black Mountain, Yale students had come to realize that Albers was a performer – 'He was a bag of tricks,' said one. 'Everything he did was very calculated. He said one time, "You're never going to be a good teacher until you're a good actor."' What they saw now was that his Teutonism was part of the act. Just as his gestures had grown ever more dramatic at Yale – leaping on tables, stamping on pictures, boxing ears – so his accent grew parodically (or self-parodically) more German. Relatively few of the many Black Mountain student memoirs mimic this accent – 'vork', 'vell', 'schtinky schtuff'. Almost all the Yale ones do (fig. 6.8).

6.8 John Cohen, Josef Albers teaching at Yale, 1955–6.

Meanwhile, Albers had been at work in his studios. Directly after Black Mountain, he had begun a series he called *Transformations of a Scheme*; machine-engraved in plastic laminate, these followed the sandblasted Bauhaus glass paintings in looking for a sculptural solution to a graphic problem. After 1950, the *Transformations* evolved into the less intricate, more elegant *Structural Constellations* (figs 6.9, 6.10). Several *Transformations* were shown at the Museum of Non-Objective Painting (now the Solomon R. Guggenheim Museum), New York, in 1949 and 1950, the latter alongside canvases by Hilla Rebay and Ilya Bolotowsky. Visitors, at least, responded well: 'Albers is an artist with the mind of a mathematician,' wrote one. In 1951, the second ever *Homage to the Square* won a purchase award at the Los Angeles County Museum of Art's 'Contemporary Painting in the United States' show, becoming the first of the series to sell (fig. 6.11). Particularly gratifying was that *Homage to the Square (II)* had been turned down for exhibition in both Philadelphia and New York. Slowly, the *Homages* emerged. One may have been exhibited as early as October 1950; an unknown example was certainly in Sidney Janis's 'American Vanguard Art for Paris' show in December 1951. In January 1952, they finally appeared as a named series in a solo exhibition, also at the Sidney Janis Gallery.

For students, Albers' studios now became places of legend. Entry was rare, stories from them alarming. His Yale studio was in the Gormenghast-like Weir Hall, a baronial extravaganza with castellated towers. One student, grudgingly asked to carry a heavy chair up to the atelier, was shown a drawing on graph paper. Asked what he saw, he stammered something about optical space. Albers, flapping his arms, cut him off with the words, 'D'you see, d'you see...a *bird*?' Although rumours of his paintings abounded, they were seldom seen; the *Homages* achieved their greatest local acclaim when eleven were stolen from Weir Hall in 1955. Richard Anuszkiewicz, whose work would eventually most resemble his master's, only saw his first *Homage* after he had left Yale for New York in 1956. Another student, who memorably recalled Albers as a cross between Bismarck and Santa Claus, was admitted to Weir Hall to photograph the new *Homages*. '[That] was the only time I saw Albers' studio,' he said, awestruck. 'It had a skylight. I just remember it was very clean.'

Fewer still penetrated the cramped, artificially lit, 'lime-washed basement *atelier*' at 8 North Forest Circle. The house above this became legendary by osmosis. Alvin Eisenman was astonished to see that the armchairs of its living room were made from the seats of a Buick – Albers, full of enthusiasm,

6.9 *Structural Constellation: Transformation of a Scheme* No.19, 1950.
Machine-engraved brown plastic laminate mounted on wood, 17 × 22½ in.
6.10 *Structural Constellation*. Machine-engraved plastic laminate mounted on wood, 17 × 22½ in.

6.11 *Homage to the Square (II)*, 1950. Oil on masonite, 33½ × 33½ in.

pressed him to visit the affluent scrapyards of Greenwich, 'because that's where *fancy* cars got in wrecks' and seats could be bought for five dollars. These were bolted to heavy wooden bases. Anni was by now becoming less mobile – '[She] had to move them from a wheelchair when she vacuumed, and that's not easy,' a bemused Eisenman recalled. '[T]he first couple of years, they didn't have much help. They were *really* poor.' 'I went out to Orange and I drove round and round,' said Steven Barbash. 'I couldn't believe that Josef Albers lived in this kind of development house. I finally knocked on the door and outside it was 1957 Connecticut, and inside it was 1932 Bauhaus.' Unlike its neighbours, the garden of Number Eight had no plants, Albers having uprooted them to reveal 'the movement of the earth.'

It wasn't only *Homages* that were being made there. In 1953, Marcel Breuer received the commission for a new monastery for what was then the world's largest Benedictine community, the abbey of St John in Collegeville, Minnesota. 'We feel the modern architect with his orientation toward functionalism and honest use of materials is uniquely qualified to produce a Catholic work,' wrote the monastery's abbot, Baldwin Dworschak. Breuer's first building, an accommodation wing for monks, was finished in 1956. A year before, he had asked Albers to design a window for the abbot's personal chapel – a small room, thirteen feet by eleven, meant for private devotion. The windows Albers made at the Bauhaus had been secular. His last – his only – religious glasswork had been *Rosa Mystica*, forty years earlier. At St John's, he could finally use some of his thwarted plans for the UN General Assembly.

6.12 Walter Rüdel, Josef Albers outside 8 North Forest Circle with Homage.

6.13 *White Cross*, 1955. Photosensitive glass.

The *White Cross Window* is as it sounds – a thin white cross, wider than tall, on a field of variegated grey. Like the hairs of a devotional gunsight, the cross – 'in the lightest white obtainable in glass' – is a focus for prayer. Of as much interest to Albers is the chequerboard glass behind it. Like the Flemish-bond brickwork of the Harvard fireplace, the panels of the window are in a set rhythm of value, size and orientation – small, horizontal rectangles of light and dark grey in the middle radiating outward to larger, vertical rectangles of mid-grey at the edge. Against the fixity of the cross, this harlequin field is in constant motion. As in Albers' Bauhaus glassworks, *White Cross* defies stained-glass tradition by ignoring structural supports – the window's pattern continues across these, each variegated pane being a single piece of glass treated with differently photosensitive dyes. This 'new form effect – differing shades touching each other without separating contours' – fulfilled the old dream of a 'single-pane glass picture'; it was made possible by Corning's new photosensitive glass. Albers' interest in the liminal, key to the *Homages*, is here explored in monochrome. *White Cross* concerns itself with duality – of light and dark, motion and stillness; a reconciliation of science and faith.

If trips home woke Albers to flaws in the German temperament, they opened his eyes to the glories of German church architecture. Using Ulm as a springboard, he had toured the country's cathedrals. To his Yale students, he now sang the unexpected praises of the Northern Baroque, twisting his arms in imitation of baldachins. As a young man at Büren, he said, he had not understood the Jesuitic beauty of the Maria Immaculata church; now, in old age, he saw it. He compared *White Cross* to the *grisaille* windows of Altenberg Abbey, even if, typically, he insisted that his own designs had been made before seeing them. In 1954, the Swiss medievalist François Bucher came to Yale with a thesis on Cistercian abbeys, Altenberg among them. He and Albers became friends. Later, Bucher would co-write a book on Albers' graphic constructions called *Despite Straight Lines* (1961).

Order by order, the church of Josef Albers' youth was reclaiming him. In 1958, the Benedictine community of St John's found itself split over the window it had commissioned from a young Polish émigré, Bronislaw Bak, for the massive, honeycombed north wall of their new abbey church. Breuer suggested approaching Albers for an alternative design. At the start, some monks objected on the grounds that in their view, the artist, if raised a Catholic, apparently lacked faith. Having never met him, they clearly derived this idea from his work: he was, said one brother, 'a technician'. Their minds were to change when Albers presented his plans to the monastery's art committee on 12 November 1959. 'He seemed quite comfortable in our midst,' one surprised monk recalled. 'He addressed us in a language that was homely, familiar, sometimes humorous.' In a masterstroke of diplomacy, Albers compared the need for the five hundred glass hexagons of the wall to work together to the cooperativist structure of a Benedictine community. The centre of the window was to be of amber yellow, 'the sun colour suspended'; the rest would be in ribbed white glass. One monk praised the design's simplicity. Another remarked that the window could be read both as a Resurrection and as a Pentecost.

Nonetheless, a vote held on 25 November went decisively against Albers' design. An embarrassed Abbot Dworschak wrote to him of his 'profound disappointment', particularly given that the two men had worked together for so long to find 'a simple, universal form [to express] the profound theological concept that we proposed'. Later, Albers turned for solace to a fellow *Bauhäusler*, Theodor Bogler, a potter who, after his wife's death in 1925, had entered the Benedictine monastery at Maria Laach in the Rhineland.

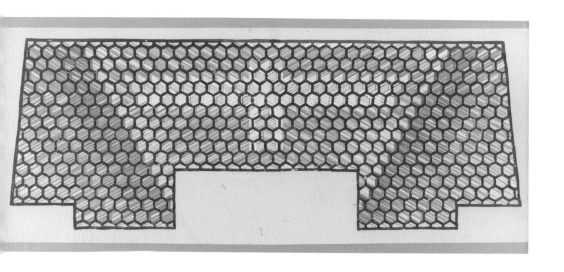

6.14 Study for St John's Abbey, North Window, Design no.4, *ca.* 1959.
Ink and collage on acetate. 9½ × 22⅖ in.

6.15 *Franciscan*, 1948. Oil on masonite.

The monk replied, encouragingly if oddly, that God, too, had measured his Creation by mass, colour and weight. The yellow-and-white design was only one of many with which Albers had experimented for the project, filling in the countless hexagons of mimeographed templates by hand with a range of colours and paints. Sketches for the St John's window see him moving back and forth between the literal – the words of the *Sanctus* picked out in the Gutenberg font he had used for *Rosa Mystica* – and the insistently abstract. Given the time and thought he had expended on the project, his reply to Abbot Dworschak's letter of regret is a model of untypical forbearance.

The monks had been wrong about Albers' lack of faith. Along with his public re-engagements with Rome had gone a private one. His wedding apart, there is no record of Albers attending Mass at the Bauhaus. In 1936, a small Catholic church had opened near Black Mountain; his close friend Jean Charlot was a regular communicant. In 1943, Charlot notes in his diary, 'Albers drives us to Mass after breakfast.' In 1948 came the painting *Franciscan*, of which Charlot wrote: 'Albers' art longs for the state of repose as does a saint for unitive vision.' These are glancing references only; the first real evidence of a religious interest comes at Yale. Marjorie Jones, head of printing at Yale University Press, took to attending Mass daily after the death of her mother. To her surprise, she found Albers at church each morning. A nun who studied at Yale recalled his 'delight that I was there, to take back some kind of good art teaching to Catholic schools'. Lois Swirnoff, *summa cum laude* Yale student and future colour theorist and Cooper Union professor, corroborates this. 'I know that toward the end of his life, [Albers] was much more interested in talking to Catholic priests about theology than he was in talking to artists,' Swirnoff says. 'You know, he was a Catholic, and I see a lot of the nesting squares in his work as a kind of ideation of the Trinity.' On his godlike status as a teacher, she is agnostic. 'I do not accept the authority of Albers because he was authoritarian,' Swirnoff notes, crisply. 'I accept the authority of Albers because he demonstrates what I, myself, have experienced, and what several thousand of my students have experienced.'

His Catholicism may explain a contradiction in him. As at Black Mountain, Albers' behaviour towards women students was sometimes inappropriate. One student, presenting her septuagenarian teacher with a piece of sculpture, found herself being kissed on the mouth. 'Then [Albers] kissed me again, and I sort of stiffened, and I thought, "If he does it again, I'm going to scream",' she said. 'It was sort of schizophrenic, because he was...very puritanical about not allowing life drawing.' This was so: Albers' students were forbidden to work from the nude. When asked why, he replied, 'Ach, it's all pornography. Those French, the Academy: it's all pornography.' His attitude to life drawing, always prudish, now became fanatical. Looking through the portfolio of one male applicant, he snapped, 'Boy, if you want to study art, come here. If you want to draw buttocks, go some other place.' Another was warned, 'Ach, boy, those bazooms vill kill you.' And yet Albers was also unusual in allowing women onto his courses at all: Yale College did not do go co-educational until 1969. Some faculty members, even in the Department of Design, discouraged female students. Nor were there women teachers, the reason for the lack of a job for Anni at Yale.

Through all this, Albers had continued to exhibit – prints at the Smithsonian and in Philadelphia, paintings in California and at the Janis Gallery in New York; both together in group shows elsewhere. The exhibition that opened in New Haven in April 1956, however, was of a different order from these. Here, at last, was a full-scale retrospective, held in what was rapidly becoming an icon of American modernism, whose design Albers had helped shape: Yale University Art Gallery. The show had been arranged by Si Sillman, a Black Mountain student and now his teaching assistant. It was Sillman who made the screen-printed *Homages* tipped into the catalogue, and who would do most of Albers' printing for the next two decades. He would teach the colour course for twenty years. 'I always remember [Albers] walking in with Si Sillman a few paces behind him, as "the boy" who took care of things,' a Yale contemporary recalled. 'Sillman would actually imitate the way [Albers] spoke,' laughed Bernard Chaet. 'He spoke English with a German accent. Albers was his father.' Yale rumour held this to be literally so, although, accent notwithstanding, Sillman had been born in Savannah, Georgia twelve years before his putative parent came to America.

The catalogue essay to 'Josef Albers: Paintings, Prints, Projects' was by George Heard Hamilton: the distinction it draws between Malevich's Platonic and Albers' Aristotelean conception of the square is impressively astute. Press reviews of the show were less so, although these were uncomprehending rather than actively hostile. *Time* magazine questioned whether 'Albers' approach [was] perhaps too basic?' before deciding, on balance, that it was not. *Art News*, meanwhile, grandly found itself 'not quite certain of the complete success of [the] laminated plastics', citing their 'uneasy feeling of three-dimensional constructions not quite at home on the two-dimensional picture plane'. That, of course, was their point; more perceptive was a comparison of Albers' working method to that of an architect. Albers, with an eye to publicity, wrote to the critic of *Arts* magazine, Leo Steinberg, praising his reviews and alerting him to the Yale show. The effect was slightly spoiled by the letter being addressed to 'Leo Stein', Albers having apparently mistaken its recipient for the brother of the novelist Gertrude. After gently pointing this out, Steinberg visited the exhibition in June, too late to review it. Given his description of the work's 'profound earnestness', this may have been just as well.

Above all, the Yale retrospective positioned Albers as an artist rather than a teacher. In private (and not always in private), Alfred Barr made it clear that he viewed Albers solely as the latter: the Yale show seemed to prove him wrong. As often, the triumph was short-lived. Albers' courting of Leo Steinberg had had an agenda: Steinberg had recently set himself up as a challenger to Clement Greenberg, stressing the control of abstract expressionist painting over its much-vaunted spontaneity. Emboldened by this assault on his nemesis, Albers, too, had gone on the offensive – the *Time* magazine reviewer described his 'deplor[ing] self-expression of the big, drippy, half-conscious sort made chic by Jackson Pollock & Co', which is to say, the sort championed by Greenberg. A month before this attack and possibly prompting it, Barr and his associate, Andrew Ritchie, had announced a series of new MoMA monograph shows called 'Works in Progress'. The first was to be of Jackson Pollock. Albers' name was not on the list. Shortly after the aggressive *Time* article, Pollock was killed in a car crash. The timing was unfortunate. In early 1957, Andrew Ritchie replaced Lamont Moore as director of the Yale University Art Gallery. Albers would not have another solo show there in his lifetime.

Not surprisingly, his dislike of Barr ran deep. When the MoMA director's daughter Victoria applied to Yale in 1958, Albers refused to interview her, deputing Bernard Chaet to do so instead. Another year would pass before he could exact revenge on Barr himself, a dish the sweeter for being served cold. In May 1959, MoMA organized an open show called 'Recent Sculpture USA'; Albers encouraged six students to submit work to it. Suspecting – probably rightly – that any link to him might result in their rejection, he advised them to send in submissions under their home, rather than their New Haven, addresses. All six were accepted. On the opening night, Albers appeared, unbidden, at MoMA. A surprised Alfred Barr waved him over to a group of sculptures all made, although he did not know it, by Yale students. 'Josef, look at this work!' he bubbled. Albers smiled a slow smile. 'Ah, Alfred,' he said. 'Ve play a joke on you.' Barr's response is not recorded.

If 1956 marked the high point of Albers as an artist, it also saw the beginning of the end of his career as a teacher. His enemies at Yale might have gone quiet, but they had not gone away. In 1954, George Howe, instrumental in hiring him, had retired as chair of the architecture department. Without Howe, things soon fell apart. His successor, Paul Schweikher, found himself attacked from all sides. In June 1956, Schweikher resigned; in September his promoter, Charles Sawyer, was sacked in his turn by Yale's president, Whitney Griswold. With Sawyer's departure, Albers was left without a protector. The statutory retirement age at Yale was sixty-eight; he had turned this the previous March. A letter from Sawyer makes it clear that he had expected Albers to stay on as head of department even so, on a salary of $10,250. The sole change would have been of his title, from professor to professor emeritus. Now Sawyer was gone. Albers' enemies circled.

In 1955, Deane Keller had written to Whitney Griswold attacking the narrowness of Yale's abstract-heavy curriculum and repeating Sir Herbert Read's dismissal of it as 'Academicism of 1954'. Now, in 1956, a second letter proposed a return to the *status quo ante*, including an intensive course in egg tempera painting. Worryingly, this was the only one of Keller's ten demands to be dismissed out of hand. By the start of the academic year 1956–7, Albers was dangerously exposed. When Gibson Danes was appointed dean of the new School of Art and Architecture, Albers was not consulted on the choice: it was Bernard Chaet who broke the news to him, pointing out Danes as he climbed from a sports car in Chapel Street. As to Charles Sawyer's departure, he read about it in the *New Haven Register*. There is little doubt that he had run his department as a fiefdom, ignoring dissent and budgets: his costly introduction of a sculpture studio in the Department of Design was widely criticized. But the broader problem was that the radicalism of Sawyer and Howe at Yale had given way to a new conservatism. A report by the National Architectural Accrediting Board in 1955–6 was strongly critical of duplication in the university's architecture department, and of confusion among students there as to what was on offer. The blame for these was laid firmly at the door of inter-departmental collaboration. The School of Fine Arts was now renamed the School of Art and Architecture, its teaching and responsibilities divided accordingly. At short notice and after a painful interview with Dean Acheson, a statesman and Yale trustee, Albers was told that his tenure would end with the academic year 1957–8.

Aside from the blow to his pride, there was the question of money. Albers may have been well paid at Yale, but he had only been on tenure for six years; not long enough to build up a pension. 'The last year was the agonizing one, because they never made it clear to him that he was leaving until the last second,' Bernard Chaet recalled. 'He called me in and he told me, "You know we're going to have to go to Mexico to live." I was in his office and some guy called him – [he and Anni] were putting in storm windows – and this guy told him that he could not pay for them gradually because of his age.' Albers had spent a decade badgering Charles Olson, his successor at Black Mountain, for money owed. When, at last, a cheque arrived, it was for $936.66. As to his paintings, the *Homages* were selling at a few hundred dollars each. The ones stolen from Weir Hall in 1955 had been valued at $300; when a young architect at Skidmore, Owings & Merrill bought a pair of 16" × 16" *Homages* in 1957, he paid $800 for the two. These bargain-basement prices were lowered still further for members of Yale faculty. '[Albers] told me in the first few years that he only ever sold about $3,000 of his paintings,' Chaet said. Ted Dreier, now working at an atomic research laboratory, wrote to Griswold and the chairman of the Carnegie Foundation, soliciting a supplement to Josef's pension. Both refused the request, Griswold noting that the Albers between them had an income of $12,000 a year – about $100,000 in today's terms. Perhaps the couple were less poor than they thought. The Ford Foundation, more munificent, sent Josef $10,000 as a grant-in-aid.

He spent the next two years teaching at Yale part-time and without status. In 1960, Griswold announced that the school would now offer graduate courses only, undergraduate art being taught by Yale College. Albers, furious, objected that 'teaching takes place at the beginning'. When his protests were ignored, he quit Yale for good. After he left, said Bernard Chaet, 'he was very lonely'; he would appear in Street Hall at night, like a ghost. Such further dealings as he had with the university were unhappy. A few months after his forced retirement, Albers was asked by Rico Lebrun, a figurative painter and visiting professor, to lecture on colour. Lebrun, said Chaet, was being 'emollient'. He lived to regret it: Albers used the talk to savage his host's work from the platform. His likely target was Andrew Ritchie, who had given Lebrun a show at the Yale gallery. When, in 1962, Albers was asked to recommend a new chair for the art department, he proposed the abstract painter Ad Reinhardt. The suggestion was ignored. Even his advice on Paul Rudolph's replacement for Street Hall ended badly, Albers' European taste for small-scale painting being blamed for the cramped studios of the new Art and Architecture Building. Attempts to mollify him met with rebuff. In 1962, he received a courteous invitation to lecture to architecture students. A note on the letter, in its recipient's hand, reads, 'I phoned the office [to] answer that I am unable to accept.' Three years later, Jack Tworkov, now chairman of the department of art, received the same answer. 'I would be content to leave [what you teach] pretty much up to you,' Tworkov had written, warmly. 'This [invitation] comes at the urging of students, faculty, and the Dean.' It was to no avail.

If Albers was gone, though, he was not forgotten. As Bernard Chaet recalled, a pro-Albers faction among Yale students now waged a guerrilla war of its own. 'They felt their father had left,' Chaet said. In May 1961, forty-two students signed a petition calling on the dean of the new School of Art and Architecture to appoint their ex-professor visiting critic in painting for the next academic year; one of the signatories was Victoria Barr. When, after three weeks, there had been no response, Albers wrote a dignified letter to his supporters. Too late, Gibson Danes reacted; an increasingly ill-tempered correspondence ensued. After its last letter, Danes issued a memo directing that Albers' Weir Hall studio be cleared by 1 September 1961.

Even with this, his memory at Yale was not erased. Seven years after his retirement, five after he had stopped teaching, Albers was still being petitioned by students to lecture. In the interim, many of the best-known American (and some non-American) artists of the late 20th century had passed through Yale, among them Chuck Close, Eva Hesse, Robert Mangold, Brice Marden and Richard Serra. Although most were not taught by Albers himself, they acknowledged his role as the abiding genius of Yale art. In terms of posterity, Albers' greatest contribution to the university came after he had left it. Robert Rauschenberg could only begin to assimilate Albers' teaching when he was no longer taught by him. The same was true of Yale students.

The British conceptual artist Michael Craig-Martin came to the university in 1961. 'Josef Albers' colour course [was] taken by many students seeking to become doctors, lawyers, scientists and stockbrokers,' he says. '[But] soft it was not.' Before Yale, Craig-Martin had never heard of Albers; he was never to meet him. Nonetheless, he recalls his 'presence and influence' as 'pervasive'. 'I realize now that [Albers' lessons] represented the summit of high-Modernist art education,' Craig-Martin says. 'Everything I know about colour comes from his course.'

Not everyone saw this at the time. 'Quite a number of my contemporaries [who] went on to become influential artists – Brice Marden, Richard Serra, Nancy Graves, Chuck Close and Robert Mangold among them – objected to [Albers'] courses, which they felt were too basic,' Craig-Martin says. Marden himself wryly recalls 'this damn Albers colour course which I just didn't understand'. At Yale, Robert Mangold was 'involved in a kind of big-scale painting which blocked me from connecting with what Albers was doing'. A decade later, he changed his mind. 'By the early 1970s, I had begun to find more and more common connections with Albers's work and my own,' Mangold says. '[My] two poles of influence...remain Barnett Newman and Josef Albers.' Richard Serra, predictably, found basic design the most useful of the Albers courses. But the colour course, too, was important, as he recalled in an interview four decades later:

> HAL FOSTER: Did the influence of Josef Albers persist when you were at Yale?
> RS: Yes, in the first year particularly. He had just retired. When I graduated, Albers asked me to help him proof his book *Interaction of Color* at the Yale University Press, because I had taught the colour course in my last year. I spent the summer proofing the book, and we would go over it together. If you taught his course, you developed an eye for things besides colour saturation, tone, equivalence and so on – subjective qualities like 'wet' and 'dry' colours. Your eyes became very attuned to seeing minute variations.
> HF: But is colour pronounced in your work?
> RS: If you think black is a colour, then it's very pronounced in my work.

'What I admired about Albers was that even though his format was strict and logical, within it there was room for play,' Serra says. 'His colour course was not taught dogmatically.... Once you understood the basic lesson that procedure was dictated by material, you also realized that matter imposed its own form on form. That's a lesson I never forgot.'

Colleagues, too, got the point. Ad Reinhardt, brought to Yale as a visiting critic, deferred to Albers as the actual innovator of a pared-down abstraction for which he himself was seen as the pioneer. 'Actually, Albers had been working symmetrically...left to right for a long time,' a modest Reinhardt observed. 'But also impersonal ideas, repetition of identical units, question of all-over surface and so on.' On Reinhardt's cartoon family tree, 'How to Look at Modern Art in America', Albers is on the left side of the radically abstract leftmost branch, above the word 'Mondrian'. Willem de Kooning, meanwhile, used his time as a visiting critic to take the Yale colour course. Bernard Chaet ascribed the change in de Kooning's palette soon afterwards to Albers' then-current fondness for pinks and ochres.

But if Albers himself noticed this change, he is unlikely to have been impressed by it. His method may have been dogmatic, but its aim was to foster difference, not likeness. Asked, in an interview in 1966, for the most important piece of advice he had given his students, he replied, 'Stay off the bandwagon.' 'Your bandwagon?', countered the interviewer. 'To follow me', said Albers, 'follow yourself.' Not everyone understood this. Robin Darwin, great-grandson of Charles and rector of London's Royal College of Art, visited Yale in 1953 while Albers was in Ulm. In Albers' own telling, the Englishman was appalled to find students competing with each other: Darwin apparently described this as 'slavery'. Albers, naturally, disagreed. 'It was', he said, 'an ethical question, not a question of competition.' He seems to have been no prouder of his putative influence on Serra or de Kooning than on any other artist. Asked to name students whose work he had particularly shaped, he countered that 'if there is any traceable influence coming from me, then it is probably from my painting as much as from my teaching. [The teaching] has reached relatively few.' The only familiar names he hazarded were those of Ray Johnson and Kenneth Noland, although these were listed alongside three other artists unknown to the canon. On Richard Anuszkiewicz, the only of his students to adopt a style something like his own, Albers was lukewarm. 'It's too easy,' he said. In their turn, Albers' most ardent defenders tended to be those whose work was least obviously like his. Michael Craig-Martin is a case in point. The most vocal of Albers' apologists from Sixties Yale, Craig-Martin is known less as a painter than as a conceptualist.

7   That Which Should Accompany Old Age

Describe me as I am – an old lunatic shut up in a basement, turning out squares all day and all night.

Josef Albers, 1970

Albers once said of his own work – and this is typical of his serious wit – 'art is not to be looked at: art looks at us'.

Max Bill, obituary of Josef Albers, Neue Zürcher Zeitung, *1976*

In 1960, a small building went up at 333 Elm Street in New Haven, around the corner from Street Hall. One storey high and of white brick, it seemed wilfully nondescript. It was. Designed by the Chinese-born architect King-lui Wu, the building was the meeting house (or 'tomb') of Manuscript, one of Yale's secretive student societies. Like most tombs, it was windowless. The wall onto Elm Street looks entirely blank, although closer inspection reveals it to be inscribed with a circle whose circumference touches pavement and roofline. This circle is so subtle as to be near-invisible. A negative, a shadow, it has been made by scraping a thin layer of mortar from between the wall's bricks. It was designed by Wu's ex-Yale colleague, Josef Albers (fig. 7.1).

It was not their first collaboration. In the five years before, Wu had commissioned fireplaces from Albers for his designs for two private houses; the square-within-square plans of these clearly echo the *Homages*. Despite the age difference – Albers was thirty years the older – the two were, and would remain, close friends. Shortly before designing the wall, Albers had been inducted into Manuscript as an honorary member. The circle hints at the society's secret insignia, the sun. But it also has a private significance. In 1950, Albers had designed a suite of windows for the UN General Assembly building (see p. 255). That design, never made, was for a circle on a white rectangle. That it should have been reused, a decade later and in such different circumstances, is notable. The purpose of the General Assembly is to be transparent; of the Manuscript tomb, opaque. The UN windows would have been hugely visible – by far the largest and most prestigious of Albers' commissions. The Manuscript circle is on an anonymous wall in an unremarkable street. Most people pass without noticing it. The circle is variously typical of Albers. The means of its making could hardly have been more minimal; it abjures waste; it refuses to distinguish between high and low. It also sets out to prove Kandinsky's dictum, much quoted by Albers, that no true work of art is ever lost. These qualities would come together again in the work he called *Manhattan*.

The Manuscript wall saw Albers revisiting a form made ten years before; in *Manhattan* he looked back nearly forty. In 1928, in Dessau, he had made a sandblasted glass painting called *City* (fig. 7.2). If its restless bands of red, white and black evoked the dynamism of a modern metropolis, the work's name – Albers called it *City*, not *Stadt* – made it clear that this metropolis was American. *City*, with its coeval series, *Skyscrapers*, sees him in the full

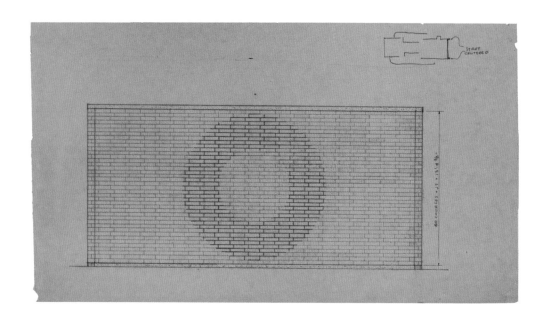

7.1 Josef Albers and King-lui Wu, preliminary drawing of the mural for Yale
Manuscript Society House, *ca.*1961. Pencil on paper, 19⅗ × 35 in.
7.2 *City*, 1928. Sandblasted opaque flashed glass with black paint, 13 × 21¾ in.

grip of *Amerikanismus*, that interwar German imagining of the United States as the embodiment of modernity. Now, three decades later, the dream that was *City* had come true.

In 1958, the architects Emery Roth & Sons were chosen to design a building next to Grand Central Terminal in New York. When the firm's plans were rejected by the developer as too dull, Richard Roth called in Walter Gropius. Gropius's design would make the future Pan Am Building among the most recognizable in New York, and the most reviled. Turning Roth's plan by ninety degrees and bulking it up to fifty-nine floors, Gropius produced an outsized concrete-clad slab that stood astride Park Avenue. 'The rightness or wrongness of...the Pan Am Building...can be summed up very briefly,' fumed one critic. 'It's wrong.' In late 1960, Gropius approached a trio of artists to produce installations for the tower for a fee of a thousand dollars each. One was Josef Albers.

It was Gropius's suggestion that Albers scale up *City*, which had been bought by the Zurich Kunsthaus earlier that year and much publicized. Albers' own idea had been to project a black-and-white slide show of *Structural Constellations* onto his allotted site in the Pan Am lobby. As this stood over a bank of high-speed escalators down into Grand Central station, and a projection would have meant leaving the lobby in darkness, Gropius gently dissuaded him. The slide show, had it happened, would have linked the famous Celestial Ceiling of Grand Central's concourse to Albers' own mural *Two Structural Constellations* (1959–60), a few blocks away in the foyer of Wallace Harrison's new Corning Glass Building (fig. 7.3). Annoyed but undaunted, he set about modifying *City* to its new scale – 8.5 × 17 metres – and new site.

Drawings and maquettes see him adding strips of colour to the thirty-five-year-old design, flattening and stilling *City* for its new life as a mural. Where the old glass painting could be taken in at a glance, *Manhattan* would be seen on the move. There was less need for it to be dynamic. Albers also decided to have *City* remade in Formica rather than glass. The Pan Am Building, then the world's largest commercial office space, housed thirty thousand workers – a quarter of a million people would pass down the escalators beneath *Manhattan* every day. Like the Statue of Liberty, past which the Albers had sailed in 1933, the mural stood at a portal to New York. In one unpublished statement on the piece, Albers rejoices that it stands 'where tens of thousands of pedestrians walk daily'. In another, he writes, simply: '*Manhattan*, 1963. My homage to the city of New York.' (fig. 7.4)

7.3 *Structural Constellations*, 1959. Vermont marble, gold leaf, 16 × 61 ft.
7.4 *Manhattan*, 1963. Formica panels, 28 × 55 ft.

The mural would remain among the city's best known public artworks for four decades. For Albers, as for Gropius, *Manhattan* sent out a coded message: its design might be old, but it was as fresh as the day it was made. This trust in the durability of modernism was to prove misplaced. In 1978, Philip Johnson's Chippendale-pedimented AT&T Building, a few blocks from Gropius's tower, marked the advent of postmodernism in America. In 1981, an ailing Pan Am sold off its New York headquarters; the famous signage on the building's roofline was quietly taken down a decade later. A decade after that, in 2000, *Manhattan* too was removed. Its disappearance went unannounced – the ex-Pan Am Building's new owners hinted, after the fact, that there had been a problem with asbestos. More likely, the work's plastic rectangles clashed with the pink marble and gilt makeover the lobby had undergone in the mid-eighties. Since Albers had assumed that *Manhattan* would one day need remaking, he had left instructions on how to do it. The point of Formica was that repairs would be cheap. *Manhattan*, though, was not replaced, and, at the time of writing, hasn't been. Its red, white and black panels are in a landfill site in Ohio.

Albers was seventy when he left Yale. He may have mourned the end of his tenure, but the years that followed would be extraordinarily prolific. At last, there was time to think and work. His mind raced back and forth between two and three dimensions, his research in one informing that in the other. As well as the Pan Am mural, he had made two others for prominent sites in New York City. With these went a two-part steel sculpture over the entrance to Paul Rudolph's new Yale Art and Architecture Building, a brick altar wall in a church in Oklahoma, and, in 1967, perhaps his most beautiful architectural work, a brick loggia wall at the Rochester Institute of Technology (fig. 7.5).

Then, too, there were books. In 1958, Albers had published a volume of drawings and verse, the former with the pared-down spareness of the *Structural Constellations*. Printing was done by a small New Haven press, in a run of five hundred copies; the book was dedicated to Anni. In 1961, it was reissued in New York. Even so, it sold badly, as Anni's chivvying letters to the publisher make clear. In 1966, sales generated royalties of $34.50. The problem, in a day before artists' books, was that how (or whether) the drawings and verse related to each other was unclear. Then, too, the poems were printed in German and English. That was part of the point: Albers was

7.5 Loggia Wall, 1967. Brick, 8 × 70 ft.

fascinated by the possibilities of translation, linguistic as graphic. Some poems were short and gnomic:

> Einer geht
> einer steht
> wer hat mehr recht
> auf den Weg
> (One man goes, another stays: who has more right to the road?)

printed, in the Bauhaus way, without punctuation. The German taste for aphorism did not touch the American imagination. And yet some poems have the sweet clarity of William Carlos Williams:

> When thinking of you
> it enters my head
>
> why now are the blueberries red
> and the black ones all eaten
>
> and the only ripened apple
> just run over by a car

Like the *Homages*, they contrive to be at once austere and romantic, radical and traditional. Albers' love of poetry ran deep, notably of the work of his fellow Westphalian Annette von Droste-Hülshoff. Droste's acute recording of natural phenomena makes her that oxymoronic thing, a romantic realist. A copy of her verse was by Albers' bedside at his death in 1976.

It was a much larger book that had by then made him famous. In May 1963, Walter Gropius wrote to thank Albers for an eightieth birthday present. 'You know of course that the [Harvard] Alumni will also give me your colossal work on colour,' Gropius goes on. 'I didn't know that you have worked already for a long time on this....I am glad indeed that you have put all your enormous knowledge on colour into such a mammoth publication.' He ends, 'Your mural in the Pan Am building is spoken of very well everywhere.'

Gropius's overblown words – 'colossal', 'enormous', 'mammoth' – seem faintly teasing. They were not, though, unwarranted. *Interaction of Color*, which appeared on Anni Albers' birthday in June 1963, was, by any measure, a big book. By far the largest then published by Yale, it weighed in at ten kilos and cost two hundred dollars – perhaps eight times as much in today's terms. The larger part of the cloth-bound box in which it came was given over to eighty Roman-numeralled folders containing copies of works which Albers had spent years tracking down. To ensure accuracy of colour, these were individually screen-printed – a task so huge that it had been shared out among three studios. Initial print tests were done by Si Sillman, using eight hundred inks; the book's design was by Norman Ives. Together, the firm of Ives-Sillman would produce Albers' catalogues for the next twenty years. The smaller part of the *Interaction* box contained the book which these images were to illustrate. This was divided into chapters dealing with the sub-categories into which he had refined his colour course in thirty years of teaching it – free studies, intersecting colours, colour instrumentation and so on. If *Interaction of Color* was a very much larger work than *Poems and Drawings*, it was not entirely unlike it. Seen on the page, its epigrammatic prose looks and reads like blank verse:

> A true middle mixture is distinguished by being equidistant
> – in light and in hue –
> from either mixture parent.

Or:

> First themes:
>
> gay — sad   young — old   major — minor
>
> More daring:
>
> bright — dull   early — late   active — passive

At its heart lay the beliefs that learning comes from doing and that visual things must be taught visually, a creed professed by Johann Heinrich Pestalozzi, the Swiss theorist whose teachings were central to the *neue Pädagogik*. 'Whether something "has colour" or not is as hard to define verbally as are such questions as "what is music" or "what is musical",' Albers writes. Published weeks after his seventy-fifth birthday, *Interaction of Color* has the feel of a *Festschrift*, a scholarly volume honouring an eminent author. It is dedicated, though, not to Josef Albers, but by him: 'This book is my thanks to my students.' None of the artwork in it is his own.

Albers' selecting of this had been extraordinary. As early as 1956, he had begun to solicit images for the new book. To Elinor Evans, an ex-Yale student, he wrote, 'Let me describe [the picture I want]: lanzeolate [*sic*] shapes of leaves are shown. Halves of them are cut in orange paper. The other half, the real leaves, are apparently covered by a transparent light blue paper strip....The transparency, of course, is a good "swindle".' His memory was, as ever, prodigious (figs 7.6, 7.7, 7.8). Two months later, he wrote to the Corning Glass Works, asking permission to use their photosensitive glass as a 'representative of so-called "volume colour"'. Other letters went to the Eastman Kodak Company, the printing ink division of the Interchemical Corporation, the Upjohn Company of Kalamazoo. Inevitably, there were delays. In April 1956, the Rockefeller Foundation had awarded Yale six thousand dollars to cover the cost of Albers' research. In December 1958, the Foundation wrote to ask when they might see results. Albers prevaricated. In the summer of 1962, students including Richard Serra set about collating the text. Finally, after seven years, *Interaction of Color* was published in a run of two thousand. Presentation copies were sent to a number of Catholic schools, including St John's and Notre Dame. Another went to a Mother Brady at Manhattanville College in Purchase, New York. The letter that accompanied all these contained the firm injunction, 'Mr Albers has stated that he does not, under any circumstances, wish to receive any acknowledgment for this gift.'

Reviews, predictably, dwelt on price and weight. The *New Haven Register* gasped, '22 Lb. Volume of Colour Studies Published by Yale to Cost $200'. The cry was taken up by the *Detroit News*, the Cleveland *Plain Dealer* and other regional papers. A more measured response came from the art press. *Arts Magazine* locates Albers' book as specifically of its day. 'The information taught to art students is even more relative than colour,' its reviewer says. 'Albers' information is relevant right now....[He] is teaching what he knows, most of which comes from his painting....It is hardly irrelevant that he is an exceptional painter.' The review is signed 'Donald Judd'. Thirty years later, Judd would recall *Interaction* as 'the last philosophy of colour, which was what it was, as well as being factual'. 'Every generation has a new idea of colour,' Judd went on. 'However, this is a generation without ideas.' He would remain among the most astute reviewers of Albers' work. After the older man's death, Judd would buy three of his paintings.

It was another reviewer who pointed to the problem with *Interaction of Color*. Although Albers examines existing theories in the book, its real point

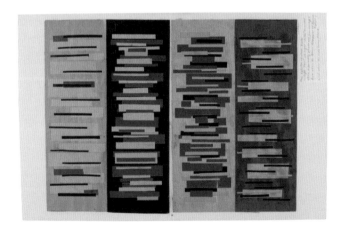

7.6 John Lockwood, proposed plate for *Interaction of Color*, Illusion of Transparence, 1950–9. Color-aid paper,
paperboard, other colored papers, 13 × 20 in.

7.7 John Lockwood, proposed plate for *Interaction of Color*, free study, 1950–9. Color-aid paper, 8 × 8⅛ in.

7.8 Kittredge, proposed plate for *Interaction of Color*, color climates, 1950–9. Color-aid paper, 20⅛ × 13⅛ in.

was as a hands-on aid to seeing. Yet *Interaction* had the feel of an art object and cost $200. The artist Edward Reep wrote:

> I joined the long line of those eagerly awaiting the arrival of [Albers'] epic book. After the initial flurry of interest had subsided, I carefully gained permission to secrete this rare prize to my own studio from our school library. There, with unbelievable reverence and freshly washed hands, I began to dissect this mysterious package.

He went on, 'One [could] hardly resist touching the velvet-like colour prints... [like running] your finger over a masterpiece when the museums guard's back is turned.' Here was the problem. *Interaction of Color* may have left Reep 'refreshed, revitalized, and strengthened', feeling that Albers 'was a giant man', but the book was hard to come by and intimidating to use. Although by 1968 all copies had sold, most had vanished into private collections or libraries, where they could be seen only under supervision. If Albers 'did much to rekindle an interest in the study and application of colour in art in the 1960s', that rekindling came about through the teaching of his students rather than *Interaction of Color*. It was with a paperback edition in 1971 that the book at last became truly popular – although this contained just ten colour plates, none with the silky exactness of Si Sillman's. Even so, the paperback has to date sold over half a million copies in fifteen languages, and, approaching its sixtieth year, continues to sell in numbers. The touring exhibition that accompanied its publication in 1963 was shown at Harvard, Berkeley and half a dozen other universities, although not at Yale. For its fiftieth anniversary in 2013, *Interaction of Color* was released as an app.

On the face of it, it is a work of uncommon modesty. At the heart of *Interaction* lies an acceptance that its author is redundant to its project. Albers does not tell the reader what to see; he merely suggests poetic (or, as Donald Judd would have it, philosophical) strategies for seeing. Unlike Goethe or Chevreul, Albers claims no unifying colour theory. Rather the opposite – his motto is: see for yourselves. As one Yale student noted, 'he sent us out all over the country virtually as missionaries, teaching colour'. *Interaction*, though, was a missal, not a bible.

7.9 Model ti244 armchair, *ca.* 1929. Laminated beech, chrome-plated tubular steel, horsehair upholstery, 28½ × 23 × 28½ in.

This self-effacement runs through Albers' work, as through his teaching. The design of the ti244 armchair may have been his, but the chair's artistry would belong to whoever assembled it. This sense that art is collaborative – that an artwork comes into being with its reception – is key to Albers' thought. The recipes on the backs of the *Homages to the Square* seem to imply that anyone might paint them, or at least repaint them. In 1969, the German-born photographer Hans Namuth filmed the eighty-one-year-old Albers in his studio at North Forest Circle. Khaki-shirted and amiable, the artist tells the world – potential forgers included – exactly how to make a *Homage to the Square*. Panels of masonite should be cut and primed like this. Underdrawing must be done with a silver pen because 'pencil schmears the line'. Drawing with stencils and rulers is just fine; paint should be laid on as thinly as possible, to allow for transparency; *et cetera*. 'It is', Albers says, insouciantly, 'like making sendviches.' You can feel his dealer shudder.

What is curious about this openness is that it seems not so much democratic as socialistic. Nietzschean to his fingertips, Albers had a deep-seated mistrust of history, and of the politics that shaped it; he was certainly *not* a socialist, and only patchily a democrat, at least in the American sense. Yale students recalled him shouting, 'Nonsense! This democracy, that all men are created equal. Nonsense, nonsense! No, all men are created differently, and they must learn to behave together.' 'There are', as one bemused student observed, 'certain social implications in there that are pretty wild.' And yet another Yale student was as foxed by Albers' writing recipes on the backs of *Homages* so that 'they could be replicated by anybody who wished to do so'. 'Democracy was a big thing with him,' the student said. 'That art should somehow be democratic, that it should be participatory. He's way ahead of a lot of the Pop artists on that one.'

On matters of politics, Anni Albers thought like her husband. In 1967, the critic Dore Ashton wrote to Josef asking him to contribute to a print portfolio called *Artists and Writers Protest Against the War in Vietnam*. Those who did included Louise Nevelson and Ad Reinhardt. Not Albers, however. By return came a reply from Anni saying, 'We, who owe our lives to an earlier US involvement prefer not to take now a political stand.' That this involvement might have been unnecessary had Germans protested against Hitler seems not to have struck her. Josef was by now a grand old man: his opinion mattered. In June 1962, he was given an honorary PhD by Yale in the same ceremony at which John F. Kennedy received an honorary Doctorate of Laws. In June

1965, a telegram arrived at North Forest Circle. It read: 'THE PRESIDENT AND MRS JOHNSON INVITE YOU TO A RECEPTION AND BUFFET SUPPER AT THE WHITE HOUSE FESTIVAL OF ARTS ON JUNE 14TH.' The poet Robert Lowell, asked to the same dinner, turned down his invitation in protest at US involvement in Vietnam. Albers attended. In 1968, Mayor John Lindsay of New York cabled to ask for a donation of work to a benefit exhibition at MoMA for the recently assassinated Martin Luther King. Albers refused.

It would be a mistake to construe this politically. His refusal to protest against Vietnam now was no more political than his denunciation of Hannes Meyer had been forty years earlier. As a Yale student, the sculptor Robert Engman recalled joining a group that wore black armbands in protest against the atom bomb. Albers, sympathetic, asked if there had been a death in Engman's family. When he explained, Albers winced, 'Since when do we wear our emotions on our sleeves?' and walked away. His distaste was not for political groups but for groups *tout court*; 'bandwagons'. This applied to art, to thought, to systematized theories of colour. Albers' individualism is one of the most singular things about him, and the most perplexing.

His refusal, or inability, to join groups grew more bothersome as groups now joined him. If leaving Yale had given him time to work, it also meant that he could no longer be dismissed by Alfred Barr and his kind as a teacher rather than an artist. In his seventies and having laboured on the same series for a decade, Albers' art began to be noticed. Suddenly, the *Homages* were everywhere. One appeared, unnamed, in a 1967 *New Yorker* cartoon; by 1973, the world-weary wife in another asks her husband, 'Bach cantatas, Barcelona chairs, Albers prints, quiche – why do our new people always turn out to be like our old people?' An advertisement for trendy shag-pile carpet included what was clearly meant to be a *Homage*, although this had been hung on its side. A *Mitered Square* appeared on a poster for the 1972 Munich Olympics. Albers initially refused the commission, until reassured that he was being invited as an American, not a German, artist. Other invitees included Robert Indiana and Roy Lichtenstein.

His new fame was fed by a series of highly publicized exhibitions, beginning with 'The Responsive Eye' at the Museum of Modern Art in February 1965. William C. Seitz, the show's curator, had been the first student at Princeton to write a thesis on Abstract Expressionism. 'The Responsive

 Olympische Spiele München 1972

7.10 Poster for Olympic Games, 1972. Screen print, 42⁷⁄₁₀ × 27⁹⁄₁₀ in.

Eye' was scholarly and encyclopedic, assembling nearly a hundred artists from all over the world. Seitz was careful not to shoehorn the visually very different work of these into a single category or tendency: the reasonable word he applied to it all was 'perceptual'. Invoking the Hering-Helmholtz debate of a century before, he suggested that 'our idea of the eye must [today] be more embracing.... The "eye" referred to in our title cannot be assumed to be identical with the anatomical orb or an inert optical instrument.' In this most scrupulously broad of senses, Albers' work might usefully be seen alongside, say, Victor Vasarely's or Bridget Riley's, even if it was not like theirs in appearance, ambition or technique.

Seitz was quick to make this clear, noting that Albers objected to the word 'optical' when followed by 'art' and that the 'delicate modulati[ons]' of the *Homages* shunned the 'dramatic manifestation [of] complementary oppositions'. The distinction was lost on reviewers. The work that caught their eye was, predictably, the most eye-catching – images that moved about, such as Riley's *Current* (1964). These quickly became the standard-bearers of the new Op Art, with Albers mustered, willy-nilly, under an illusional flag. When, later in 1965, *The Nation* magazine reviewed 'Josef Albers: The American Years' at the Washington Gallery of Modern Art, it was with the headline, 'His Art Deceives the Eye of the Beholder: Josef Albers, Father of Op Art, Proves He's No Swindler'. The *Herald Tribune* at least recognized that the 'distinction [of his art lay] not in *trompe l'oeil*, but in [an] immaculate, not to say consummate sense of style and order'; although the effect was spoiled when the reviewer, unable to pass up a handy assonance, dubbed Albers a 'top pop of op'.

Op was not the only case of mistaken identity in his work. *The Washington Daily News*, noting Albers' 'strong German accent', listened bemused to his objection to the term 'hard edge' as applied, indiscriminately, to the *Homages*. 'My paintings have hard edges and soft edges,' Albers complained. The piece ran under the headline, 'None So Blind as He That Will Not See'. There was no fighting back. In *Yale Scientific*, Albers argued, articulately, that 'just as colour itself alters, so do its boundaries vary from clashing to merging, from vibrating to vanishing contours....[The] recent art label *hard-edge*...is meaningless.' The magazine was not widely read in the art world, though. The first paragraph of his article paraphrased an earlier poem:

Optical painting
is just as senseless, as unscientific
as acoustical singing
or haptic modelling.
It is parallel to such redundancies as
wood carpentering
or stone masoning
or textile carpeting.

Forty years after his death, his art is still blithely assigned to Op, Hard Edge Painting or Minimalism, although it properly belongs to none of these.

A more useful response came in 1968, in an exhibition curated by John Coplans and called 'Serial Imagery'. This noted that the show's Arp-like *Treble Clef* gouaches were eight from a series of eighty, made between Berlin and at Black Mountain, of which Albers had destroyed more than half (figs 7.11, 7.12). The show's *Variants* and *Homages* were seen in the same light, the latter being further divided into sub-series based on variations of a single colour such as red or yellow. The work's seriality lay not just in its repetition over time but its employment, for each series, of a consistent underlying module. While noting that Albers 'predicated some twenty years in advance of [Frank] Stella the use of combined symmetrical and non-symmetrical structures in a single painting', 'Serial Imagery' did not mistake his art for minimalism. The last word was left to the artist himself: *In visual formulation there is no final solution therefore I work in series.*

For twenty years, the Albers had lived in the same small house in North Forest Circle. To its improbable door had come the good and great. In 1951 alone, the visitors' book was signed by John Cage, Willem and Elaine de Kooning, Mary Callery, Buckminster Fuller and Charles and Ray Eames. These would be followed by Naum and Miriam Gabo, the Breuers, the Gropiuses, Henri Cartier Bresson and the Earl of Snowdon. When the couple did decide to sell up, it was for the most pragmatic of reasons – that Josef wanted a larger studio, and understood that he could afford one. In May 1970, the Albers moved two miles down Route 34, from the suburb of West Haven to the neighbouring Orange. The road between them led handily to the Merritt Parkway, linking New Haven to New York. At last, in his eighties, Josef treated himself to a

7.11 *Treble Clef G, A*, 1932–5. Gouache on paper, 15 × 10 in.
7.12 *Treble Clef G, I*, 1935. Gouache and pencil on paper, 15 × 10³⁄₁₀ in.

Mercedes Benz, the kind of car whose seats he had previously bought from scrapyards. Every time he drove it home from the city, he would guffaw at the green roadside sign that read, 'This is Orange'.

If the new house, 808 Birchwood Drive, was somewhat larger than the old, it was hardly grander. Built the year before and clad in grey shingle, its split-level ranch style was an answer to North Forest Circle's Cape Cod. As before, plants around the house were removed to expose its foundations – among those who were struck by this was Joseph Hirshhorn, who, with his wife, Olga, were to be among Albers' most significant collectors. That the cook at the Hirshhorn estate in Greenwich made proper *Kartoffelpuffer* (potato pancakes) only added to their attractions. Proximity to Route 34 apart, the appeal of the new house lay in its large, windowed basement, taken over by Josef as a studio. Here, he continued to make *Homages*, now helped by Albert Powell, a Yale technician who supplemented his income by mowing the lawns of professors. As Josef got older, it was Powell, from St Kitts, who sized and cut the masonite panels. In the basement, too, Albers worked on architectural commissions – murals in Germany and Kansas in 1972, and

7.13 Ruth Wurcker, Josef Albers' *Wrestling* sculpture, 1976.

Wrestling (1976), a sculpture for an insurance building in Sydney by his former Black Mountain student Harry Seidler (fig. 7.13). *Wrestling* was to be his first commission in Australia, and his last architectural work.

Anni's domain was upstairs. Now too frail for the loom, she had given up weaving for printmaking. A workroom on a level with her bedroom was another of the house's attractions. The large sitting room beyond these was filled with Josef's work, objects by students, items of Josef's furniture and the odd piece of modernist design. Otherwise, it was furnished from catalogues – as Anni delighted in pointing out, its white vinyl sofas came from Bloomingdales. There were fewer visitors now. The most regular was King-lui Wu, with his wife, Vivian, and their three children, much loved by Josef and Anni. 'We called them Uncle Albers and Auntie Albers,' the youngest, Mai-Tse Wu, recalls. 'They never corrected us. Every year, they gave us the same Christmas present – a can of Planters Mixed Nuts each, wrapped in tissue paper and yarn.' Like many wives of her day, Anni was an enthusiast of drip-dry fabrics. There was a potted palm on the coffee table in the sitting room, linoleum and Formica in the kitchen. The couple were in bed by nine, in their studios at nine the next morning. Birchwood Drive was a cul-de-sac. Josef, now in his eighties, would walk around this on a daily constitutional. Still trim, he would wear the grey flannel jacket he had had made for himself in Chile in 1953, over faded khaki trousers and shirt and vinyl slippers. He chatted to neighbours' children, who took to the grandfatherly old man with white hair and red cheeks. It was a typical life in suburban America.

If the house in Orange was modest enough, it marked a new sense in its owners of financial security. On quitting Yale twelve years before, Josef had fretted that he and Anni would pass an impoverished old age in Mexico. In the interim, honours had accrued – honorary doctorates, White House dinners, the Fine Arts Medal of the American Institute of Architects, membership of the US National Institute of Arts and Letters. Recognition came, too, from abroad. When they visited Bottrop in 1960, Josef had shown Anni his childhood house, the schools where he had taught and the restored St Michael's church: then they had got into their rented Opel and sped away. 'Für einen Tag in Bottrop' – 'In Bottrop for one day' – read a wounded local headline. Now, in 1968, Albers' eightieth birthday saw him belatedly honoured in his own land. Besides a German edition of Eugen Gomringer's monograph, there was a doctorate from the University of Bochum, a one-man show at the Münster Landesmuseum, a whole room at Documenta in Kassel

7.14 Henri Cartier-Bresson, Josef Albers at home, 1968, Connecticut.
7.15 Henri Cartier-Bresson, Anni and Josef Albers at home, 1968, Connecticut.

and the North Rhine-Westphalia Grand Prize for Painting. Feted on a visit home in November by the mayor and Minister President, Albers tactfully ascribed the rarity of his appearances to his fear of flying. Two years later, he was made a freeman of Bottrop. Two years after that, he made the city the first gift of his work; a process that would lead, in 1983, to the opening of the Josef Albers Museum.

For all Albers' new-found celebrity, as an article in *Vogue* noted, his prices had remained 'niggardly'. At an auction at Parke Bernet in New York in early 1970, a 48-inch *Homage* sold for ten thousand dollars. A de Kooning in the same sale went for four times as much, a Warhol for six. Although Albers was recognized (or misrecognized) as a leading figure in various fashionable movements, his own work remained relatively unfashionable. The reasons for this were suggested by his exclusion from the MoMA touring exhibition, 'New American Painting', in 1958. Albers' paintings, while made in America, looked un-American, which is to say small-scale and measured. If de Kooning was Dutch, he ranked with Jackson Pollock as a pioneer of that robustly American thing, abstract expressionism. Then again, there was the problem of age. Warhol was forty-one at the time of the Parke Bernet sale, Albers eighty-two. The idea that an old man could make new art taxed the art world's imagination.

The number of paintings emerging from his studio did at least compensate for their price. Between January and May 1967 alone, Sidney Janis sold twenty *Homages* for a total of $68,000. Alongside the income from these went another from screen prints, now published by Ives-Sillman in runs of a hundred or more. In 1973, the firm would produce *Formulation : Articulation*, a set of two boxed portfolios each containing thirty-three handsomely screen-printed folders of work from Albers' fifty-year career – early glass paintings, *Treble Clefs*, *Transformations*, *Variants*, *Homages to the Square*. But the feeling persisted that his work was undervalued in terms both of its price and its critical reception. As the *Vogue* article put it, it was a 'scandal that Albers [had] never been offered a full-dress retrospective exhibition at any of the four New York major museums'. In the year he and Anni moved house, this was to change.

Shortly after shooting his film, Hans Namuth introduced Albers to Lee Eastman. Eastman was an extraordinary figure, a New York entertainment lawyer who numbered Frank Sinatra among his clients. When he met Albers, Eastman was acting for Paul McCartney in the break-up of the Beatles; McCartney had married Eastman's daughter, Linda, shortly before. The lawyer's peerless eye for business was matched by another for art. At his death in 1991, his collection would include works by Giacometti, Matisse and Picasso, although its greatest strength was in post-war American painting – Mark Rothko, Robert Motherwell and, preeminently, Willem de Kooning. Uniting his passions for litigation and painting, Eastman had become de Kooning's lawyer in 1958. In conversation with Albers, Eastman had asked whether his dealer had ever been audited. Anni was 'horrified'. For Josef, Sidney Janis was 'part of the family'.

The two had met in 1948, when Janis's gallery was new and Albers struggling to find a dealer. He would be by no means the most successful Janis artist: the gallery represented, among others, de Kooning, Rothko and Gorky. If prices for Albers' works had not risen remarkably, though, they had at least done so steadily – sufficient, when multiplied by numbers sold, to provide maker and dealer with an income. Given Albers' capacity for work and the speed with which *Homages* were produced, this arrangement suited both well enough. Janis had also introduced Albers to buyers who would be his most loyal and discriminating, among them James and Lillian Clark, Texas-based collectors of Mondrian, Léger and Brancusi. The pair of paintings subtitled *For J. H. Clark* (1961) remain among the most beautiful of the *Homages*. It was through Janis, too, that Albers met Joseph Hirshhorn, whose extraordinary purchase in 1968 – Bauhaus glassworks, early self-portraits, *Structural Constellations*, *Homages* and more – form the core of the Hirshhorn Museum's current collection, and changed Albers' fortunes forever. The problem, at the Janis Gallery, was of over-supply. As with any commodity, the market for paintings is easily saturated. As long as *Homages* were piled high and sold (relatively) cheap, their price would not rise. This committed Albers to a Stakhanovite output in old age. Lee Eastman, from the sharper world of show business, understood the value of rarity. At some point, he explained it to Albers.

This was not all he explained. By December 1970, the lawyer had been through Janis's books. The gallery was holding money back: Eastman committed them to paying Albers $100,000 against an unspecified larger sum.

Two months later, Janis was ordered to hand over all its remaining work to a new Albers foundation. Early in 1971, he writes to Albers that he has 'had lunch with Henry'. 'We must', Eastman says, 'proceed with the catalogue immediately,' as Henry is leaving for Italy. 'Henry' was Henry Geldzahler, curator of the new 20th-century department at the Metropolitan Museum of Art. In 1969, Geldzahler had organized the Met's first ever contemporary show, 'New York Painting and Sculpture: 1940–1970', a runaway success. Albers had had thirteen works in the exhibition, in a room devoted solely to them. Now, he was to have a full monograph show of his own, the first at the Met of a living artist.

This alone might have boosted demand for his paintings, and with it their prices. What Eastman did next was a classic piece of market-making. Just as Albers' work was about to take off, he withdrew it from the market. Later, he explained his strategy to the *New York Times*. 'Albers's paintings became unavailable, and then they were like black tulips,' Eastman said. 'Everybody wanted one.' The next year, a Toronto dealer called Jack Pollock – Eastman described him as 'friendly' – paid $40,000 for a *Homage*, setting a new record for Albers at auction. This was four times what the Parke Bernet painting had gone for, six times the price typically charged by Sidney Janis. Paradoxically if predictably, demand for Albers' work shot up. The gallerist Denise René, who represented him in Paris, reported that 'people [were] beginning to fight for [*Homages*] because they [were] not available'. Albers, at eighty-three, found himself nudged towards stardom.

The attractions of a Met show were clear. As Geldzahler put it, 'A painting by Willem de Kooning hanging fifty yards from a roomful of Rembrandts is judged according to the artist's highest ambition.' 'Albers was German,' adds another observer. 'Being in a *historisches museum* meant everything to him.' Why Geldzahler was so keen on the show is another matter. In his writing on 'New York Painting and Sculpture', Albers' name isn't even mentioned. Perhaps, bringing contemporary art to a historical museum, Geldzahler saw the old *Bauhäusler* as having feet handily in both camps. By 1971, the title of Albers' article '*Historisch oder jetzig?*' – 'Historical or Modern?' – might equally have applied to its author. The number and prices of Albers' works also meant that he was more likely to donate them – Eastman's letter about Geldzahler had noted that the curator expected a *quid pro quo* 'gift to the Metropolitan of 20 paintings and as much graphic work as possible'. At his second meeting with Geldzahler, Albers had turned up with a package under his arm. This held the glass painting *Pillars* (1928). 'Nine thousand dollars,' Albers had snapped. The museum, sensibly, bought it. Ninety-eight of the hundred paintings in the Met show would come, free, from the artist's own collection.

Another explanation for Geldzahler's zeal may have been professional unscrupulousness. For two years, a young Guggenheim curator, Margit Rowell, had travelled to New Haven each Saturday to see Albers in his studio. The interviews were to lead to a monograph by Harry N. Abrams, who would publish *Formulation : Articulation* in 1972. 'Around five, we'd go up to the kitchen, where Anni would feed us industrial pastries from the day-old shelf at the supermarket,' Rowell laughs. In May 1970, she wrote to Albers, expanding her brief. 'I would', she said, 'like very much to hold a major retrospective exhibition of your work at the Guggenheim Museum in 1972.' Before asking her director's approval, would Albers be interested? He replied that he would.

In September, Thomas Messer, the Guggenheim's director, wrote to Albers that he had 'thought for some time that a Josef Albers Retrospective at the Guggenheim Museum would be an important event'. The date he proposed was autumn 1972, 'since it would take that long to complete a retrospective with the care and thoroughness that you would insist upon'. Albers must certainly have discussed this with Lee Eastman, and Eastman with Henry Geldzahler: Geldzahler later spoke of Eastman's 'forceful intervention' in the matter. At any rate, the retrospective went to the Met, and in autumn 1971, making a show at the Guggenheim impossible. From initial discussion to opening night took nine months. 'It was a shame,' Rowell says, 'because Albers' work would have looked great at the Guggenheim – the tension between the circle and the square, the building's European scale.' In January 1972, Rowell published an article in *Artforum* based on her interviews with Albers. Acute, engaged and well researched, this quoted its subject discussing the influence on his early work of Munch and Van Gogh. Albers did not like his art being analysed in this way: his furious annotations on his copy of the article suggest that he saw, too late, how far he had let down his guard. Rowell's book on Albers was never published.

The Metropolitan exhibition opened on 19 November 1971 and ran for seven weeks. Geldzahler's oddly bloodless catalogue essay sets out to reconcile what it calls the 'antagonistic [strands of] Science and Poetry' in Albers' work. In its 'stripped and repeated images', it says, 'there is no place

JOSEF ALBERS AT THE METROPOLITAN
MUSEUM OF ART NOV 19 1971–JAN 9 1972

7.16 *Josef Albers at the Metropolitan Museum of Art, P-Yellow*, 1971. Screen print, 28½ × 21 in.

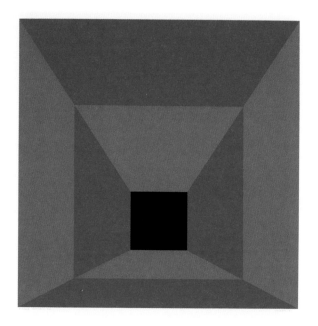

JOSEF ALBERS AT THE METROPOLITAN
MUSEUM OF ART NOV 19 1971-JAN 9 1972

7.17 *Josef Albers at the Metropolitan Museum of Art, P-Black*, 1971. Screen print, 28½ × 21 in.

to hide'. To this is added the surprising observation, 'All is out in the open for everyone to see.' Reviews in the art press were scarce. The show did, though, get three notices in the *New York Times*, including one that found its subject 'never unduly modest' and repeated Rauschenberg's description of him as 'impossible'. The canard of Albers' German accent was again trotted out. A more intelligent response came from the critic John Canaday, who noted that the *Homages* 'could be hung by the hundreds instead of the dozens...to the increasing advantage of each'. While allowing that Albers might be seen 'historically and technically [as] a parent of both optical and minimal art', Canaday sees his work as more 'contemplative' than either. Peter Schjeldahl, customarily astute, agreed. Albers' 'use of colour', he said, 'has to do with quite a lot more than dazzlements of the optic nerve'. 'The more one sees of his *Homages*,' Schjeldahl goes on, 'the more inexhaustible the possibilities of this quiet, squares-within-squares motif come to seem.'

If Albers was edging towards fame, his work was being seen by the famous. The playwrights Edward Albee and Mike Nichols, cartoonist Saul Steinberg and painter Jasper Johns now owned his work. Politicians, too, took note. In 1975 came talk of a wall painting for the new German chancellery in Bonn. Described by Chancellor Helmut Schmidt as having 'all the charm of a Rhineland savings bank', this stark building, in its occupant's view, needed softening. Schmidt earmarked Albers' mural for the cabinet meeting room, overruling television crews who argued for fumed oak. The new building's iconography was politically vexed: Schmidt saw the Bauhaus, and thus Albers, as antidotes to *Entartete Kunst*. As often, the plan came to nothing. In this case, though, the reason was not money or aesthetics, but the artist's death.

Among the most fervent of Albers' new admirers was Maximilian Schell. An actor, linguist and musician, the Swiss-Austrian Schell was a man of huge culture. Exiled from Nazi Vienna as a child, he was, in his thirties, best known for such work as *Judgment at Nuremberg* (1961). He wrote to Albers in late 1969 to enthuse about *Despite Mist* (1967), the *Homage* diptych he had just bought from Janis. 'You cannot imagine my joy at being able to take your wonderful painting home with me to Europe,' Schell says. 'I admire your art so much, and this picture particularly, that I know it will have a profound influence on my work.' His tastes did not run only to *Homages*. At the same time as *Despite Mist*, Schell had bought the *Variant* painting *Chalk Green Facade* (1958). Had

Albers ever designed for the stage? he asks. He could imagine his paintings linking Shakespeare's world to their own.

Back home in Munich, he wrote to Janis: 'I would...appreciate it if you would let me know about the other Albers which I saw in your gallery. I am so fascinated by this painter that I would like to have a representative collection of his work.' In 1971, Schell would buy three more *Homages*: *Speech* (1965), *R-J3* (1968) and *Profuse* (1969), the first two in contrasts of red, the last of yellow. In 1972 came another eight. To Lee Eastman, now handling sales, Schell explained that he wanted to 'create in Munich a sort of Albers-Foundation', opening his house to the public. To Albers himself, he wrote as a friend. Schell's letters to the old man are filial and gossipy. In February 1976, he writes from the Chateau Marmont in Los Angeles to say that Josef 'has a huge new fan: Jon Voight, one of the best young American actors (he won the New Yorker Critics' Prize for *Midnight Cowboy*)'. 'I miss my home very much, especially your paintings,' Schell ends. 'I miss them a lot.' He apologizes for not stopping in at Orange on his way back to Germany, but hopes to visit on his return to America. He did, although Albers was no longer there to greet him.

If Mammon now figured more prominently in Albers' life, God remained quietly present. From the Benedictine abbey of Gerleve in North-Rhine-Westphalia came letters from Fr Rupert Overlack, a young priest who had seen Albers' show in Münster. Albers' sister, Frau Marx, had spoken to him at the opening – 'She and her husband know my family well,' the priest says. 'Every time I'm in Münster, I drop in for a "seeing lesson". Such clarity and purity radiate from your paintings that one is struck dumb.... Is it possible to say that they demand a *metanoia*? Is that going too far?' A *metanoia* is a spiritual conversion through repentance: it is an intriguing reading. Albers' warm reply directs the priest to his *Graphic Tectonics*, two of which, he points out, are named for antiphons from the Mass.

Letters came, too, from Fr Josef Tenorth, a pupil of Albers' during his nine months in Bottrop in 1924. Now a parish priest, Tenorth recalls being made to paint on *Butterbrotspapier* – greaseproof paper – 'pictures not of what was, but of what was beautiful'. 'Unlike the other teachers, you had your hair cut short and suit buttoned up, so there was no need for a tie,' Tenorth writes. 'I can still remember your prudent step, and unusual way of dealing with us children. There was something uncomfortable, and compelling, and furious, about it which I have never forgotten – back then, it was entirely new.' The priest's life has been hard. Conscripted in the Wehrmacht as an ordinand, he was badly wounded in 1945. Now, he is diocesan head of social work in Aachen, a job he finds 'physically and mentally grinding'. 'Your book of drawings and words [*Despite Straight Lines*] is a wonderful help,' he writes to Albers. 'Its infinite harmony and beauty. Once more, I thank you! To me, your work is a meditation.'

Religion came in unexpected guises. In 1965, an Essen self-portrait had been stolen from the college in Hartford, Connecticut, where Albers was giving a trio of lectures called *Search Versus Re-Search*. A day later, an anonymous tip-off led police to the lithograph, in the confessional of a Catholic church.

Four years later, the Chicago publisher Marshall Field commissioned the graphic designer Bradbury Thompson to devise a new Bible. Thompson, in turn, approached Albers. By May 1972, his contribution had been agreed. The art director of Field Enterprises writes to Norman Ives to confirm this. There are to be three Albers frontispieces, one to each of the new Bible's volumes – *Introitus*, *Seclusion* and *Ascension*, all based on works which 'originally appeared in 1942 as zinc lithographs in black ink'. The next letter agrees the fee Albers has demanded for his designs, 'namely, six copies of the Limited Edition and [a] reasonable number (or ten) from the Deluxe Edition' of the Bible. There was to be no cash payment. As Alvin Eisenman recalled, Albers had been offered 'several thousand dollars' for his work. He wryly refused it, saying, 'I need all the credit in that department I can get.'

This was not the end of the story. In early 1974, Field's art director, Gordon Kwiatkowski, wrote to Albers asking for an answer to a proposal he had discussed with Norman Ives, that another set of frontispieces be designed for a planned second printing of the Bible. Perhaps, the letter asks, Albers might 'sanction new colour schemes and size changes' for the prints already used? The writer also thanks him for 'the beautiful *Homage to the Square* print...[which] will remain one of the most sacred of my possessions'. The letter ends, 'Mr Albers, I was so happy to have received it because I sensed it was a personal gesture on your part.' Albers' furious row of penned question marks makes it clear that this was not the case. When a reply came, it was from Lee Eastman.

7.18 *Introitus*, 1942. Screen print, 10⁹⁄₁₀ × 6⅛ in.
7.19 *Seclusion*, 1942. Screen print, 7⁹⁄₁₀ × 8¼ in.
7.20 *Ascension*, 1942. Screen print, 10⁹⁄₁₀ × 6⅛ in.

Field Enterprises' hapless director had walked into a minefield. Eight months before, in June 1973, Alvin Eisenman had asked Albers to back Norman Ives' promotion from adjunct to full Yale professor. Albers' response had been fulsome. Ives, he said, had been his student and colleague, but most of all his 'collaborator' – 'a successful and respected maker and designer, and outstanding in his own work.' Ives got the job. Four months later, though, things had changed. In October, Eastman wrote to Ives-Sillman accusing them of overcharging Jack Pollock, the 'friendly' Toronto dealer who in 1972 had quadrupled the baseline price for *Homages*. Ives, wounded, wrote back to dispute this. 'You are aware of the many services we render to Josef,' he ended, 'Both willingly and lovingly.' But Ives-Sillman could not work at a loss. After this, things quickly fell apart.

In November 1973, Eastman wrote sharply, 'I do not think either of you still grasp [*sic*] what this is all about.' In January 1974, his tone was frostier: 'Josef Albers would very much like to receive payment forthwith of the sum of $10,000.00 which he loaned you some time ago as evidenced

7.21 John T. Hill, Portrait of Josef Albers in front of Washburn College Bible print.

by a note dated May 27, 1971.' By March, Albers' twenty-year association with Ives-Sillman was over. From then on, his printing would be done by a studio in New York. Eastman's reply to Kwiatkowski's letter about the new Bible was abrupt. Albers' work would longer be *pro bono*: 'I take it this is a commercial venture. I would like therefore to know...what remuneration he is to receive.' Soon after, the project was shelved. Thompson's book would finally appear as the Washburn College Bible, three years after Albers' death (fig. 7.21).

There is no question that Albers' finances and standing improved greatly in the last years of his life. But success came at a cost. It was the ingenuity and devotion of Sillman and Ives that had produced the catalogue to Albers' 1956 Yale show, which in turn led to their mutual masterpiece, *Interaction of Color*. For twenty years, the meticulous register of Albers' prints was owed to the same source. Sillman had arranged the 1956 show at Yale; he and Ives had hung the one at the Met. More, the two men had looked on Albers as a father, and he them, bemusedly, as sons. Now they were cut out of his life, and no longer executors of his will: 'We eliminated Ives and Sillman,' as Eastman wrote. Nothing in the sources suggests wrongdoing on their part. At worst, an over-identification with Albers had led them to take him for granted. His dismissal of them was harsh. As Bernard Chaet said, 'The way he handled Sillman and Ives was horrible. They gave their lives to him, and he threw them out of his house.'

His treatment of Sidney Janis was little better. Albers clearly felt betrayed by Janis's holding back of money, although this was fairly common practice in commercial galleries and had, in any case, been dealt with. His treatment of his old friend was inexplicably severe. In May 1972, Janis wrote to Albers suggesting a double exhibition of his work with Mondrian's. 'I feel this... should finally confirm [your] artistic position in Twentieth Century Art,' Janis says. Albers' reply to this olive branch was less curt than cruel: 'Dear Sidney, permit me to answer your recent letter briefly. I am not interested. Good luck. Yours, Albers.' Janis wrote again, reminding Albers of the 'pioneer work we have so painstakingly done over the past twenty-five years...[when] others consistently ignored your paintings'. Albers' margin notes are ungrammatical with rage: 'When did you send my paintings go to Europe? I remember that you send Kollection to London and Basel not was my paintings sent there from you.' Janis tried one last time. 'I remember [in 1948] how difficult it was to get people to see the originality and importance of your paintings which to me was so clearly evident....[R]egardless of belated recognition, no one is more gratified over it than I.' After that, the correspondence ends.

And yet Albers was capable of great loyalty, and of inspiring it. His friendship with Franz Perdekamp lasted half a century, with the Wu family to the end of his life. In his eighties, he corresponded with boys he had been at school with in Büren seventy years before. In 1967, Thornton Wilder wrote to him, 'If I was among the first to acknowledge the master's genius, I wish also to be accounted among the most enduring and faithful.' Buckminster Fuller celebrated Albers' eighty-sixth birthday by writing, 'While you are not my blood brother, you are a beloved friend. You 86, I 78. Who do I thank that I had the extraordinary fortune to know and become a friend of Joseph [*sic*] Albers.'

In the archive of the Albers Foundation in Connecticut is a file marked 'I Remember'. This contains scraps of paper on which, in English and German, Albers has jotted vignettes of his life, each headed with the titular words. None is dated, although, as most are in biro, they are clearly post-war. Some are droll – the author's first impressions of American bicycles, for example, with their 'lack of straight horizontals'. Most, though, recall snubs and subsequent retribution.

There is the rejection of *Homage to the Square 2* in New York, followed by its award in Los Angeles; Charles Sawyer cutting the word 'constellation' from Albers' description of their new Yale department, only later to reinstate it; one of his Bauhaus typefaces being rejected for publication and then used; '2 superior academicians' at Black Mountain mocking his now-famous term 'thinking in situations'; and so on. Who these notes were written for is difficult to say. Their lack of formality suggests messages in bottles from Albers to himself. Some stories are repeated two or three times, as he tries to get their narrative and phrasing *just right*. The impulse to record, to write down, seems understandable in one cut off from his own past and tongue. What is sad about the notes is their suggestion of a man who saw the world as unkind.

On Friday 19 March 1976, Albers turned eighty-eight. That morning, he 'felt a sharp pain'. Anni, worried, called the doctor: Josef was taken to the Yale-New Haven Hospital and kept in for tests on his heart, although the pain faded. He was an irascible patient – by the following Thursday, he was ready to come home: Vivian Wu had offered to collect him. As Anni made breakfast at Birchwood Drive, the telephone rang. Just after dawn, in his sleep, Josef had died.

His will had been clear: 'I direct that my funeral be in accordance with the rites of the Roman Catholic Church, in all quietness without music, flowers or participation by the public in any manner.' He and Anni had chosen their plot in Orange Cemetery five years before, next to a path so that she could drive in after going to the post office and sit by his grave in the car. Rather than being at its head, Albers' gravestone was set parallel to the road. His funeral was held by a young priest at the parish church, Holy Infant, two days after his death. Anni apart, there were seven mourners, among them Anni's brother, Hans Farman, King-Lui and Vivian Wu, and Lee Eastman.

Si Sillman had written to Anni the day after Josef's death: 'The news... brought a sense of loss and saddness [*sic*] impossible to describe.' For Norman Ives, 'His presence was totally positive, both morally and spiritually.... He discovered that little-known secret: simplicity.' Telegrams and letters arrived from Marcel Breuer, the Feiningers, Max Bill; Mayor Teddy Kollek of Jerusalem, Chancellor Helmut Schmidt, and the president of West Germany, Walter Scheel. Hans Namuth, in block capitals, wrote, 'I had always thought that Josef would live forever – and now that he is dead I know: he will.' From a little girl on Birchwood Drive came a pencilled note on pink paper: 'Dear Mrs Albers, I'm very sorry that your husband past away. He was a very nice man. Everytime he walked up and down the street he was so kind and nice. He drew the most beautiful paintings. My Brother, sister and I will miss him very much walking + talking with us!'

Obituaries, predictably, dwelt on Albers at the Bauhaus. 'One of the last Bauhaus giants', announced the Toronto *Globe and Mail*; the *Ruhr-Nachrichten* led, not entirely accurately, with *Der letzte Bauhausmeister*. The London *Times* noted, 'The paintings by which he will be remembered were all done after the age of 60.... These were the long series of pictures which he called *Homage to the Square*...a seemingly inexhaustible sequence.' 'For Albers,' the piece went on, 'colour was an analogy of human behaviour and this led him to a belief in the inescapable moral function of art.' Max Bill, in the *Neue Zürcher Zeitung*, mentioned the commission for the cabinet meeting room in Bonn. 'We may assume that this, imagined by Helmut Schmidt and widely considered to be the crowning achievement of Albers' career, will certainly be brought to fruition,' Bill said. It never was. The *New York Times* quoted Albers on his art: 'Just putting colours together is the excitement of it. What interests me is the way they marry, interpenetrate and produce the baby, the colour that is their product together.'

His memorial service was held on 23 April, in the lecture hall of Louis Kahn's Yale University Art Gallery. Dogwood was in bloom: baskets of it were banked on the stage, where a string quartet played Charles Ives. Chester Kerr, director of the Yale University Press, stood to deliver an address. 'At Yale today, we rejoice in the eternity of Josef Albers,' Kerr said, 'and in his impact on the worlds we value.' He joked that Albers had died peacefully in his sleep, 'or was it furiously?' Then he quoted Anni. 'Josef has done his share on earth. Now he deserves a rest.'

Notes
Select Bibliography
Collections
Exhibitions
Picture List
Index

Notes

The acronym JAAF refers to the Josef and Anni Albers Foundation, Bethany, Connecticut. The acronym JAAFA refers to the Foundation's Archives. Other sources of primary material, such as the Bauhaus-Archiv and Yale libraries, are indicated in the relevant footnotes.

Introduction: *Homages to the Square*

p. 18 'Art is there lest we perish...' G. Colli and M. Montinari (eds), *Sämtliche Werke: Kritische Studienausgabe* (Berlin: W. de Gruyter, 1980ff), 16 [40] 13: 500.

'Art must do more than Nature...' Quoted in Grace Glueck, 'Each Day, Another Albers Pancake', *New York Times*, 5 December 1971, p. 24.

'He liked the square for its simplicity...' Richard Anuszkiewicz interviewed by Frederick Horowitz, 1996. All Horowitz interviews cited are held at the JAAFA.

p. 19 'In the summer of 1950...' JA, undated and unpublished interview with Margit Rowell, *ca.* 1969–70.

'Malevich invented the square...' Paul Westheim, 'Bemerkungen zur Quadratur des Bauhauses', *Das Kunstblatt* VII (1923), p. 319ff.

p. 20 'post-painterly abstraction...' The term comes from the exhibition 'Post-Painterly Abstraction', organized by the most famous American critic of the day, Clement Greenberg, at the Los Angeles County Museum of Art in 1964.

'Its imagining of an art of...' Sol LeWitt, 'Paragraphs on Conceptual Art', *Artforum* 5 no. 10, June 1967, pp. 79–83.

'I was in awe of him just for...' Charles Wilson interviewed by Horowitz, 1 April 1993.

'Despite their obvious likenesses...' Numbers from the *catalogue raisonné* of Albers' paintings, currently being compiled by Dr Jeannette Redensek at the JAAF in Bethany, CT.

p. 23 '*Homage to the Square (A)*' The work is now in a private collection in New York.

'nerves [became] still more sensitive' From interviews with JA by Irving Finkelstein, taped in support of his PhD thesis (1965); tape 2, side B, track 1. Courtesy of the JAAF.

'From this full stop Albers...' Michel Seuphor, 'The Perfect Square' in Eugen Gomringer et al., *Josef Albers: His Work as Contribution to Visual Articulation in the Twentieth Century* (New York: George Wittenborn Inc., 1968), p. 184.

'As to the artist himself, he said...' JA interviewed by Finkelstein.

'Usually, I do not try to do...' Ibid.

'Another student recalled Albers expressing...' Mark Johnson interviewed by Horowitz, 28 September 2001.

'One such is the small work, eleven...' Catalogue 1950.1.10, collection of the JAAF.

'By 1960, Albers had settled on...' See transcript of JA interviewed by Jane Fisk McCullough, December 1965, JAAFA 67.7.

p. 25 'The fourth, central square is...' For an analysis of the dimensions of the *Homages*, see, *inter alia*, Werner Spies, *Albers* (New York: Harry N. Abrams, Inc., 1970).

'Much has been written on the...' See, for example, Hans Joachim Albrecht, *Farbe als Sprache: Robert Delaunay, Josef Albers, Richard Paul Lohse* (Cologne: Verlag M. du Mont Schauberg, 1975).

'A formula that would guarantee...' Thus, for example, his interest in colour blindness. The undiagnosed tritanopia of Eric Bentley, a colleague at Black Mountain College, was a source of fascination to Albers. Eric Bentley, pers. comm., 21 January 2017.

'As *Newsweek* perceptively put it...' Douglas Davis, *Newsweek*, 18 January 1971, pp. 77–8.

p. 26 '*Cerulean blue shade*' Grumbacher's Pre-Tested Oil Paint.

'*Varnished with Eonite*' A wood varnish made by the Sears Corporation. Due to its tendency to discolour, Albers stopped using Eonite in 1959. See Patricia Sherwin Garland, 'Josef Albers: His Paintings, Their Materials, Technique and Treatment', *Journal of the American Institute for Conservation* 1983, vol. 2, no. 2, pp. 62–7.

p. 27 'This, later, would land conservators...' Ibid.

'At seventy, he published a collection...' *Poems and Drawings* (New Haven: Readymade Press, 1958).

'As that tireless cosmopolitan Count Harry...' Harry Graf Kessler, *Gesichter und Zeiten: Erinnerungen* (Frankfurt am Main: Fischer, 1921), p. 210.

p. 28 'To be new, of necessity, meant...' The term 'master of suspicion' was coined by the French philosopher Paul Ricoeur to describe the work of Nietzsche, Freud and Darwin; see Ricoeur, *Freud and Philosophy: An Essay on Interpretation* (New Haven: Yale University Press, 1970).

'Albers, intrigued at the gap...' These were Grumbacher, Lucien Lefebvre-Foinet and Shiva.

p. 30 'The book in which the poems...' Eugen Gomringer, *Constellations* (Esslingen: Bechtle Verlag, 1954).

'In the year the older man turned...' Gomringer, *Josef Albers: His Work*.

'This set out its stall as a...' A notice on the flyleaf points out that it was written 'in consultation with Josef Albers'.

'While he notes that, as the...' Gomringer, *Josef Albers: His Work*, p. 8.

'If the notion of a kinship between...' Albers would not have liked the comparison. His friendship with the architect Philip Johnson faded in part over Johnson's defence of 'novelties...[such as]...the Lichtensteins and all this, you know? Which I have no sympathy for, not one millimetre.' JA interviewed by Finkelstein, tape 2, side B, track 1.

p. 31 'Among the *Homages*' ancestors in...' See Wilhelm Flitner, *Erinnerungen, 1889–1945* (Paderborn: Ferdinand Schöningh, 1986), pp. 290–1.

'no smock, no skylight, no studio...' Elaine de Kooning, 'Albers Paints a Picture', *Art News* 49, no. 7, November 1950, pp. 40–3, 57–8.

'The now popular concept of serial...' Lucy Lippard to JA (quoting him), letter confirming quotations, 14 February 1967, JAAFA Box 6 Folder 20. Albers' remarks appeared, edited, in Lippard's article 'Homage', *Art in America*, Summer 1967, p. 52.

p. 32 'Working on a table made for...' Leo Steinberg, *Other Criteria* (New York: Oxford University Press, 1972).

p. 34 'I'm not paying "homage to the square"!' In Neil Welliver, 'Albers on Albers', *Art News* 64, no. 9, January 1966, p. 69.

'What he liked about the square...' John H. Holloway and John A. Weil, 'A Conversation with Josef Albers', *Leonardo*, vol. 3, 1970, pp. 459–64.

'Cartier Bresson, the well-known French…' Ibid. p. 463.

'Albers' friend, the Gestalt psychologist…' Rudolf Arnheim, *The Power of the Center: A Study of Composition in the Visual Arts* (Oakland: UCLA Press, 1988).

p. 41 'In Albers' first year at the Bauhaus…' André Gide, 'Notes to Angèle', *Nouvelle Revue Française*, March–June 1921, quoted in Theodore Ziolkowski, *Classicism of the Twenties: Art, Music and Literature* (Chicago: University of Chicago Press, 2015), pp. 12–13.

'It is just a demonstration how colour…' JA interviewed by Finkelstein, tape 1, side B, track 1.

'At eighty-one, filmed in the suburban…' Hans Namuth and Paul Falkenberg, *Josef Albers: Homage to the Square*, film (1969).

p. 42 'Often I have to paint a picture…' In Katharine Kuh, *The Artist's Voice: Talks with Seventeen Artists* (New York: Harper & Row, 1962), p. 20.

'When I destroy…I feel clean' JA interviewed by Rowell.

'In the early sixties, Albers painted…' *Homage to the Square: Despite Mist* now belongs to the French collector François Pinault.

p. 43 'Colours, he said, appeared to him…' Kuh, *The Artist's Voice*, p. 20.

'When you go downstairs [to the basement]…' JA interviewed by Sevim Fesci, New Haven, CT, 22 June–5 July 1968, Oral History Interviews, Archives of American Art, Smithsonian Institution.

'I mean, you are going like a horse through life' Herbert Bayer interviewed by Arthur A. Cohen, 3 November 1981–10 March 1982, Oral History Interviews, Archives of American Art, Smithsonian Institution.

'When a student translated a passage…' Sheldon Nodelman interviewed by Horowitz, 2 December 2004. The article was presumably Jean Clay's 'Trois étapes d'une logique' in *Réalités*, March 1968, pp. 64–9.

p. 44 'I lead the spectator from…' JA interviewed by Rowell.

'We believe…that [the] desire…' JA, 'Historisch oder Jetzig?', *Junge Menchen* no. 8, November 1924, p. 171.

He who sees better, who discerns…' JA, *Interaction of Color* (New Haven: Yale University Press, 1963).

'You may buy here brown and…' Anonymous, '"Cheating" Art Lovers Makes Life Exciting For Albers,' *New Haven Register*, 22 February 1959.

'Colour is fooling us all the time…' JA interviewed by Fesci.

1 Am Anfang

p. 46 What difference does it make if…' JA, unpublished interview by Margit Rowell, 25 June 1970.

p. 47 'It was the Feast of St Joseph…' Birth certificate held in Josef Albers Papers MS32, Yale Manuscripts and Archives, Sterling Library, Yale University.

'The spelling of the second…' Registration, Rektoratschule.

'Lorenz Albers had arrived in Bottrop…' Einwohnermeldekarte von Lorenz Albers, Stadtarchiv Bottrop.

p. 48 'In 1890, when Lorenz and Magdalena…' Richard Charles Murphy, *Gastarbeiter im Deutschen Reich: Polen in Bottrop, 1891–1933* (Wuppertal: Peter Hammer Verlag, 1982).

'Even my spit was black…' Nicholas Fox Weber, *The Bauhaus Group: Six Masters of Modernism* (New Haven: Yale University Press, 2011).

p. 49 'By 1915, the year Josef Albers would…' Friedrich Heckmann, *Ethnische Minderheit, Volk und Nation* (Stuttgart: Ferdinand Enke Verlag, 1993).

'The town was not alone in experiencing…' Robin Lenman, *Artists and Society in Germany, 1850–1914* (Manchester: Manchester University Press, 1997).

'What made Bottrop unique was…' John J. Kulczycki, *The Foreign Worker and the German Labour Movement: Xenophobia and Solidarity in the Coal Fields of the Ruhr, 1871–1914* (Oxford: Berg, 1994).

'The Polish immigrants had to be housed…' Murphy, *Gastarbeiter im Deutschen Reich*.

p. 50 'The house at 18 Horsterstrasse…' Willy Jeger, *Bottrop Gestern: Anekdoten, Geschichten und Bilder aus der guten alten Zeit* (Gummersbach: Gronenberg, 1979).

p. 51 'But those with lesser land…' For a contemporary analysis of this process, see Gustav von Schmoller, 'What We Mean by the Middle Class' (1897).

'So great and rapid had been…' Max Jürgen Koch, *Der Bergarbeiterbewegung im Ruhrgebiet zur Zeit Wilhelms II (1889–1914)* (Düsseldorf, 1954).

'In Bottrop, members of the Polish…' Koch, *Bergarbeiterbewegung*.

'At intervals throughout Josef Albers' youth…' Kulczycki, *The Foreign Worker*.

'The dangers were as much spiritual…' Erik Grimmer-Solem, *The Rise of Historical Economics and Social Reform in Germany, 1864–1894* (Oxford: Clarendon Press, 2003), p. 98.

p. 52 'The building trades, with their…' Robert Michels, *Die deutsche Sozialdemokratie*. In *Archiv für Sozialwissenschaft und Sozialpolitik XXIII* (1906), pp. 509–17; Shulamit Volkov, *The Rise of Popular Antimodernism in Germany: The German Master Artisans, 1873–1896* (Princeton: Princeton University Press, 1978).

'The guild's mission, as its statutes…' Johannes Geurts (ed.), *Fünfzig Jahre Malerinnung Bottrop* (Bottrop: W. Postberg, 1955).

'At its first meeting, on 11 October…' Ibid. Lorenz would eventually become chairman in 1918, a difficult year when he stood unopposed.

'My father was quite musical…' From interviews with JA by Irving Finkelstein, taped in support of his PhD thesis (1965). Courtesy of the JAAF. A further detail of the life of an apprentice in a master's household is spelled out in the memoir of Gerhard Richter – no relation – who would be Albers' student at the Bauhaus from 1928–9. Of his own master, a cabinetmaker in Leipzig called Ramin, Richter said: 'This man was wonderful. He was very strict; he often beat me a little. In my contract is written that the master has the right to punish; that was written in my contract, so I got some sometimes – on my back.' From Martha Lange, Session with Gerhard Richter, former Bauhaus student, in 'The Bauhaus, Dessau and Berlin: Two Recollections', *Design Issues* vol. v, no. 1, Fall 1988, pp. 35–44 (Cambridge, MA: MIT Press).

p. 53 'He is recorded as living…' Max Albers is assumed to be the author of a painting of a pig farm now in the Josef Albers Museum in Bottrop. It was once mistakenly attributed to his nephew.

'The only proof of Lorenz Albers' existence...' Josef Albers Papers MS32, Box 28, Folder 266, Yale Manuscripts and Archives, Sterling Library, Yale University.

'A painter like my father did...' From an interview with JA by Jean Clay, *Visages de l'art moderne* (Lausanne: Editions Rencontre, 1969), p. 67. Quoted in Nicholas Fox Weber, *The Drawings of Josef Albers* (New Haven: Yale University Press, 1984), p. 2.

p. 54 'Gropius said, several times...' JA interviewed by Finkelstein.

p. 55 'As a child, my main fun...' JA interviewed by Sevim Fesci, New Haven, CT, 22 June–5 July 1968, Oral History Interviews, Archives of American Art, Smithsonian Institution.

'A more intimate memory of his mother...' Pete and Elizabeth Jennerjahn interviewed by Frederick Horowitz, 7 December 1995, p. 35.

'Perhaps it was overlain by another...' The death certificate lists her time of her death – 5:30 in the afternoon – but gives no cause.

p. 56 'Colours that he himself excluded...' JA interviewed by Finkelstein, tape 2, side B, track 1.

p. 57 'In 1963, when Albers was seventy-five...' George Rickey, *Constructivism: Origins and Evolution* (New York: George Braziller, 1967).

'I happened to have with me...' Letter, JA to George Rickey, 28 May 1963, JAAFA Box 8, Folder 4.

'In even older age, Albers identified...' To Nicholas Fox Weber.

p. 58 'This was a forbidding place...' Joachim Bolik, *Das alte Bottrop in Bildern* (Gummersbach: Gronenberg, 1986).

p. 59 'In time, it would settle...' It was finally underpinned in the 1960s, when in danger of collapse.

'Lorenz's name is not among the...' Geurts, *Fünfzig Jahre Malerinnung Bottrop*.

'I cannot cope with the burden...' Personalakten Signatur 7739/Heinrich van Bömmel, Münster Landesarchiv.

'The town's population was not just...' Murphy, *Gastarbeiter im Deutschen Reich*.

'Male elementary schoolteachers in Wilhelmine Germany...' For an analysis of this, see Marjorie Lamberti, *The Politics of Education: Teachers and School Reform in Weimar Germany* (New York: Berghahn Books, 2002).

p. 60 'You have to fulfill all the demands...' JA interviewed by Fesci.

p. 61 'The photograph of Lorenz in a...' Geurts, *Fünfzig Jahre Malerinnung Bottrop*.

'Albers' repeated insistence that his...' Weber, *The Bauhaus Group*.

'But it also makes Lorenz...' It is, perhaps, worth noting that Allied propaganda in the Second World War spread the idea that Adolf Hitler (1889–1945) was a house painter rather than an artist, the first being an ignoble profession, the second noble. Hannah Arendt accepted this in her book *The Origins of Totalitarianism* (1951). It has subsequently been proven that Hitler never worked as a house painter: cf. Norman Stone, *Hitler* (1980).

'Seventy years later, Josef Albers...' JA interviewed by Fesci.

p. 62 'They were boarded with suitably...' A bigger, ugly school was built in 1907. Albers was lucky to have missed it.

'Children even came to school in them...' Heinrich Feldmann, *Lehrerausbildung vor dem ersten Weltkriege in der Präparandenanstalt Langenhorst* (1982), p. 9.

'In summer, they ate strawberries...' Ibid.

'The headmaster, Fr Keller, in his...' *Handbuch für den Unterricht in der Biblischen Geschichte*, Aschendorff (Münster, 1909).

'One form teacher, Wilhelm Dortmann...' *Stahls Heimatrechenbuch mit Raumlehre für das südliche Westfalen*.

p. 63 'Unusually for a Prussian-run school...' Feldmann, *Lehrerausbildung*.

'A contemporary, Heinrich Mevenkamp, recalled...' See Hildegard Stratmann, *Lehrer werden: Berufliche Sozialisation in der Volksschullehrer-Ausbildung in Westfalen (1870–1914)* (Münster: Waxmann, 2006), p. 176.

'Friedrich Wilhelm Foerster, a Berlin...' Friedrich Wilhelm Foerster, *Schule und Charakter: Beiträge zur Pädagogik des Gehorsams und zur Reform der Schuldisziplin* (Zurich, 1907).

'The day when could they be dismissed...' Andrew Donson, *Youth in the Fatherless Land: War Pedagogy, Nationalism, and Authority in Germany, 1914–1918* (Cambridge, MA: Harvard University Press, 2010), p. 25.

p. 65 'Not for nothing was Büren known...' Reminiscences of Büren are contained in letters to Albers from two schoolmates, Franz Schröder and Heinrich Finger, in the JAAFA.

'Not for nothing was Büren known...' Fritz Bause papers, JAAFA catalogue no. 2016.40.1 / JA OS Box 27.

'There were only four hours...' Stratmann, *Lehrer werden*.

'The food was notoriously grim...' Schröder and Finger letters, JAAFA.

'For all that, academic standards at...' Stratmann, *Lehrer werden*.

'Albers' own record at the school...' Fritz Bause, in his scrapbook of Büren alumni, JAAFA.

p. 66 'His performance in singing and...' Landesarchiv NRW, Münster: B 124 Provinzialschulkollegium Münster, 1.1.1 Kathol Lehrerseminar Nr. 801: Die Aufnahme der Zöglinge, Bd. 12.

'Nevertheless, he managed to pass his teacher's exams...' Personalakt Josef Albers, Stadtarchiv Bottrop.

'Albers left for Bottrop to take...' Ibid.

'Having criticised a girl student...' Letter, JA, *Meine lieben Klassenkuppels*, 2 February 1957, JAAFA Box 3, Folder 37.

'Fifty years later, Josef Albers would...' JA in the *Dülmener Heimatblätter*, 31 May 1959.

p. 67 'It has to be said that there...' Dülmen Stadtarchiv, Amt A176.

p. 68 'The subtleties of these maps...' For more on the importance of maps in pre-Great War Germany, see Jason D. Hansen, *Mapping the Germans: Statistical Science, Cartography, and the Visualization of the German Nation, 1848–1914* (New York: Oxford University Press, 2015).

'I sat there as long as I could...' JA interviewed by Finkelstein, tape 2, side B, track 2. It is clear, from later correspondence with his friend Franz Grosse Perdekamp, that Albers used 'Pinakothek' to mean the Alte (or Old) Pinakothek, which housed Bavaria's collection of Old Masters.

'In that year, Hugo von Tschudi...' Wilhelm was fervently anti-modernist. In his *Rinnsteinrede* (Gutter) Speech of December 1900, he said: 'We, the German people, have preserved the ideal of purity which other peoples have lost....But if, as now happens again and again, art insists on showing misery in all its grim reality, then it sins against the German people.'

'Gerard, deeply conventional, set to work...' For details of the commission, see James J. Sheehan, *Museums in the German Art World: From the End of the Old Regime to the Rise of Modernism* (Oxford: Oxford University Press, 2000).

p. 69 'With only the exterior finished...' See Monika Lahme-Schlenger, 'Karl-Ernst Osthaus und die Folkwang-Idee', in Henrike Junge-Gent et al., *Avantgarde und Publikum: zur Rezeption avantgardistischer Kunst in Deutschland 1905–1933* (Cologne: Böhlau Verlag, 1992).

'The red of the flowers, the dark...' Ernst Lorenzen, *Westfälisches Kunstblatt* jg. 2 nr. 9, June 1909.

'In the year he finished Osthaus's...' For Van de Velde's Nietzscheanism, see Elie Haddad, 'In Nietzsche's Shadow: Henry van de Velde and the New Style in Architecture', *Architectural Theory Review* vol. 10, issue 2 (2005).

'Coming home [from Munich in September 1908]...' JA interviewed by Finkelstein, tape 2, side B, track 2.

p. 70 'Its inventory catalogue of 1912...' See Mario-Andreas von Lüttichau and Sandra Gianfreda (eds), *The Ecstasy of Colour: Munch, Matisse and the Expressionists* (Göttingen: Museum Folkwang, 2012), pp. 13–16.

'As we shall see, sixty years later...' Margit Rowell, 'On Albers' Color', *Artforum* 10, January 1972, p. 26ff.

2 The World Outside: Berlin and Munich

p. 73 'The image – dated, signed 'Albers' and...' For more on this, see Nicholas Fox Weber, *The Drawings of Josef Albers* (New Haven: Yale University Press, 1984).

'Its clearest echoes are of...' Albers' correspondence from 1916 onwards suggests that he travelled to Düsseldorf regularly, often for the theatre.

'The room with the view of...' The house, like most of Stadtlohn, was destroyed by Allied bombing in 1945.

'In an inversion of the usual order...' Chronik der Schule zu Stadtlohn, S. 84; quoted in a letter from Ulrich Söbbing, Stadtlohn city archivist, 12 January 2015.

p. 75 'Accounts show payments for them...' Letter, Ulrich Söbbing, 12 January 2015.

'On 23 September 1911, Albers...' Personalakt Josef Albers, Stadtarchiv Bottrop.

'the entry for 10 July 1913 records that...' Protokollbuch Josefschule, Stadtarchiv Bottrop, signature S1, no. 24.

'He was to report back to his...' Personalakt Josef Albers, Stadtarchiv Bottrop.

'It is often said I studied at the...' From interviews with JA by Irving Finkelstein, taped in support of his PhD thesis (1965); tape 2, side B, track 2. Courtesy of the JAAF.

p. 76 '[He rejects] immediate perception...' Cited in Donald E. Gordon, *Expressionism: Art and Idea* (New Haven: Yale University Press, 1987), p. 175.

'Although Albers later recalled an...' George Heard Hamilton, catalogue to 'Josef Albers: Paintings, Prints, Projects', exhibition at Yale University Art Gallery, 25 June – 18 April 1956, p. 5.

'a real training in a very old...' JA interviewed by Sevim Fesci, New Haven, CT, 22 June – 5 July 1968, Oral History Interviews, Archives of American Art, Smithsonian Institution.

'[Herwarth] Walden of the 'Storm' Gallery...' Ibid.

p. 77 'At the exhibition, there was a painting...' JA, undated and unpublished interview by Margit Rowell, *ca.* 1969–70.

'Yet, fifty years later, he would...' JA interviewed by Finkelstein, tape 1, side B, track 1.

p. 78 'The records of the Royal Art School...' It is now part of the Berlin University of the Arts.

'The records of the Royal Art School...' Berlin: Otto Stollberg, 1928.

'His death certificate lists his trade...' Josef Albers Papers, Yale Manuscripts and Archives, Sterling Library, Yale University.

p. 81 'The war years apart, they would write...' These letters (hereafter cited as 'JA to FP' and vice versa) are in the possession of Perdekamp's grandchildren in Recklinghausen. Copies are in the archives of the JAAF, with translations by Ingrid Eumann.

'When, in 1974, Albers' wife Anni...' Albers in conversation with Nicholas Fox Weber, 1976.

'In a later one from Hohenhonnef, Albers...' Letter, JA to FP, 15 March 1916.

p. 82 'He was tuberculous [and so] got...' JA interviewed by Finkelstein, tape 1, side B, track 2.

'He would also be denied their heroism...' From the Schulchronik Altenbergen, 1917.

'Albers' official leave of absence...' Personalakt Josef Albers, Stadtarchiv Bottrop.

p. 83 'He needs 'the two portraits' at once...' Letter, JA to FP, 13 October 1916.

'You draw like a coal miner.' H. Daniel Butts interviewed by Frederick Horowitz, 20 July 1995.

'The linocut he made from this...' For a chronology of Albers' drawings, see Weber, *Drawings of Josef Albers*. For a chronology of the prints, see Brenda Danilowitz, *The Prints of Josef Albers: A Catalogue Raisonné, 1915–1976*, revised edn (Manchester and New York: Hudson Hills Press, 2009). It should be noted (cf. Weber, *Drawings of Josef Albers*) that Anni denied that this drawing was a self-portrait. She appears to have been mistaken.

p. 89 'Up to this point, he says, he...' *Der Golem*, film, dir. Paul Wegener and Henrik Galeen (Germany, 1915).

'The hero of Meyrink's novel suffers...' Gustav Meyrink, *Der Golem* (Leipzig: Kurt Wolff, 1915).

'One film in particular, the Danish-made...' *Verdens Undergang*, film, dir. August Blom (Denmark, 1916).

p. 92 'My friend, Perdekamp...he might have...' JA interviewed by Finkelstein, tape 1, side B, track 2.

'There are quick pen and ink...' *Glück auf!* is a traditional miners' greeting, wishing luck in the finding of a new lode of coal; the school stood on a street of the same name, opposite St Michael's church. It was later renamed the Albrecht Dürer Schule, and then, in 2014, closed down.

'More brightly, Molitor recalls Albers' lessons...' Molitor's correspondence with Albers is in the JAAFA.

'In the place of book-lessons on...' Heinrich Wolgast, *Das Elend unserer Jugendliteratur* (Hamburg: Selbstverlag, 1899).

p. 95 'With many school administrators off...'
For the evolution of *Heimatkunde*, see Jennifer
Jenkins, *Provincial Modernity: Local Culture and Liberal
Politics in Fin-de-Siècle Hamburg* (Ithaca: Cornell
University Press, 2003); Elizabeth Boa, *Heimat –
A German Dream: Regional Loyalties and National
Identity in German Culture, 1890–1990* (Oxford:
Oxford University Press, 2000); and Celia Applegate,
A Nation of Provincials: The German Idea of Heimat
(Berkeley: University of California Press, 1990).
For German elementary schools in the First World
War, see Andrew Donson, *Youth in the Fatherless Land:
War Pedagogy, Nationalism, and Authority in Germany,
1914–1918* (Cambridge, MA: Harvard University
Press, 2010).
'In 1908, the Jugendstil artist August Endell...' August
Endell, *Die Schönheit der Großen Stadt* (Stuttgart:
Streeker & Schröder, 1908).
'Along with this, Endell championed a new...' 'Um die
Schönheit', in *Pan* magazine (Berlin, 1899); cited in
Shearer West, *The Visual Arts in Germany, 1890–1937*
(Manchester: Manchester University Press, 2000).
'Out went distant vistas of spires...' Ludwig Meidner,
'Introduction to the painting of the metropolis' /
Anleitung zum Malen von Großstadtbildern, *Kunst
und Künstler* 12 (1914), pp. 299–301. Cited in West,
The Visual Arts in Germany.
'The truly modern artist sees the...' Piet Mondrian,
'Dialogue on the New Plastic', quoted in Charles
Harrison and Paul Wood, *Art in Theory 1900–2000:
An Anthology of Changing Ideas* (Hoboken, NJ: Wiley
Blackwell, 2002), p. 284.
'He did so, he said...' JA interviewed by Finkelstein.
'One wonders if he can have seen...' This is now at the
Los Angeles County Museum of Art.
p. 97 'Philip Franck, a friend of Max Liebermann...' JA,
unpublished interview by Margit Rowell, 14 April 1971.
'His Berlin certificate qualified him...' JA interviewed
by Finkelstein.
'Lithographs are originals. In them...' 'Zur Einführung!',
Der Bildermann 1, no. 1 (5 April 1916); quoted in Peter
Paret, *The Berlin Secession: Modernism and Its Enemies in
Imperial Germany* (Cambridge, MA: Harvard University
Press, 1980), p. 240.
'As a result, they had become very...' See Hans-
Wolfgang Singer, *Die moderne graphik* (Leipzig:
E. A. Seemann, 1914).
'Kollwitz, Nolde, Schmidt-Rottluff, Corinth...' See Robin
Lenman, *Artists and Society in Germany, 1850–1914*
(Manchester: Manchester University Press, 1997),
pp. 169, 170.
p. 99 'The lithographs he made of these...' JA interviewed
by Fesci.
'I did a series of landscapes, of miner...' JA interviewed
by Finkelstein, tape 1, side B, track 2.
'Even so, he said, the Dutchman...' Ibid.
'It was to him that Albers attributed...' Ibid.
'Another student at Essen recalled...' Quoted in
Klaus Timm, *The Teaching of Josef Albers*, thesis
(Hamburg, 1961).
p. 103 'It is good to breathe new...' Letter, JA to FP, 23
October 1917.

'My home town, Bottrop, has a very...' JA interviewed
by Finkelstein.
p. 106 'and maybe they, too, will feel...' Letter, JA to FP,
22 June 1917 (author's translation).
p. 107 'Before leaving Bottrop, though, he...' Letter,
JA to FP, 25 April 1917.
'Her veneration in Germany went...' See Fr Alfons
Maria Weigl, *Mary, 'Rosa Mystica':
Montichiari-Fontanelle* (1974).
p. 108 'That the priest asked an unknown...' He would pay
for this in the Second World War, arrested in his new
parish in Stadtlohn for handing out anti-Nazi leaflets.
Albers' window was destroyed by Allied bombing on
16 September 1942. A copy of the original was installed
in St Michael's to celebrate the centenary of the church
in 2012.
'I thought it wiser to place the order...' Karl Emsbach and
Max Tauch, *Kirchen, Klöster und Kapellen im Kreis Neuss*
(Cologne: Rheinland-Verlag, 1986), pp. 166–9.
'Albers' letters to Gottfried Heinersdorff...' These are in
the Archiv der Vereinigten Werkstätten für Mosaik und
Glasmalerei Puhl & Wagner Gottfried Heinersdorff,
Berlinische Galerie, Museum für Moderne Kunst,
Berlin. Copies held at the JAAF.
p. 109 'The window's feel is not so much...' Given the war,
it is, of course, impossible that Albers can have seen
this, even in reproduction.
p. 110 'In one, dated 26 March, Albers writes...' Letter,
JA to FP, 26 March 1918. This is presumably the Dr
Brinkmann who organized Bottrop's choir in 1916,
serving as the town's deputy mayor and then joint
mayor from 1916–20.
'Albers, witheringly, tells him that...' Ibid.
'In that same year, Kandinsky's Blaue Reiter...' For the
later Munich Secession, see Lenman, *Artists and
Society in Germany*.
p. 112 'He is only allowed to bring coal...' Albers later
introduced Karsch to Franz Perdekamp; the couple
would marry in 1922. Perdekamp family legend has
it that Karsch and Albers had previously been lovers,
although there is no supporting evidence for this.
'In any case, Albers did not know...' Cf. Fesci and
Finkelstein interviews.
p. 114 'As early as 1900, Henry van de Velde...' In Eva
Mengden, *Franz von Stuck, 1863–1928: A Prince of Art*
(Cologne: Taschen, 1995), p. 36.
'Hugo von Hofmannsthal noted his...' Hugo von
Hofmannsthal, 'Franz Stuck', *Neue Revue*, 1894, p. 197,
in *Prosa I, Gesammelte Werke* (Frankfurt am Main:
S. Fischer Verlag, 1950).
'It was Stuck who advised Kandinsky...' See Maria Makela,
*The Munich Secession: Art and Artists in Turn-of-the-
Century Munich* (Princeton: Princeton University Press,
1990), p. 110.
'Even at the Bauhaus, when it...' Mengden, *Franz von
Stuck*, p. 88.
'in cold and warm[...]I believe it's true.' JA interviewed
by Finkelstein, tape 2, side B, track 2.
'For Hans Hofmann, whose private...' Ibid.
p. 116 'Stuck insisted that students paint shadows...'
Hans Purrmann, 'Erinnerungen an mein Studienzeit',
in *Werk* XXXIV, 11 (November 1947), pp. 366–72.

'Nonetheless, it was Max Doerner and not...'
JA interviewed by Finkelstein.
'When Albers was his student, Doerner...' Max
Doerner, *Malmaterial und seine Verwendung im Bilde*
(Munich: F. Schmidt, 1921).

3 A Man of Glass: Weimar

p. 119 'In 1920, the Bauhaus was...' It had opened on
1 April 1919.
'There is no difference between the artist...' *Manifesto and
Programme of the Staatliche Bauhaus* (Weimar, April 1919).
'A circular came into my hands...' Quoted in Neil Welliver,
'Albers on Albers', *Art News* 64, no. 9, January 1966,
pp. 48–51, 68–69.
p. 120 'It must have been a bitter...' Personalakt
Josef Albers, Stadtarchiv Bottrop.
'To limit their possible influence...' Minutes of the
Weimar *Meisterrat*, 13 March 1922.
p. 122 'Itten was a *Quatschkopf*.' Unpublished interview
by Margit Rowell, 25 June 1970.
'To this faint praise was added the...' Ibid.
'Although he wrote to Franz Perdekamp...' Letter,
JA to FP, 10 January 1921.
'Possibly the flat was like fellow Bauhäusler Lydia...'
Lydia Driesch-Foucar, *Erinnerungen an die Anfänge
der Dornburger Töpferwerkstatt d. Staatl. Bauhauses
Weimar 1920–1923*, Bauhaus-Archiv, Berlin.
'With no money to have coal delivered...' Walter Gropius,
confidential memorandum to the Student Council,
14 October 1919; quoted in Frank Whitford, *The Bauhaus:
Masters and Students by Themselves* (London: Conran
Octopus, 1992), p. 43.
p. 123 'While she saw this as positive...' Gertrud Arndt
papers, Mappe 1, Bauhaus-Archiv, Berlin.
'The stranger wordlessly handed him...' Marcel Breuer,
quoted in Nicholas Fox Weber, *The Bauhaus Group:
Six Masters of Modernism* (New Haven: Yale
University Press, 2011), p. 291.
'So I went [to Weimar] and submitted...' From interviews
with JA by Irving Finkelstein, taped in support of his PhD
thesis (1965); tape 2, side B, track 2. Courtesy of the JAAF.
'He is there first as a student...' See Klaus-Jürgen Winkler
(ed.), *Bauhaus-Alben 3* (Weimar: Verlag der Bauhaus-
Universität, 2008), and *Bauhaus-Alben 4* (Weimar:
Verlag der Bauhaus-Universität, 2009).
'Albers would later maintain that Itten...' JA interviewed
by Sevim Fesci, New Haven, CT, 22 June – 5 July 1968,
Oral History Interviews, Archives of American Art,
Smithsonian Institution.
'We made wood sculptures, we sawed...' Fritz Kuhr, quoted
in the memoir of Gustav Hassenpflug (1947), Bauhaus-
Archiv, Berlin.
p. 125 'Its gridded mount is off-the-peg...' JA interviewed by
Finkelstein, tape 2, side B, track 2.
'Gertrud Arndt recalled asking for paper...' Arndt papers,
Bauhaus-Archiv.
'Few works caught their eye...' Minutes of the Weimar
Meisterrat, 25 March 1921.
'It was my dream...' JA interviewed by Rowell, 25 June 1970.
p. 129 'It was given rooms in a lodge...' Ibid.
'The accompanying Curriculum for the...' See Winkler,
Bauhaus-Alben 3, p. 154.

'Stained glass, she said, was...' Diary entry for 1 November
1919; quoted in Monika Stadler (ed.), *Gunta Stölzl:
Bauhaus Master* (Berlin: Hatje Cantz, 2009), p. 49.
'He was accepted as a student...' See Winkler, *Bauhaus-
Alben 3*.
'Relics of the *Glasmalereiwerkstatt* are rare...' These
are illustrated in Rolf Bothe et al., *Das frühe Bauhaus
und Johannes Itten: Katalogbuch anlässlich des 75.
Gründungsjubiläums des Staatlichen Bauhauses in Weimar*
(Berlin: Hatje Cantz Verlag GmbH+C, 1994), pp. 272–3.
p. 130 'Many other of his pieces are lost...' In Winkler,
Bauhaus-Alben 3.
'Usually dated 1923 and later destroyed...' This had been
turned into a classroom by 1930. The window was
probably lost then.
'In 1921, before his fall from grace...' See Klaus Weber,
'Kunstwerk – Geistwerk – Handwerk: Die Werkstätten
in den ersten Jahren des Bauhauses', in *Das frühe
Bauhaus und Johannes Itten* (Berlin: Hatje Cantz
Verlag GmbH+C, 1994), pp. 228–9.
'Surprisingly, given his Expressionist leanings...'
From Itten's *Mein Vorkurs am Bauhaus* (1964), quoted
in Weber, 'Kunstwerk – Geistwerk – Handwerk'.
'And there was a window...' undated letter, cited in
Weber, 'Kunstwerk – Geistwerk – Handwerk', p. 229
and p. 280 n. 49.
'The window presumably predates these appointments...'
For Itten's replacement by Schlemmer, see Volker Wahl
(ed.), *Die Meisterratsprotokolle des Staatlichen Bauhauses
Weimar 1919 bis 1925, Veröffentlichungen aus thüringischen
Staatsarchiven 6* (Weimar: Böhlaus Nachfolger, 2001),
p. 156. Schlemmer's tenure in the glass painting
workshop was brief; on 2 October 1922, he was replaced
as *Formmeister* by Paul Klee, presumably leaving him
free to concentrate on the new theatre workshop.
'The window's chequerboard pane is...' 'Flashed' glass
is glass of one colour which has been dipped into a
molten bath of another, coating the original pane
in a thin, contrasting film.
'Albers recalled travelling to the glass...' He identified
the town to Margit Rowell (JA interviewed by Rowell,
25 June 1970).
p. 132 'I was asked to get material...' JA interviewed
by Finkelstein, tape 2, side B, track 2.
'Your request is not as easy as...' From Josef Albers
papers, Mappe 9, Bauhaus-Archiv, Berlin.
'Re. Albers...interesting and worthwhile possibilities
and paths.' Entry dated 20 February 1923 in Archiv der
Vereinigten Werkstätten für Mosaik und Glasmalerei
Puhl & Wagner Gottfried Heinersdorff, Berlinische
Galerie, Museum für Moderne Kunst.
p. 133 'In the month of Albers' first letter...' Van Doesburg's
wife, Nelly, insisted that Gropius had offered her
husband a post at the Bauhaus when they met
at the architect Bruno Taut's house in 1919 or 1920.
By the time the couple finally made it to Weimar,
the position had been filled. See Reyner Banham,
Theory and Design in the First Machine Age (Westport:
Praeger, 1960), p. 191.
'Soon, twenty-five students were on Doesburg's...'
See *Guide, Theo van Doesburg Archive*, archive of Theo
van Doesburg and his wives, Rijksdienst Beeldende

Kunst/Netherlands Office for Fine Arts, The Hague (1991); 9A Special themes/Projects, 1217 mf. 270, p. 78.

'Anything important and progressive, any new...' In Walter Dexel's obituary for Van Doesburg, 1931; cited in letter from Karl Peter Röhl to Constanze Hofstaetter, undated, Bauhaus-Archiv, Berlin.

p. 134 'Doesburgian students soon set themselves up...' See *Karl Peter Röhl: Aquarelle. Zeichnungen. Druckgraphik 1919–1961*, Kunsthalle and Schleswig-Holsteinischer Kunstverein, Kiel (1979), p. 21. KURI was an acronym from the German words for 'constructive, utilitarian, rational and international'.

'In mechanical production, the spiritual intention...' *Bouwkundig Weekblad* no. 28, 9 July 1921, p. 180.

'Each evening,' he crowed to a friend...' Theo van Doesburg, letter to Antony Kok, 7 January 1921.

'What the Bauhaus in Weimar, with its...' In the *Grosse Berliner Kunstausstellung*, September 1921.

'We wanted [Van Doesburg] either to run...' René Halkett, 'When I was at the Bauhaus', House Magazine of BASF Aktiengesellschaft *BASF No. 1, 1977*, Ludwigshafen.

'What the Cross was to early...' Recalled by Hans Richter in 'Easel – Scroll – Film', *Magazine of Art*, 1952.

p. 136 'The Bauhaus, said the sheet, remained...' *Mécano* 4/5 (1923).

'Many use the *Lokus* [lav]...' Gerhard Marcks, *Erwähnenswertes aus meinem Leben* (1922), Bauhaus-Archiv, Berlin: 2013/9.40, Mappe 1.

'The Bauhaus lends itself readily to...' In Tut Schlemmer (ed.), *The Letters and Diaries of Oskar Schlemmer* (Evanston, IL: Northwestern University Press, 1990), p. 117.

'It is noticeably like Peter Keler's...' Since neither window had been made for the 1923 Bauhaus Exhibition, neither had the better claim to being reproduced in *Staatliches Bauhaus in Weimar, 1919–1923*. The upper window presumably was chosen as being the more attractive image.

p. 137 'Van Doesburg, he said, had...' Welliver, 'Albers on Albers'.

'I knew Van Doesburg personally...' JA interviewed by Rowell, 25 June 1970.

p. 138 'We were all interested in Van Doesburg's...' In the *Journal of Architectural Education* vol. xviii, no. 2, September 1963.

'It was necessary to revive...no means involved in this.' Quoted in Hans Maria Wingler, *Das Bauhaus: Weimar, Dessau, Berlin 1919–1933* (Cologne: Verlag Gebr. Rasch und C. und M. DuMont, 1962), pp. 62–3.

'He had also been entrusted with a budget...' Letter, JA to FP, undated, 'Meine liebe Kumpels'.

'His Fagus factory had been a masterpiece...' Nikolaus Pevsner, *Pioneers of Modern Design* (London: Faber, 1936).

p. 140 'In 1922, Gropius found his old...' Werner Graeff, *Mit der Avantgarde*, in *Kunstverein für die Rheinlande und Westphalen* exhibition catalogue (Düsseldorf, 1962).

'Among charges levelled at the director...' This was Itten's secretary, Lotte Hirschfeld; both accusations were true.

'Even apprentices and journeymen, such as Albers...' Minutes of the meeting of the Masters of Form and Craft, 14 October 1922; in Volker Wahl (ed.), *Die Meisterratsprotokolle des Staatlichen Bauhauses Weimar 1919 bis 1925* (Weimar: Böhlaus Nachfolger, 2001), p. 249.

'As to Schlemmer's question...' ThHStA Weimar Staatliches Bauhaus Weimar 12, sheet 209.

p. 141 'Klee, he later said, left him...' See JA interviewed by Fesci.

'Since Mr Itten cannot return to...' Josef Albers personal papers, Sterling Library, Yale University.

'Among other complaints were that its students...' There were seventeen Jewish *Bauhäusler* at the time.

'That he was fully aware of these designs...' JA interviewed by Rowell, 25 June 1970.

'I had in mind to study with...' Breuer was by then the junior master in charge of the carpentry workshop.

p. 142 'Breuer went from wood to bent metal...' Martha Lange, Session with Gerhard Richter, former Bauhaus student, in 'The Bauhaus, Dessau and Berlin: Two Recollections', *Design Issues* vol. v, no. 1, Fall 1988, 35–44.

'The reading room was now reinvented...' In fact, the room was not ready in time for the opening of the show. See Walter Passarge, 'Die Ausstellung des Staatlichen Bauhauses in Weimar', in *Das Kunstblatt* VII (Potsdam, 1923).

'As one critic put it...' Arthur Korn, *Glass in Modern Architecture*, transl. Dennis Sharp (New York: Barrie & Jenkins, [1928] 1968).

'In the same way, the counterpoised...' In 'Werkstatt-Arbeiten des Staatlichen Bauhauses zu Weimar', in *Neue Frauenkleidung und Frauenkultur*, 1925, pp. 2–3.

'*Das Werk* in Zurich noted...' Ibid. p. 41.

p. 144 'Wagenfeld's famous lamps might be described...' In the catalogue to the 1929 Leipzig Spring Fair.

'Paul Scheerbart, an apostle of the...' Paul Scheerbart, *Glasarchitektur* (Glass Architecture), 1914.

'Stained glass was the old method...one piece.' JA interviewed by Finkelstein, tape 2, side B, track 2.

p. 145 'Albers, pragmatically, proffered...' See Anna Rowland, 'Business Management at the Weimar Bauhaus', *Journal of Design History* vol. 1, no. 3/4 (1988), 153–75.

'Shortly afterwards, he was told to.' For this, see e.g. Walther Scheidig, *Crafts of the Weimar Bauhaus, 1919–1924: An Early Experiment in Industrial Design* (London: Studio Vista, 1967), pp. 27–9.

'Gropius called the students present...' JA interviewed by Finkelstein. Albers' classroom was Room 39.

'Gropius, for his part, recalled merely...' In Herbert Bayer, Walter Gropius, Ise Gropius (eds.), *Bauhaus 1919–1928*, exhibition catalogue (New York: Museum of Modern Art, 1938), p. 17.

'As Herbert Bayer recalled...' Herbert Bayer interviewed by Arthur A. Cohen, 3 November 1981–10 March 1982, Oral History Interviews, Archives of American Art, Smithsonian Institution.

p. 146 'Thirty years later and a professor...' Paul Zelanski interviewed by Frederick Horowitz, 8 July 1996.

'When you relate me to Moholy...' JA interviewed by Finkelstein, tape 1, side B, track 2.

'Asked whether it was Gropius who...' Ibid.

'He had presented his request for leave...' Personalakt Josef Albers, Stadtarchiv Bottrop.

'Pleading letters from Gropius cut no ice...' In Albers papers, Bauhaus-Archiv, Berlin.

p. 147 'As Albers would later gleefully recall...' Josef
Albers, undated handwritten note in file 'I Remember',
JAAFA; cited in Frederick A. Horowitz and Brenda
Danilowitz, *Josef Albers: To Open Eyes* (London:
Phaidon, 2006).

'Albers began his *Vorkurs,* she said...' Etel Fodor Mittag,
in the film *Bauhaus: Modell und Mythos,* dir. Kerstin
Stutterheim and Niels Bolbrinker (Germany, 1998).

'The problem with this, when applied...' Walter Gropius,
'Umlauf an den Meisterrat vom 13.2.1923', Bauhaus-
Archiv, Berlin.

p. 148 'I opposed that sentimental self-expression...'
JA interviewed by Finkelstein, tape 2, side A, track 1.

'As one Bauhäusler recalled...' Wolf Hildebrandt, in
Bauhaus: Modell und Mythos.

'A Dutch student solemnly listed the...' Jan van der
Linden papers, Bauhaus-Archiv, Berlin.

'Nor, for all his focus on...constructional thinking'
Albers, 'Werklicher Formunterricht', *bauhaus*
nos. 2–3 (1928).

'But his exploration of the...' Ibid.

p. 149 'Practice of course also played...' Gustav
Hassenpflug memoir.

'This is what has made the...' JA interviewed by Fesci.

'Quietly tenacious, Fleischmann, known as Anni...'
Quoted in Weber, *The Bauhaus Group.*

'To her surprise, one was for her...' Ibid.

'He incorporated the Bauhaus idea...' Ute Ackermann
interviewed by Frederick Horowitz, 15 April 1999.

p. 150 'Besides the peasant woman...named Mara' She
has been identified as Mara Utschkunowa (later Auböck,
1895–1987), who took Itten's *Vorkurs* at the Weimar
Bauhaus in 1921.

'three shining days...island of Sylt.' Albers refers to having
lately turned 33, which dates the letter to mid-1921.

'First, there was an essay called...' JA, 'Historisch oder
Jetzig?', *Junge Menschen* no. 8, November 1924, p. 171.

'The following month, the school's frugal...' See
Magdalena Droste, *Bauhaus 1919–1933* (Berlin:
Taschen/Bauhaus-Archiv, 2006), p. 113.

4 Student to *Meister*: Dessau and Berlin

p. 153 'In December 1924, in a letter...' Letter, JA to FP,
5 December 1924.

'Later, Gropius was to recall that...' Quoted in Nicholas
Fox Weber, *The Bauhaus Group: Six Masters of Modernism*
(New Haven: Yale University Press, 2011), pp. 309–10.

'The school's main attraction had been...' Gropius would
only finally open this in 1927.

'The Haus am Horn was to be...' Magdalena Droste,
Bauhaus 1919–1933 (Berlin: Taschen/Bauhaus-
Archiv, 2006).

'More generous funding allowed the...' The others were
Hinnerk Scheper (mural painting), Marcel Breuer
(cabinetmaking), Herbert Bayer (advertising and
typography) and Joost Schmidt (sculpture and lettering).
Gunta Stölzl (weaving) would join them in 1927.

'At least as attractive was Gropius's...' From the *Frankfurter
Zeitung,* 31 October 1927; quoted in Droste, *Bauhaus
1919–1933,* p. 122.

p. 154 'Their wedding, a Roman Catholic nuptial...'
Weber, *The Bauhaus Group.*

'He will not be bringing his new...' Letter, JA to FP,
31 July 1925.

'Initially dismissing textiles as 'sissy', she...' Anni Albers
interview, 5 July 1968, Oral History Interviews, Archives
of American Art, Smithsonian Institution.

p. 155 'The factory aesthetic of Gropius's...'
Burgkühnerallee is now called Ebertallee.

'The six other *Meisterhäuser* were for...' In Dessau,
the school was reincorporated as a *Hochschule für
Gestaltung,* or College of Design, with a status below
that of a university. Its masters now became professors.

'Albers, like other junior masters...' Walter Gropius,
Bauhausbauten Dessau, Bauhausbücher 12 (1930), p. 14.

'Floors being segregated by gender...' Marcel Breuer
and his first wife, Marta Erps, also lived in the
Prellerhaus, as did Marianne and Erik Brandt and
Alfred and Gertrud Arndt.

'If Gropius's designs for the *Meisterhäuser*...'
Gropius, *Bauhausbauten Dessau.*

p. 156 'That the *Meisterhäuser* were part-prefabricated...'
For more on this, see Wolfgang Thöner, 'Model Houses
and Artists' Colony: The Design and Construction of the
Masters' Houses,' in *The New Masters' Houses in Dessau
1925–2014: Debates, Positions, Contexts,* Edition Bauhaus
46 (2017), pp. 33–46.

'Schlemmer professed himself worried by...' See Elaine
S. Hochman, *Bauhaus: Crucible of Modernism* (New
York: Fromm International, 1997), p. 194.

'The young masters make very...' Ise Gropius's diary
(1924–8), microfilm reel 2393, Walter and Ise Gropius
papers, Archives of American Art, Smithsonian
Institution.

'In the weeks after...Ottens and Schmidt.' See Barry
Bergdoll, 'Bauhaus Multiplied', in Barry Bergdoll
and Leah Dickerman, *Bauhaus 1919–1933: Workshops
for Modernity* (New York: Museum of Modern Art,
2009), p. 55.

'The prefabricated structures, Breuer pointed...'
Marcel Breuer, 'Das "Kleinmetallhaus Typ 1926"',
in *Offset: Buch und Werbekunst* 7, 1926, p. 371ff.

p. 157 'Art and technology are *not* a new...' Georg
Muche in *bauhaus* no. 1 (1926).

'This left Moholy-Nagy...' As described by Paul
Citroën, ironically, in his 1946 memoir.

'Why did you ask so...had no answer.' Nina Kandinsky,
Kandinsky und ich (Munich: Kindler, 1976).

'The director himself had now acquired...' Three years
earlier, Gropius had written to Ford asking for $3,000
to fund the Haus am Horn. See Peggy Deamer (ed.),
Architecture and Capitalism: 1845 to the Present (London:
Routledge, 2013).

'Painting, the fine arts, would not...' See Siegfried Ebeling,
Space as Membrane (1926), trans. Pamela Johnson
(London: Architectural Association, 2010).

p. 158 'A copy of *Der Raum als Membran*...' Cf. *The Dessau
Bauhaus Building* (Dessau: Stiftung Bauhaus Dessau,
1989), p. 89.

'Mies van der Rohe, the school's third...' On Mies's reading
of Ebeling, see Fritz Neumeyer, *Mies van der Rohe on the
Building Art* (Cambridge, MA: MIT Press, 1991).

'Ebeling's essay "Cosmological Space-cells: Thoughts"...'
Siegfried Ebeling, 'Kosmologische Raumzellen. Ideen

zur Ethik des konstruktiven Denkens', *Junge Menschen* no. 8, November 1924.

'We do construction experiments with straw...' Letter, JA to FP, 22 April 1928.

'Thus the school's partnership with Junkers...' For more on this, see e.g. Walter Scheiffele, *Bauhaus, Junkers, Sozialdemokratie: Ein Kraftfeld der Moderne* (Berlin: form + zweck verlag, 2003).

'Hajo Rose, a student on Albers' preliminary...' Hajo Rose, 'In Vorkurs with Joseph Albers'; notes by Isolde Rose from a lost manuscript, Bauhaus-Archiv, Berlin.

p. 159 'Ominously, this was not to be...' See minutes of the Weimar Bauhausrat, 24 April 1924.

'This need to appear functional is behind...' *Offset Buch und Werbekunst* 7, 1926. Albers' project is on p. 401ff.

'The project's unnamed client was...' Albers was not the only Bauhaus master to feel the pressure to build. The 1931 construction trade fair, the Deutsche Bauaustellung, included a tiled music room by Kandinsky. He was listed in the accompanying catalogue as an architect.

'In that year, 1926, Ullstein had...' Advertisements for these featured an exemplary housewife named Brigitte, under the slogan 'Sei sparsam, Brigitte – nimm Ullstein-Schnitte!' ('Be thrifty, Brigitte – use Ullstein patterns!').

'The best-known of these, for a...' Toothpaste exercised a curious hold over the Bauhaus imagination. Moholy's article in *Offset*, 'Fotoplastische Reklame' ('Photoplastic Advertising'), was admiringly illustrated with an American advertisement for Kolynos.

p. 160 'Albers could turn out architectural *Denkspiele*...' From Angelika Weißbach (ed.), *Wassily Kandinsky: Unterricht am Bauhaus, 1923–1933* (Berlin: Gebr. Mann Verlag, 2015), p. 13.

'Forty years later, in America...' Josef and Anni Albers interviewed by Martin Duberman, 11 November 1967; transcript, BMC Interviews, Martin Duberman Collection, Western Regional Archives, State Archives of North Carolina (NCWRA).

p. 161 'The letters would, of course, be...' An earlier set of opaque white glass letters, made up of ten elements, is in the design collection of the Museum of Modern Art in New York. Made by Metallglas A. G. in Offenburg and presented to the museum by Albers, it is dated 1923. This seems incorrect. The letters probably date from 1925, and are referred to by Albers in an unpublished essay; JAAFA Series IIb, Box 43, Folder 25.

'Time is money: events are determined...' This was also illustrated in *Offset*. JA, unpublished essay, JAAFA Project File 43, Folder 19.

p. 162 'Broadly, *Schablonenschrift* – made up of...' This first claim was not quite true. Like Bayer's *Universalschrift* – the type of the Bauhaus building's famous sign – *Schablonenschrift* only works on a large scale and at a distance. As a print type, it is hopeless.

p. 163 'That Albers cut out and kept...' They are now in the JAAFA Box 51 Folder 3.

'The following year, he boasts to Gottfried...' Handwritten letter, JA to Gottfried Heinersdorff, 16 October 1928; Bauhaus-Archiv, Berlin.

'The cup is a standard laboratory...' See the catalogue to the 14 December 2006 Design and Design Art sale at Phillips, lot no. 24.

'One handle is set vertically...' Although this was clearly meant as a prototype – only four were made, one given as a present to Herbert Bayer – the cup never went into production.

p. 164 'Where they score over Breuer's tables...' By 1929 it had become clear that making furniture in wood cost around half as much as making it in tubular steel.

'Stained glass was the old method...' From interviews with JA by Irving Finkelstein, taped in support of his PhD thesis (1965). Courtesy of the JAAF.

p. 165 'So I learned to sandblast...' JA interviewed by Fesci.

'I have to cover that glass in...' JA interviewed by Finkelstein, tape 2, side B, track 2. The firm he used was Rudolph Sandbläserei; see letter, JA to Gottfried Heinersdorff, 16 June 1927.

'I took [the glass]...which was simple.' JA interviewed by Finkelstein.

p. 167 'As a result, similar elements...' This phenomenon had been noted by the German meteorologist Wilhelm von Bezold in the late 19th century.

'Despite this rectangular, frontal and...' In the Zuercher Kunstgesellschaft Jahresbericht, 1960.

'I called it the Thermometer...the Thermometer style.' JA interviewed by Fesci.

'That is the stubbornness...It is studies.' JA interviewed by Finkelstein.

p. 169 'Only in March 1930, after a decade...' See letter from Dr Rammelt, registry inspector to the Government of Anhalt, to JA in Berlin, 24 December 1932.

'Furnishing an apartment is always...' Letter, JA to FP, 17 January 1929.

'On Kandinsky's birthday, 4 December, Josef...' Letter, Anni Albers to Wassily and Nina Kandinsky, 22 November 1934, JAAFA.

p. 170 'Our standard dance...' Kandinsky, *Kandinsky und ich*.

p. 171 'The Albers now had a house...' For more on this, see Wolfgang Thöner et al., *The New Masters' Houses in Dessau: Debates, Positions, Contexts* (Dessau: Edition Bauhaus 46, 2017).

'Featherdown quilt and an Egyptian...' This Egyptian figure was a copy from the Pergamon Museum, a present from Josef on her 24th birthday.

p. 173 'Albers foolishly fooled around...And architecture tells us nothing of amour.' In the film *Bauhaus: Modell und Mythos*, dir. Kerstin Stutterheim and Niels Bolbrinker (Germany, 1998); (author's translation).

'Like Anni, Berger was *haute bourgeoisie*...' Anni suffered from Charcot-Marie-Tooth Disease, a hereditary motor disorder first described in 1886. It is not known when she was diagnosed with the disease.

'In March 1930, he wrote to her...' In Otti Berger papers, Bauhaus-Archiv, Berlin: BHA 2014129.1,2.

'The girl was their maid, Charlotte Hesse...' These are in the archives of the Bauhaus Stiftung Dessau under Hesse's married name, Lohmann; inv. no. I 2759.

p. 174 'The one that survives, *Dom auf Schwarz*...' Both were broken en route to America in 1933, *Dom auf Grau* irreparably.

'the activation of negatives...' *Bauhaus: Zeitschrift für Gestaltung* no. 2/3, 1928, pp. 3–7.

'What is sickening here...' Otti Berger papers.

'These...considered in building.' Quoted in Theo van Leeuwen, *Introducing Social Semiotics* (London: Routledge, 2004), p. 71.

p. 176 'In 1927, Meyer had written that...' Hannes Meyer, 'Curriculum Vitae 1927', in Lena Meyer-Bergner (ed.), *Hannes Meyer: Bauen und Gesellschaft: Schriften, Briefe, Projekte* (Dresden: VEB Verlag der Kunst, 1980), pp. 27–32.

p. 178 'After a time, there were increasingly...' Max Schmeling, German world heavyweight boxing champion, 1930–2.

'Early in 1930, Meyer's sidekick...' Original collage lost. This copy is in the Ernst Kállai papers at the Bauhaus-Archiv.

p. 179 'In the second, the *Vorkursmeister* appears...' This was published in Wulf Herzogenrath, *Josef Albers und der 'Vorkurs' am Bauhaus (1919–1933)*, Wallraf-Richartz-Jahrbuch vol. 41 (1980), pp. 245–77.

'If ostensibly light-hearted, Kállai's humour...' Kállai seems to have had a personal animus against Albers. In 1929, he attacked the headquarters of the Ullstein publishing company as 'kitsch arts-and-crafts'. Albers had made a suite of windows for the building the year before; his mother-in-law was an Ullstein.

'H[annes] M[eyer] wonders whether...' Otti Berger papers.

'As early as 1923, the critic Walter...' Walter Passarge, 'Geistesgeschichtliche Anmerkungen zur Kunst des Nachexpressionismus', *Das Kunstblatt* 13, Berlin (1929), pp. 263–72.

p. 180 'The Model ti244 armchair (1929)...' This was shown in Dessau, at the Grassi Museum in Leipzig, and in Berlin.

'In March 1929, he persuaded Hannes Meyer...' See Rasch's speech to the Kongreß der Tapetenfabrikanten, Baden-Baden, 1952.

'It was he who oversaw the...' For wallpaper production at the Bauhaus, see Peter Hahn et al., *Bauhaustapete: Reklame & Erfolg einer Marke* (Dessau: Stiftung Bauhaus Dessau, 1995).

'Attached to a set of samples given...' Harvard Art Museums Collection, Busch-Reisinger Museum, object number BR49.286.A-K.

p. 182 'Yesterday Engemann...' Friedrich Engemann (1898–1970), architect and deputy director of the Bauhaus.

'Only Kuhr...' Fritz Kuhr (1899–1975), painting student.

'and Heiberg...' Edvard Heiberg (1897–1958), Norwegian architecture teacher.

'(and perhaps Hilberseimer)' Ludwig Hilberseimer (1885–1967), architecture teacher.

'Gunda' Gunta Stözl.

'...Why starting at the highest salary?' Letter, JA to Ludwig Grote, 20 June 1930. For more on this correspondence, see Eva Forgács, 'Between the Town and the Gown: On Hannes Meyer's Dismissal from the Bauhaus', *Journal of Design History* vol. 23, no. 3 (2010), pp. 265–74.

'Here, the atmosphere is very tense...' Letter, JA to FP, 21 June 1930.

'On 29 July 1930, Hesse summoned...' Thirty years later, Grote would write to Albers about the sacking, insisting that Meyer had admitted planning to move the Bauhaus

to Moscow. From the tenor of the letter, Albers seems not to have known this. Letter, Ludwig Grote to JA, 31 October 1963, JAAFA Box 4 File 22.

'Despite the director's attacks on art...' This ran from April 1929 to August 1930 and visited Zurich, Bern and four German cities.

'Later, Albers would recall the cause...' JA interviewed by Finkelstein, tape 2, side B, track 2.

p. 183 'With Kandinsky, Albers fretted that the new...' For a discussion of this see Magdalena Droste, *Hannes Meyer 1889–1954. Architekt Urbanist Lehrer* (Berlin: Wilhelm Ernst & Sohn Verlag, 1989), p. 165.

'Every Bauhäusler...will know, that...' In the Otti Berger papers. The typewritten proclamation is dated 13 August 1930; it was written by Erich Borchert (1907–44), a protégé of Hinnerk Scheper's, one of a number of *Bauhäusler* who had left for the Soviet Union.

'Gropius's advice was unhesitating...' Gropius had suggested Mies as his own successor in 1928. Mies had turned the job down.

'Mies, wrote Albers to Perdekamp...' Letter, JA to FP, 29 March 1932.

p. 184 'Mies felt that Albers's basic course...' Howard Dearstyne Papers, Josef Albers (1929–45) subject file, Library of Congress Rare Book and Special Collections Reading Room, p. 94.

'By 1932, Albers could write to Perdekamp...' Letter, JA to FP, 29 March 1932.

p. 185 'Where the Thermometer paintings had been...' *Stufen* was broken in transit to America in 1933. This version, *Steps in Grey*, was remade in New York in 1935.

'Wittgenstein's meditations on the duckrabbit' In Ludwig Wittgenstein, *Philosophical Investigations* (1953). See also Introduction to this book, p. 36.

'Soon a letter arrived from the...' Josef Albers Papers, Yale Manuscripts and Archives, Sterling Library, Yale University.

p. 188 'Two years after they had...' The building, at 28 Sensburger Allee, still stands.

'This they set about painting white...' See Weber, 'Anni Albers', in *The Bauhaus Group*.

'I can't pay the rent...make few plans.' Letter, JA to FP, 10 June 1933.

'Barr would later recall...' Quoted in Bergdoll and Dickerman, *Bauhaus 1919–1933*. In fact, Barr seems to have got his dates wrong. Lyonel Feininger's diary entry for 6 December 1927 reads, 'This morning I spent almost two hours with two charming young American academics (Harvard men).... [One], whose name is Alfred Hamilton Barr, Jr., bought a watercolour of mine.' See June L. Ness (ed.), *Lyonel Feininger* (New York and Washington, DC: Praeger Publishers, 1974), p. 160.

'How do you like Hannes Meyer?...' Letter, Alfred Barr to JA, 24 February 1933, JAAFA.

'On 11 April, Mies stepped from...' See Mies van der Rohe, 'The End of the Bauhaus', *Magazine of the North Carolina State College School of Design* vol. 3, no. 3, Spring 1953, pp. 16–17.

'A search of the school found communist...' For more on this, see Peter Hahn et al., *Bauhaus Berlin: Auflösung Dessau 1932; Schliessung Berlin 1933; Bauhäusler u. Drittes Reich* (Berlin: Weingarten and Bauhaus-Archiv, 1985).

'Minutes record that...' Bauhaus Dessau minutes,
  20 July 1933.
'I would be grateful...' Bauhaus Dessau minutes,
  29 June 1933.
p. 189 'The Bauhaus is no more and...' Letter, JA to
  Frantisek Mokry, 22 August 1933, JA Briefe Mappe 7,
  Bauhaus-Archiv, Berlin.
'I haven't made any glass pictures since...' Letter,
  JA to Paul Citroën, 3 July 1933.
'In August, a letter arrived from...' Letter dated 17 August
  1933 in Josef Albers papers (MS 32), Manuscripts and
  Archives, Yale University Library, Box 1 Folder 14.
'Josef telegraphed...Come anyway.' JA and AA interviewed
  by Duberman, p. 2.
'On 30 August, they sent a cautious acceptance...'
  Letter, JA to Philip Johnson, JAAFA.
'He mentions that he and Anni have...' Letter,
  JA to Ludwig Grote, 21 September 1933, JAAFA.
p. 192 'In 1939, he was made *Zellenleiter...*' Personalakten
  Signatur 7739/Heinrich van Bömmel, Münster
  Landesarchiv.
'After the war, a court found him...' See *Schicksale der
  Jüdischen Coesfelder zwischen Bedrohung und Ermordung,
  1919–1945*, Stadtarchiv Coesfeld, pp. 151–2.
'The chief architect of the camp...' Ertl is listed as having
  studied *Material- und Werklehre bei Herr J. Albers*, with
  further training under Albers following his diploma;
  Bauhaus-Diplom no. 50, 9 June 1931.

5 *Amerika:* **Black Mountain College**
p. 194 'Art is performance.' In Grace Glueck,
  'Each Day, Another Albers Pancake', *New York Times*,
  5 December 1971, p. 24.
p. 195 '[Josef] says that art must have freedom...'
  See Mary Emma Harris, *The Arts at Black Mountain
  College* (Cambridge, MA: MIT Press, 1987), p. 9.
'After celebrating their first Thanksgiving...'
  Barbara ("Bobbie") Dreier interviewed by
  Frederick Horowitz, Black Mountain College
  Reunion Interviews, 18 October 1995.
'He was also the nephew of Katherine...' Dreier had
  lectured at the Berlin Bauhaus in January 1933, at the
  invitation of Kandinsky. See Margret Kentgens-Craig,
  The Bauhaus and America: First Contacts, 1919–1936
  (Cambridge, MA: MIT Press, 1999), p. 95.
'We didn't know about...And that's what happened.'
  Theodore Dreier interviewed by Martin Duberman,
  Black Mountain College Reunion Interviews, 1995.
'When we came across this word...' Anni Albers
  interviewed by Martin Duberman, 1967,
  State Archives of North Carolina (NCWRA).
'As soon as he saw photographs...' Quoted in Katherine
  Chaddock Reynolds, *Visions and Vanities: John Andrew
  Rice of Black Mountain College* (Baton Rouge: Louisiana
  State University Press, 1998), p. 106.
'Relieved, Rice answered...' J. A. Rice interviewed by
  Martin Duberman, 1967, State Archives of North
  Carolina (NCWRA).
'Four months later, the Albers...' Typically of Black
  Mountain College, even this is disputed. Rice
  later recalled collecting the Albers himself:
  see Rice interviewed by Duberman.

p. 196 'In New York, they had been warned...'
  AA interviewed by Duberman.
'The place's oddity was confirmed...' Ibid.
p. 197 'accommodation and food very good...'
  The rooms, numbers 273 and 274, were at the
  westernmost end of the second floor of Lee Hall.
'a lot of the feel of the bauhaus...' The Albers had been met
  on the quay in New York by four Bauhaus artists, among
  them the American *Bauhäusler* Howard Dearstyne.
  In Albers–Kandinsky correspondence, JAAFA.
'Three years later, in an article...' Louis Adamic,
  'Education on a Mountain', *Harper's*, April 1936.
'Drawing on German theory, Dewey had...' John Dewey,
  Art as Experience (New York: Capricorn Books, 1939).
'The college was to be...' Copy of letter, John Dewey to JA,
  18 July 1940; sent by JA to J. B. Neumann.
p. 198 'Although Anni's letter drew happy parallels...'
  J. A. Rice, 'Black Mountain College Memoirs', ed.
  William C. Rice, *Southern Review*, XXV, July 1989,
  pp. 573–85.
'Black Mountain, it was said...' Mary Emma Harris
  and Ilya Bolotowsky interview, Black Mountain
  College Research Project.
'ALBERS: This is really what...' JA and AA interviewed
  by Duberman, 1967, State Archives of North Carolina
  (NCWRA).
'I would like a dentist also...' Minutes of the Black
  Mountain Faculty meeting, 28 September 1936;
  Western Regional Archives, State Archives of
  North Carolina (NCWRA).
'Soon after, they left to work for...' They never made it.
  To Albers' fury, and despite having no legal right to
  the name, Moholy had opened a design school called
  'the New Bauhaus' in 1937. It went bust in 1938, its
  founder having gambled its capital on the Chicago
  stock exchange.
p. 199 'Regretfully, the letter said...' Letter, Robert
  D. Leigh, president of Bennington College, to JA,
  5 April 1934; in Josef Albers Papers (MS32),
  Manuscripts and Archives, Yale University Library.
'Albers testily wrote back...' Letter, JA to Walter
  Gropius, 11 October 1937, Gropius Papers,
  Houghton Library, Harvard.
'One peppy student said...' Ted Dreier interviewed
  by Horowitz, 18 August 1996.
'ALBERS: [He] told this lady [...] MRS ALBERS: Alice.'
  JA and AA interviewed by Duberman.
'As a result of Albers' inability...' Jacob Lawrence
  interviewed by Horowitz, 19 July 1997.
'Albers, she said, "had a wonderful...' Bobbie Dreier
  interviewed by Horowitz.
p. 200 'My English was good...into his translations.'
  AA interviewed by Duberman.
'At the end of about three weeks...Cut the translation.'
  Rice interviewed by Duberman.
'Eventually we said...We got it, you know.' Bobbie
  Dreier interviewed by Horowitz.
'You saw things. I've never forgotten...' Rice interviewed
  by Duberman.
'I am doing a lot of work...' Letter, JA to Wassily
  Kandinsky, dated '27.IV.1934', in *Kandinsky–Albers. Une
  correspondance des années trente* [Kandinsky–Albers:

Correspondence in the 1930s], *Cahiers du Musée national d'art moderne*, special issue/archives, December 1998.

'Ten had arrived in America...' See inventory sent to JA by John Becker, dated 25 January 1934, JAAFA.

'His ex-student Howard Dearstyne...' Howard Dearstyne Papers, Josef Albers (1929–45) subject file, Library of Congress Rare Book and Special Collections Reading Room, pp. 132–3.

'He himself took a more sanguine view...' From interviews with JA by Irving Finkelstein, taped in support of his PhD thesis (1965); tape 2, side B. Courtesy of the JAAF.

'In Spring, there will be a so-called...' Letter, Marcel Breuer to JA, undated (but clearly 1935), JAAFA Box 2 Folder 4. The works to which Breuer refers are the ones left in Germany.

p. 201 'Mr Albers's abstractions never transcend...' 'New Outbreaks of Abstraction Continue', *New York Times*, 15 March 1936.

'Most of the people who come...' Fifteen woodcuts were shown at the Addison Gallery in Andover, MA, in January 1935. The curator was Charles Sawyer, who would later bring Albers to Yale.

'The curator of another show was...' The show, 'Josef Albers', was at the Phillips Gallery, Exeter, NH, in 1939. See letter, Thomas Folds to JA, 14 November 1971, JAAFA Box 24 Folder 3.

'Typical of the press Albers received...' 'Is It a Show Case?', *Des Moines Tribune*, 23 January 1945.

'Poor Barr, who believes only in...' Letter, JA to Wassily Kandinsky, Kandinsky Correspondence, JAAFA.

'Albers' argument that the Bauhaus was...' Letter, JA to Janet M. Henrich, 19 November 1937, Registrar Files (Exhibition #82), Museum of Modern Art.

'He is always frank...not always right.' JA, unpublished note in file 'I Remember', JAAFA.

'A mild consolation was that the writer [...] a great guy!' Wilder later described himself as an 'enraptured pupil' of Albers. See letter, Thornton Wilder to JA, 6 May 1967, JAAFA Box 11 Folder 46.

'Another was that a Bauhaus glass piece...' JA interviewed by Finkelstein. Another glass painting, *Overlapping* (1927), survived both the Nazis and Communists in what would become the East German city of Erfurt. The first regime viewed the work as handicraft, and thus allowable; the second as materially too valuable to destroy.

'By the 1940s, the glass paintings...' See, for example, Elizabeth Jennerjahn's recollection of these in Mervin Lane (ed.), *Black Mountain College: Sprouted Seeds: an Anthology of Personal Accounts* (Knoxville: University of Tennessee Press, 1990), p. 132.

'Anni described the Bauhaus as...' AA interviewed by Duberman.

'As Josef ruefully wrote to Kandinsky...' JA to WK, 6 February 1935; in *Friends in Exile*, op. cit., p. 56.

p. 202 'We are very far away here...' JA to Jean Arp, 17 May 1934; in Josef Albers Papers (MS32), Manuscripts and Archives, Yale University Library.

'To Georges Vantongerloo, also in Paris...' JA to Georges Vantongerloo, 28 May 1935; archive, Max Bill Georges Vantongerloo Stiftung, Zumikon, Switzerland.

'I have read through...beautiful for you there.' Paul Guermonprez, in reply to a letter from JA, dated 24 April 1935, JAAFA.

'Albers' woodcuts had been shown...' 'Siliographie recenti di Josef Albers e di Luigi Veronesi', Galleria del Milione, Milan, 23 December 1934–10 January 1935.

'But as you are only making small...' Letter, Baroness Rebay to JA, 12 March 1940, JAAFA Box 8 Folder 35.

'It is just that my statement...' Letter, JA to FP, 3 September 1934.

'he had noticed the crossed arms...' William Darr interviewed by Frederick Horowitz, 14 June 1996.

p. 203 'Anni added, quietly...' JA and AA interviewed by Duberman.

'In 1939, the couple were naturalized...' They were naturalized separately, Anni on 21 May and Josef on 22 November.

'To get them was a job of the hell...' Letter, JA to Frederick Mangold, JAAFA Box 38 Folder 4. Albers was being optimistic. That August, an official from the Department of Immigration visited Black Mountain to warn Anni that her parents would be deported if they came to America without a visa.

'In all, fifty-two refugees from Hitler...' From Frederick Horowitz interviews, JAAFA.

'On his letter to Albers is...' Guermonprez, a member of the Dutch Resistance, was shot by the Gestapo in June 1944.

'There were as few rules as possible...' Mary Caroline Richards, *Opening Our Moral Eye: Essays, Talks and Poems Embracing Creativity and Community* (Herndon, VA: Lindisfarne Books, 1996), p. 67.

'He put on a real performance...a theatrical entrance.' Jane Slater Marquis interviewed by Frederick Horowitz, 6 and 14 February 1996.

'A fellow student agreed...' Vera Baker Williams interviewed by Frederick Horowitz, 27 July 2004.

p. 205 'I don't think I've ever seen an instructor...' Elaine de Kooning quoted in Lane, *Sprouted Seeds*, p. 249.

'a circle is red, a square is blue' JA interviewed by Finkelstein.

'but got little further than the French...' Michel Eugène Chevreul, *De la loi du contraste simultané des couleurs et de l'assortiment des objets colorés* (1854).

'They were male and female of the...' Don Page interviewed by Frederick Horowitz, 11 February 1996.

'I found my ideas were absolutely...' John Cage interview, 2 May 1974, Oral History Interviews, Archives of American Art, Smithsonian Institution.

'Robert Wunsch, a Southerner, drama teacher...' Alfred Kazin, *New York Jew* (New York: Knopf, 1978), p. 105.

'Every time the fire would spring...' Clark Foreman interview, 16 November 1974; Interview B-0003, Southern Oral History Program Collection (#4007), University Library, University of North Carolina at Chapel Hill.

p. 208 'The day after Hitler became German chancellor...' See William S. Powell (ed.), *Dictionary of North Carolina Biography* (Chapel Hill: University of North Carolina Press, 1996).

'The Albers also faced the intractable...' For more on this, see e.g. Marjorie Lamberti, 'The Reception of Refugee Scholars from Nazi Germany in America: Philanthropy and Social Change in Higher Education', *Jewish Social Studies* vol.

12, no. 3, Spring–Summer 2006, pp. 157–92; and Gabrielle Edgcomb, *From Swastika to Jim Crow: Refugee Scholars at Black Colleges* (Malabar, FL: Krieger Publishing Co., 1993).

'coming together, standing together, working together...' From the leaflet announcing the new logo, signed by JA, dated March 1935, JAAFA Box 40 Folder 20.

p. 209 'Josef's painting *Lozenge Horizontal* came joint...' For the winning entry, see <http://ncartmuseum.org/art/detail/the_carpenter> (accessed 26 November 2017).

'When, in the war, a Black Mountain...' See Harris, *The Arts at Black Mountain College*, p. 67.

'You can't talk to a German about liberty...' Rice interviewed by Duberman.

'The Ku Klux Klan's antipathy...' See, for example, the experience of the YWCA's Camp Merrie-Woode, described in Dorothy Height, *Open Wide the Freedom Gates: A Memoir* (New York: Public Affairs, 2003).

'Typical, if inaccurate, is the idea...' Elliot Weinberger quoted in Lane, *Sprouted Seeds*, p. 77.

'The German phenomenologist, Erwin Straus, predicts...' In the view of one scholar, it was Straus who was most resistant to the idea of integration at Black Mountain; this is borne out by the college minutes. See Stephen J. Whitfield, 'The South in the Shadow of Nazism', *Southern Cultures* vol.18, no. 3, Fall 2012.

'Albers, by contrast, is mild...' Minutes, Board of Fellows and Faculty Meetings vol. iv, 25 January 1944; NCWRA.

'Only in September, when Black Mountain...' Alma Stone Williams had attended the first Summer Session in 1944.

p. 210 'Rice says all the time...the artist say it?' JA interviewed by Finkelstein.

'In 1936, the Yugoslav writer Louis...' Adamic, 'Education on a Mountain'.

'That Adamic would later describe...' Louis Adamic, *My America, 1928–1938* (New York: Harper & Bros., 1938), p. 637.

'In January 1938, he wrote to Rice...leave of absence.' Letters dated 28 January, 1 February and 1 March 1938, all in JA papers, JAAFA Box 38 Folder 4.

'That autumn, Albers wrote to Lawrence Kocher...' Letter, Lawrence Kocher to JA, 21 October 1937, JAAFA Box 5 Folder 45.

p. 211 'His suggestion was a Bauhaus quartet...' Gropius and Breuer had gone to Harvard in 1937.

'Albers, who had intended the cottage...' JA interviewed by Finkelstein.

'This was furnished with wood-and-leather...' See Edward DuPuy interviewed by Mary Emma Harris, BMC Research Project Papers, NCWRA.

'Visiting students thought of the room...' Patricia Lynch Wood interviewed by Horowitz.

'There are cabbages and onions...' 'Black Mountain College Bulletin', vol. v, no. 4, May 1947.

p. 212 'When he went to Lake Eden five years...' See William McCleery interviewed by Mary Emma Harris, BMC Research Project Papers, NCWRA.

'He trained you to be so skilled...' Marilyn Bauer interviewed by Horowitz.

'I don't think there was one single comment...' Ati Gropius interviewed by Frederick Horowitz, Black Mountain College Reunion Interviews.

p. 213 '[Albers] would come in...' Mary Phelan Bowles interviewed by Horowitz, Black Mountain College Reunion Interviews.

'In faculty meetings, he now sang...' See Faculty Meeting Minutes, 19 October 1936; NCWRA.

'Elaine de Kooning was astonished...' See Lane, *Sprouted Seeds*, p. 249.

'The Japanese American artist Ruth Asawa...' Ruth Asawa interviewed by Horowitz.

'Along with disorientation went repetition...' Bobbie Dreier interviewed by Horowitz.

'I exclaimed at his patience in making...' Grace Alexander Young, 'Art as a Fourth "R"', *Arts and Decoration*, January 1935.

'Within a year, Albers was painting...' Albers later subtitled the work *Christmas Shopping*.

p. 215 'To a later generation of students, at Yale...' Allan Ludwig interviewed by Horowitz, 14 June 1996.

'For a lib'ral gets no exercise...' The words were by William McCleery, the music by John Evarts; typewritten script in JAAFA JA 41.4.

'Mexico was cheap: although, after...' See JA correspondence, JAAFA Box 33 Folders 5–7. Albers was the only ex-Bauhaus master to take a pension from the Nazis.

'Mexico was also accessible by the couple's...' The car, a second-hand college vehicle, was deducted from Albers' salary at the cost of $350.

'To Kandinsky he wrote...' Albers' enthusiasm did not extend to contemporary Mexican art. Muralists such as Diego Rivera, he said, made 'propaganda'; to which he added, 'Communist, of course.'

'We checked [Lake Eden] for a site...' Letter, JA to FP, 17 September 1937.

p. 216 'It was Kocher's questioning of the quality...' Letter, Lawrence Kocher to JA, 1 October 1937.

'While the future abstract expressionists...' The Albers' early proselytizing of Mexico had repercussions beyond the college. In 1936, John Graham, a friend and fellow member of the recently formed Association of Abstract Artists, moved there. In 1937, he published his study of primitive (including Mayan) art, *Systems and Dialectics of Art*, hugely influential on the future abstract expressionist painters.

'The Greeks enslaved their neighbours, so...' Seymour Rogoff interviewed by Horowitz, 20 October 1996.

'This back-and-forth between line and colour...' He made the drawings for these while teaching a summer school at Harvard in 1941. As we shall see, these periods at Harvard were enormously important to the development of his work.

'*Equal and Unequal* (1939) has the look...' *Equal and Unequal* would hang in Anni's bedroom for fifty years.

'Since January [I've been painting] only...' Letter, JA to FP, September 1947.

p. 219 'Twenty years later, he would claim...' See Introduction, p. 34.

'There was no mistaking what the *Adobes*...' See Brenda Danilowitz et al., *Anni and Josef Albers: Latin American Journeys* (Berlin: Hatje Cantz, 2007), p. 144.

'So, too, with the Mexican collages...' See Kiki Gilderhus in ibid. p. 123ff.

'Bobbie is "Böbbschen", Josef is sleepless...'
Letter, JA to Bobbie Dreier, 9 July 1934, JAAFA.

'we remember his...above all his daddy' In JA professional papers, JAAFA Box 39 Folder 9.

p. 224 'It ends Benedicamus Domino!' i.e., thanks be to God.

'It is signed "Anni's husband".' Letter, JA to Betty Seymour, JA correspondence with individuals, JAAFA.

'John Andrew Rice recalled overhearing them argue...' Rice interviewed by Duberman.

'Your paintings are your children...forgo having children.' Ruth Asawa and Albert Lanier interview, 21 June–5 July 2002, Oral History Interviews, Archives of American Art, Smithsonian Institution.

'Elain Schmitt recalled him jiggling...' Elaine Schmitt interviewed by Mary Emma Harris, BMC Research Project Papers, NCWRA.

'...Nancy Smith being groped...' Nancy Smith interviewed by Frederick Horowitz.

'Letters to Slats were signed...' Marquis interviewed by Horowitz.

'This was the culture of Black Mountain College...' Harris, The Arts at Black Mountain College, p. 78.

'As to Anni, her response to...' Beth Moffitt interviewed by Horowitz, 4 January 1997.

p. 225 'I liked the rigid and the things...' Asawa and Lanier interview, Archives of American Art.

'I was willing to submerge any desires...discipline I came for.' Quoted in Calvin Tomkins, Off the Wall: A Portrait of Robert Rauschenberg (New York: Picador, 2005), p. 23.

'There is no extraordinary without the...' Quoted in the catalogue essay to 'Josef Albers: Paintings, Prints, Projects' (New York: Clarke & Way, 1956).

'Years later...entire visual world.' Tomkins, Off the Wall.

'Repeated, among other places, in his...' William Grimes, 'Kenneth Noland, Abstract Painter of Brilliantly Colored Shapes, Dies at 85', New York Times, 6 January 2010.

'Actually, I studied with him just for half...' Kenneth Noland interviewed by Paul Cummings, 1971, Oral History Interviews, Archives of American Art, Smithsonian Institution.

'Albers' teaching, he said, was...' Kenneth Noland quoted in Lane, Sprouted Seeds, p. 212.

'To Leonard Billing, a student...' Leonard Billing interviewed by Horowitz.

p. 226 'Black Mountain wore...It wore everybody out.' Gropius interviewed by Horowitz, p. 3.

'Finally, after sixteen years...' JA and AA interviewed by Duberman, p. 35.

'The least thing had to be discussed...' Ibid.

'Economics was now taught by Karl...' See Harris, The Arts at Black Mountain College, pp. 111, 113.

'That was like the Bauhaus!...' JA interviewed by Horowitz. As Albers admitted, we have now only...' Letter, JA to Theodore Rondthaler, 4 November 1948, JAAFA Box 8 Folder 49.

p. 227 'And now we will see...' Typewritten copy in BMC teaching series, JAAFA Box 41 Folder 5.

'Two students writing under the pseudonym...' One of the authors, Jerrold Levy, was Herbert Bayer's stepson; the other was Richard Negro. See Alessandro Porco (ed.), Poems by Gerard Legro (Toronto: Bookthug, 2016).

'It was tacked to the college...' See Lane, Sprouted Seeds, p. 264.

'Albers, delighted at the Schwindel...' Ilya Bolotowsky interviewed by Mary Emma Harris, BMC Research Project.

'This morning I hate it...' Leo Lionni, Between Worlds: The Autobiography of Leo Lionni (New York: Knopf, 1997), p. 165.

'As a future colleague at Yale was to put it...' Alvin Eisenman, BMC Alumni Panel Discussion, University of North Carolina Asheville, 29 April 2000. Eisenman's wife, Hope Greer, was a student at Black Mountain.

p. 229 'First mention of them comes in January...' Minutes of BMC faculty meetings, January 1944.

'Black Mountain is trying to do an...' Letter, JA to Clarence N. Pickett, 24 April 1944; BMC papers, NCWRA.

'The FSC referred him to the...' The Fund was set up by Julius Rosenwald, co-owner of Sears, Roebuck & Co., to promote education for African Americans in the rural South. It was particularly active in North Carolina.

'The teacher was Jacob Lawrence...' Letter, JA to Fred G. Wale, 9 April 1946; Black Mountain correspondence, Papers of the Rosenwald Fund, John Hope and Aurelia E. Franklin Library, Fisk University. One of the more persistent Black Mountain myths is that Albers hired a private railway carriage to spare the Lawrences the humiliation of a segregated Southern train. Given the parlous state of BMC finances, this story seems remarkable; there is no documentary evidence to support it.

'If we are disappointed not to find Greek...' JA, unpublished writings, JAAFA Box 80 Folder 29.

'He wrote to the Museum of Modern Art...' Letter, JA to Museum of Modern Art, 4 February 1943; BMC papers, NCWRA.

'Like all teachers at the summer...' This was of eight gouaches, borrowed from the Downtown Gallery in New York.

'Yet, in Lawrence's memory...wonderful experience for me.' Jacob Lawrence interviewed by Horowitz, 19 July 1997, p. 2.

'Any form [of art] is acceptable...' Katharine Kuh, 'Josef Albers', in The Artist's Voice: Talks with Seventeen Artists (New York: Harper and Row, 1962), p. 12.

'As to summer students, they were...' See Harris, The Arts at Black Mountain College, p. 100.

'So, too, the teachers...' Letter, JA to Karl With, 12 February 1945, JAAFA Box 11 Folder 55.

p. 230 'As M. C. Richards remembered it...' M. C. Richards interviewed by Martin Duberman, State Archives of North Carolina (NCWRA).

6 Ends and Beginnings: Yale

p. 232 'It would not be an exaggeration...' In Michael Craig-Martin, On Being an Artist (London: Art Books Publishing Ltd., 2015), p. 50.

'He had a lot of sons and...' Robert Slutzky interviewed by Frederick Horowitz, 10 May 1996.

p. 233 'the students are beginning to come...' Letter, JA to FP, 27 December 1950.

'"That", he ends, "is all we know...' Letter, JA to FP, 10 May 1949.

'After Cincinnati, he would teach for a...' From interviews with JA by Irving Finkelstein, taped in support of his PhD thesis (1965); tape 2, side A, track 1. Courtesy of the JAAF. Holty was artist-in-residence at the University of Georgia at Athens from 1948–50. He and Albers were early members of American Abstract Artists.

'During the 1950 summer vacation...' See David Harvey interviewed by Horowitz, 29 September 1996.

p. 234 'His arrival, Sawyer drily recalled...' Charles Sawyer interviewed by Frederick Horowitz, 10 November 1995.

'George Heard Hamilton, professor of art history...' George Heard Hamilton, unpublished interview, 3 June 1992, JAAFA Box 4 Folder 31.

'The art historian Robert Rosenblum, then a Yale...' Robert Rosenblum, 'Reflections on the Tremaine Collection', in *The Tremaine Collection: 20th Century Masters/The Spirit of Modernism* (Hartford, CT: Wadsworth Atheneum, 1984).

'Work in the exhibition came from...' The painting was bought in May 1945 and exhibited as *The Flying Man*. It had earlier hung in the shared Albers/Dreier drawing room at Roadside Cottage.

'It might interest you that [*Flying*]...' Letter, JA to S. R. Naysmith, 1 May 1945, JAAFA Box 24 Folder 7.

'The work's graphic potential was clear...' Letter, S. R. Naysmith to JA, 13 December 1945, JAAFA Box 24 Folder 7. The work was reproduced without Albers' permission. Citing advice from Herbert Bayer, he asked for a $1,000 royalty payment. Miller, having consulted their lawyers, sent $150, which JA returned uncashed.

'Having work in the Miller collection...' Letter, S. R. Naysmith to JA, 23 January 1946, JAAFA Box 24 Folder 7.

'As Emily Tremaine, wife of the owner, told *Newsweek*...' *Newsweek*, 19 January 1948.

p. 236 'Any design connected with an architectural...' JA in Eleanor Bittermann, *Art in Modern Architecture* (New York: Reinhold Publishing Co., 1952), pp. 148–9.

'All three men went to see him...' Sawyer interviewed by Horowitz. This was presumably Holty's flat at 90th Street and Madison Avenue. Sawyer and Howe visited together, Kahn separately: see Alvin Eisenman interviewed by Horowitz, 5 May 1995.

'Albers' and Kahn's paths had crossed...' JA interviewed by Finkelstein, tape 2, side A, track 1.

'Both had written for a book called...' Paul Zucker (ed.), *New Architecture and City Planning: A Symposium* (New York: Philosophical Library, 1944). Albers' essay was 'The Educational Value of Manual Work and Handicraft in Relation to Architecture' (1940); Kahn's was 'Monumentality'.

p. 237 'The two men had also shown together...' 'Five American Printmakers', Philadelphia Art Alliance, 11 February–16 March 1947.

'In February 1948, Albers had had a letter...' Letter, Charles Sawyer to JA, 12 February 1948; Josef Albers Papers (MS 32), Yale Manuscripts and Archives, Yale University Library. The committee was the University Council for Art and Architecture. For more on this, see Robert Stern, *Pedagogy and Place: 100 Years of Architecture Education at Yale* (New Haven: Yale University Press, 2016), p. 95. See also Eeva-Liisa

Pelkonen, 'Toward Cognitive Architecture', in *Louis Kahn –The Power of Architecture* (Weil am Rhein: Vitra Design Museum, 2012), p. 133ff.

'In October 1949, a second letter...' Josef Albers Papers (MS 32), Yale Manuscripts and Archives, Yale University Library.

'Albers joined them.' For more on this, see Sarah Williams Goldhagen, *Louis Kahn's Situated Modernism* (New Haven: Yale University Press, 2001); also 'Student Architects, Painters, Sculptors Design Together', *Progressive Architecture* no. 30 (April 1949).

'Nine months later, he frets that...' Letter, JA to FP, 21 September 1951. Variegate photosensitive glass had been developed by the Corning Glass Works in 1949. The process was publicized in e.g. S. D. Stookey, 'Photosensitive Glass', in J. Alexander, *Colloid Chemistry*, vol. vii, p. 697 (New York: Reinhold, 1950).

p. 238 'It never did. In March 1952...' Letter, FP to JA, 31 March 1952. Lisbet Marx *née* Albers lived in Bottrop, the last of the family to do so. Since 1939, Perdekamp had been director of the Vestischer Museum in nearby Recklinghausen.

'Wallace K. Harrison, the UN's chief architect...' Howard Dearstyne Papers, Josef Albers (1929–45) subject file, Library of Congress Rare Book and Special Collections Reading Room. Dearstyne was working as an architectural designer for Harrison & Fouilhoux at the time.

'In 1950, Harrison himself designed...' Originally Three Mellon Bank Centre, this has since been renamed 525 William Penn Place.

'The Harrison papers contain a sole reference...' Wallace K. Harrison Papers, Box 16 Folder 3, Avery Architectural and Fine Arts Library, Columbia University.

'All that survives otherwise is...' JAAFA, outsized architectural studies.

'The General Assembly Building would open...' 'Glass and the United Nations', *Corning Glass Works Gaffer*, October 1952, pp. 3–6, 9, 10.

'The General Assembly glass, though...' This was presumably the victim of US congressional cost-cutting; the Léger murals had been paid for privately by Nelson Rockefeller. For more on the UN project, see Victoria Newhouse, *Wallace K. Harrison, Architect* (New York: Rizzoli, 1989), chapters 12 and 13.

'That gallery's stepped-back facade relates...' Kahn also consulted Albers on the building's 'grey and tan' colour scheme. See 'Conversation with Bernard Chaet', 4 March 1992, JAAFA. Despite this, Albers never liked the building.

'Later, Kahn would describe his design...' In Louis I. Kahn, Heinz Ronner and Sharad Jhaveri, *Louis I.Kahn: Complete Work 1935–1974* (Boulder: Westview Press, 1977).

'George Howe's successor at the architecture...' Robert Paul Schweikher, oral history interview by Betty J. Blum, Art Institute of Chicago, 1984.

p. 240 'Although Albers' plans for the General...' See Newhouse, *Wallace K. Harrison*, p. 129.

'The dual appointment of Albers as...' See letter, Charles Sawyer to JA, 16 June 1950, Josef Albers Papers (MS 32), Yale Manuscripts and Archives, Yale University Library.

'The *New York Times* noted that painting...' 'Will Serve as Chairman of New Art Unit at Yale', *New York Times*, 16 July 1950.

'A view long held within its walls...' See for example Deane Keller in 'Conversation with Bernard Chaet', 4 March 1992, JAAFA.

'Some of the old guard jumped...' Letter, Lewis York to President Charles Seymour, 9 May 1950, Yale Manuscripts and Archives, Yale University Library.

'Offered a post, he had appeared...' Sawyer interviewed by Horowitz.

'To me, the composition presents...' Bittermann, *Art in Modern Architecture*, p. 149.

'The Dean of the School of Design...' See e.g. letter, Walter Gropius to JA, 16 March 1950, Josef Albers Papers (MS 32), Yale Manuscripts and Archives, Yale University Library. For more on Hudnut, see Jill E. Pearlman, *Inventing American Modernism: Joseph Hudnut, Walter Gropius, and the Bauhaus Legacy at Harvard* (Charlottesville: University of Virginia Press, 2007).

p. 241 'Lest malcontents ambush him, he ran...' Eisenman interviewed by Horowitz.

'You I don't want. You can stay...' Paul Zelanski interviewed by Horowitz, 8 July 1996.

'When, in answer to the question...get his money back.' Alfred Hammer interviewed by Horowitz, 8 June 1996.

p. 242 'As ever, Albers wore a grey flannel...' William Werner interviewed by Horowitz, 1 December 2003.

'Finally, he said...' Robert Birmelin, pers. comm., 18 February 2017.

'One student whose work began to show...' William Bailey interviewed by Horowitz, 26 September 1995.

'Another recalls James Brooks being introduced...' Ken Resen, pers. comm., 9 February 2017.

'Irwin Rubin, poached from Cooper Union in 1952, remembered...' Irwin Rubin interviewed by Horowitz, 7 July 1997.

'because your ears would stay red...' See Zelanski interviewed by Horowitz.

'One Second World War veteran...' Julian Stanczak interviewed by Horowitz, 22 August 1995.

'If [a student painting]...You go find your own.' Rubin interviewed by Horowitz.

p. 243 'Irwin Rubin joked that unfortunates given...' Ibid.

'Wags circulated a Yale *Ten Commandments*...' JAAFA Box 41 Folder 9(1). Commandment VI was 'Thou shalt not do messy painting'; VIII, 'Thou shalt not express something.'

'If you can't take it here...' Anne Locks Brody interviewed by Horowitz, 19 October 1996.

'To Neil Welliver, he once confided...I was on my own then.' Neil Welliver interviewed by Horowitz.

'The year before coming to Yale...' These were 'Albers: Paintings in Black, Grey, White' (Egan Gallery, 24 January–12 February 1949) and 'Albers: Paintings Titled "Variants"' (Sidney Janis Gallery, 24 January–12 February 1949).

p. 244 'Albers must be accounted another victim...' Clement Greenberg, 'Review of Exhibitions of Adolph Gottlieb, Jackson Pollock, and Josef Albers', *The Nation*, 19 February 1949.

'He knew everything that you had done...' Steven Barbash interviewed by Horowitz, 8 June 1996.

'You'd never know when he'd be there...' Allan Denenberg interviewed by Horowitz, 9 June 1996.

'Called the Hochschule für Gestaltung...' In March 1949, Albers and Bill had shown together at Galerie Gerd Rosen in Berlin.

'In March, Albers had a letter from...' Letter, United States International Information Administration to JA, 16 March 1953, JAAFA Box 35 Folder 12. Albers was on a lecture tour of Chile and Peru when the inital letter arrived in West Haven, thus delaying his reply.

'This was followed by an anguished letter...' Letter, JA to Harold E. Howland, 16 September 1963.

'Weimar and Dessau now lay in...' Rudolf Ullstein had confirmed the destruction of the last in a letter of 12 April 1950, JAAFA Box 11 Folder 11. There was, Ullstein said, no money for *Luxusreperatur* (luxury repairs).

p. 245 'They wrote to each other almost...' Letter, JA to Anni Albers, JAAFA.

'The following year, Franz Perdekamp shifted...' 'Westfälische Kunst der letzten 50 Jahre', Recklinghausen, 1951.

'Choosing his words with care...' Letter, JA to FP, 20 August 1951.

'The next month, in what was...' Letter, JA to FP, 21 September 1951.

'Shouldn't the people in charge...the Fatherland has changed.' Unidentified local paper, undated, 1952; from cutting in Albers scrapbook, Museum of Modern Art archives.

'As Albers wrote in his report...' 'Report on a Course in Basic Drawing, Design and Color given at the Hochschule für Gestaltung in Ulm', 20 January 1954, JAAFA Box 35 Folder 17.

'At Ulm, as at Black Mountain...' Ibid.

p. 246 'Bill's successor was to reinvent the school...' Tomás Maldonado, 'Inaugural speech of the Rector of the HfG', 5 October 1964.

'Worse still, Ulm students now viewed...' See Paul Betts, *The Authority of Everyday Objects: The Cultural History of West German Industrial Design* (Berkeley: University of California Press, 2004), p. 169ff.

p. 247 'From somebody who was there when...' Rubin interviewed by Horowitz.

'And he actually apologized to us...' Ibid.

'To another, he said...' Allan Ludwig interviewed by Horowitz, 14 June 1996.

'Relatively few of the many Black Mountain...' It was widely thought at Yale that Albers played up his accent so that students would supply words for which he seemed to be groping: see Robert Reed interviewed by Horowitz, 2 May 2003.

p. 249 'Several *Transformations* were shown at the Museum...' Loan exhibition, 11 October 1949–15 February 1950.

'Visitors, at least, responded well...' Hostess Reports, Museum of Non-Objective Painting, 1–7 March 1950.

'One may have been exhibited as early...' 'An Exhibition of Josef Albers: Paintings and Prints', The Bookbuilders Workshop, Boston (9 October 1950–?) may have included a *Homage*.

'In January 1952, they finally appeared...' 'New Work by Josef Albers: Homage to the Square and Transformation of a Scheme', 7–26 January 1952. Two more *Homages* were in 'Two exhibitions: Naum Gabo and Josef Albers', Arts Club of Chicago, 29 January–28 February 1952.

'Although rumours of his paintings abounded...' Charles Perry interviewed by Horowitz, 24 June 1996.

'Richard Anuszkiewicz, whose work would eventually...' Richard Anuszkiewicz interview, 28 December 1971, Oral History Interviews, Archives of American Art, Smithsonian.

'It had a skylight. I just remember...' Orr Marshall interviewed by Horowitz, 31 May 1996.

'Fewer still penetrated the cramped...' Letter, JA to FP, 20 August 1951.

p. 252 '[She] had to move them...They were *really* poor.' Eisenman interviewed by Horowitz.

'I went out to Orange...it was 1932 Bauhaus.' Barbash interviewed by Horowitz. The house was actually in nearby West Haven; Barbash seems to have confused it with the Albers' later home.

'Unlike its neighbours, the garden of...' Letter, JA to FP, 20 August 1951.

p. 253 'This "new form effect – differing shades...' JA on *White Cross*, JAAFA Box 57 Folders 6–7.

'*White Cross* concerns itself with duality...' The window was moved in the 1990s; it is now in a guest bedroom.

p. 254 'As a young man at Büren...' See Albert Sangiamo interviewed by Horowitz, 11 May 1996.

'He compared *White Cross* to the...' See Neal David Benezra, *The Murals and Sculpture of Josef Albers*, Outstanding Dissertations in the Fine Arts (New York and London: Garland Publishing Inc., 1985), p. 68.

'In 1954, the Swiss medievalist François...' *Die Zisterzienserabtei Notre-Dame de Bonmont im Zusammenhang mit der burgundisch-transjuranischen Gruppe* (University of Berne, 1955).

'He and Albers became friends...' François Bucher and JA, *Despite Straight Lines* (New Haven: Yale University Press, 1961).

'Having never met him, they clearly...' For the history of this debate, see Hilary Thimmesh, OSB, *Marcel Breuer and a Committee of Twelve Plan a Church: A Monastic Memoir* (Collegeville, MN: St John's University Press, 2010), p. 82ff.

'He addressed us in a language...' Ibid. p. 97.

'Another remarked that the window could...' Ibid. p. 99.

'An embarrassed Abbot Dworschak wrote...' All St John's correspondence in JAAFA Box 57 Folders 6–7.

p. 257 'The monk replied, encouragingly if oddly...' Letter, Father Theodor Bogler to JA, 30 April 1967, JAAFA Box 1 Folder 54.

'Given the time and thought he had...' Letter, JA to Abbot Baldwin Dworschak, OSB, 7 December 1959, JAAFA Box 57 Folder 6.

'In 1936, a small Catholic church...' St Margaret Mary Catholic Church in Swannanoa, NC.

'Albers' art longs for the state...' Jean Charlot, 'Nature and the Art of Josef Albers', *College Art Journal* vol. xv, no. 3, p. 190ff (1956).

'To her surprise, she found Albers...' See Eisenman interviewed by Horowitz.

'A nun who studied at Yale...' Linae Frei interviewed by Horowitz, 28 September 1996. Frei later taught art at St Xavier University, Chicago.

'I accept the authority of Albers because...' Lois Swirnoff interviewed by Horowitz, 24 February 1996.

'It was sort of schizophrenic...' Beth Moffitt interviewed by Horowitz, 4 January 1997.

p. 258 'When asked why, he replied...' Sangiamo interviewed by Horowitz.

'Another was warned...' Neil Welliver interview, 14 November 1996, Oral History Interviews, Archives of American Art, Smithsonian Institution.

'The exhibition that opened in New Haven...' 'Josef Albers: Paintings, Prints, Projects', Yale University Art Gallery, 25 April–18 June 1956.

'I always remember [Albers] walking...' John T. Frazer interviewed by Horowitz, 30 May 1996.

'Sillman would actually imitate the way...' Bernard Chaet interviewed by Horowitz, 4 March 1992.

'Yale rumour held this to be literally...' Ken Resen, pers. comm.

'*Time* magazine questioned whether...' 'Think!', *Time* magazine, 18 June 1956, p. 80.

'*Art News*, meanwhile, grandly found...' Michael Loew, 'Albers: Impersonalization in perfected form', *Art News* vol. 55, no. 2, April 1956.

p. 259 'Albers, with an eye to publicity...' Letter, JA to Leo Steinberg, 30 April 1956, JAAFA Box 10 Folder 23.

'Given his description of the work's...' Letter, Leo Steinberg to JA, 12 June 1956, JAAFA Box 10 Folder 23.

'Alfred Barr made it clear that...' See, for example, Eisenman interviewed by Horowitz.

'Albers' courting of Leo Steinberg...' For more on this, see Michael Hill, 'Leo Steinberg vs. Clement Greenberg, 1952–72', *Australian and New Zealand Journal of Art* vol. 14, no. 1, pp. 22–9.

'When the MoMA director's daughter...' Chaet interviewed by Horowitz.

p. 260 'Barr's response is not recorded.' Robert Engman interviewed by Horowitz, 28 February 1996. The show ran from 13 May–16 August 1959.

'In June 1956, Schweikher resigned...' Letter, Bob Osborne to Whitney Griswold, 6 May 1957; Griswold Papers Box 25 Folder 232; Yale Manuscripts and Archives, Yale University Library. See also Bernard Chaet, unpublished interview, JAAFA, pp. 13–16.

'The sole change would have been...' Papers, Provost's Office 1947–60, Box 3; Yale Manuscripts and Archives, Yale University Library.

'Worryingly, this was the only one...' Letter, Edgar S. Furniss to Whitney Griswold, 3 February 1956; Griswold Papers Box 25 Folder 232, Yale.

'...it was Bernard Chaet who broke...' Bernard Chaet, unpublished interview, JAAFA.

'As to Charles Sawyer's departure...' Eisenman interviewed by Horowitz.

p. 261 'At short notice and after a painful...' Bernard Chaet, unpublished interview, JAAFA.

'Albers had spent a decade badgering...' See letter, JA to Charles Olson, 11 May 1957, JAAFA Box 38 Folder 9.

'The ones stolen from Weir Hall...' Letter, JA to Sidney Janis, 10 February 1957, JAAFA Box 20 Folder 18.

'Both refused the request, Griswold noting...' Letter to Ted Dreier from Griswold's executive assistant, Catherine J. Tilson, 8 March 1960; Griswold Papers Box 25 Folder 232, Yale.

'The Ford Foundation, more munificent...' Ford Foundation Archives, Visual Artists 1958 Programme for Grantees, Box 3023/SK 34385.

'When his protests were ignored...' Chaet interviewed by Horowitz.

'After he left, said Bernard Chaet...' Ibid.

p. 262 'He lived to regret it: Albers...' Ibid.

'The suggestion was ignored.' Memo, Alvin Eisenman to Whitney Griswold, 14 June 1962; Griswold Papers Box 26 Folder 239, Yale.

'Even his advice on Paul Rudolph's...' See Stern, *Pedagogy and Place*. Albers' *Repeat and Return* (1963), a sculptural line drawing in stainless steel, hangs above the entrance; the building is now known as Rudolph Hall.

'A note on the letter...' Letter, Charles H. Brewer, Jr. to JA, 12 June 1962, JAAFA Box 41 Folder 6.

'They felt their father had left...' Bernard Chaet, unpublished interview, JAAFA.

'After its last letter, Danes issued...' JAAFA Box 19 Folder 16.

'Even with this, his memory...' See, for example, a petition of 101 students sent to JA by Stephanie Tevonian, JAAFA Box 41 Folder 6.

'In the interim, many of...' Albers' influence was not all positive. So claustrophobic did Close and Serra find the studios in Paul Rudolph's new building that they decamped to a property in Wells Street. See Stern, *Pedagogy and Place*.

p. 263 '[But] soft it was not.' Craig-Martin, *On Being an Artist*.

'Everything I know about colour...' Richard Cork, *Michael Craig-Martin* (London: Thames & Hudson, 2006), p. 17.

'Marden himself wryly recalls...' Brice Marden interview, 3 October 1972, Oral History Interviews, Archives of American Art, Smithsonian Institution.

'[My] two poles of influence...' Robert Mangold, pers. comm.

'I spent the summer proofing the book...' As Serra graduated from Yale in 1964 and *Interaction of Color* was published in April 1963, his memory is presumably at fault. Proofreading must have been done in 1962.

'RS: If you think black is a colour...' Richard Serra in conversation with Hal Foster, *Richard Serra: The Matter of Time* (Bilbao: Guggenheim Museum, Steidl Publishers, 2005).

'His colour course was not taught...' Kynaston McShine, *Richard Serra Sculpture: Forty Years* (New York: Museum of Modern Art, 2007), pp. 17–18.

p. 264 'But also impersonal ideas, repetition...' Ad Reinhardt interview, *ca.* 1964, Oral History Interviews, Archives of American Art, Smithsonian Institution.

'On Reinhardt's cartoon family tree...' First printed in *PM*, 2 June 1946; reprinted in *Art News* 60, 1961.

'Bernard Chaet ascribed the change in...' Chaet interviewed by Horowitz.

'Asked in an interview...follow yourself.' Neil Welliver, 'Albers on Albers', *Art News* 64, January 1966, p. 48ff.

'Albers, naturally, disagreed...' JA interviewed by Finkelstein, tape 1, side A, track 1. Darwin allowed that the 'intellectual' teaching at Yale might produce 'a more

self-contented and acceptable member of society...[but] not great art, or anything like it'. Quoted in Alex Seago, *Burning the Box of Beautiful Things: The Development of a Postmodern Sensibility* (Oxford: Oxford University Press, 1995), p. 149.

'The only familiar names he hazarded...' Letter, JA to George Rickey, 28 May 1963, JAAFA Box 8 Folder 44.

7 That Which Should Accompany Old Age

p. 266 'Describe me as I am...' Sam Hunter, 'Josef Albers Modern Icons', draft typescript, JAAFA Box 100 Folder 10. Published as 'Josef Albers: "Prophet and Presiding Genius of American OP Art"', *Vogue* (US), October 1970, pp. 70–3, 126–7.

p. 267 'In the five years before, Wu...' i.e., the Rouse (1955) and DuPont (1959) Houses, both in Connecticut.

'Shortly before designing the wall...' See Steven Parks et al., *Manuscript Society (1953–2002)* (New Haven: Phoenix Press).

'It also sets out to prove Kandinsky's...' See, for example, JA, 'On the Way', in Société International d'Art XXe Siècle, Paris (1966).

'In 1928, in Dessau, he had made a sandblasted...' Albers seems to have made two examples of *City*, one 28 × 55 cm, the other 33 × 55³⁄₁₀ cm. The first remained in Germany in 1933 and is now in the Kunsthaus Zurich. The other was badly broken in transit to America; what remains of it is in the collection of the Albers Foundation.

p. 269 'When the firm's plans were rejected...' For more on this, see Meredith L. Clausen, *The Pan Am Building and the Shattering of the Modernist Dream* (Cambridge, MA: MIT Press, 2004). The building is now called the Met Life.

'The rightness or wrongness...It's wrong.' James T. Burns, in *Progressive Architecture*, April 1963.

'In late 1960, Gropius approached...' The others were Richard Lippold and Gyorgy Kepes.

'It was Gropius's suggestion that...' See Neal David Benezra, *The Murals and Sculpture of Josef Albers*, Outstanding Dissertations in the Fine Arts (New York and London: Garland Publishing Inc., 1985), pp. 105–45.

'The slide show, had it happened...' In 1960–61, Albers had also made a mural called *Two Portals*, based on the *Homages to the Square*, for the lobby of the Time & Life Building on Sixth Avenue, another Harrison commission.

'Drawings and maquettes see him adding...' See, for example, the painted paper collage, *Maquette for Pan Am Building Mural*, in the Yale University Art Gallery collection.

'Albers also decided to have *City*...' See correspondence between JA and Debell & Richardson, Inc., JAAFA Box 43 Folder 15.

'In another, he writes, simply...' Both in JAAFA Box 51 Folder 17–18.

p. 271 'Its red, white and black panels...' For more on this see Charles Darwent, 'Rebuilding Manhattan', *The Art Newspaper* no. 263, December 2014.

'In 1958, Albers had published a volume...' JA, *Poems and Drawings* (New Haven: Readymade Press, 1958). The press was an unsuccessful venture into publishing by George Heard Hamilton.

'In 1966, sales generated royalties...' Letter, George
   Wittenborn to JA, 13 February 1967; letter, Anni Albers
   to George Wittenborn, Inc., 5 May 1964, JAAFA Box 69
   Folder 3.
p. 273 'Your mural in the Pan Am building...' Letter, Walter
   Gropius to JA, 25 May 1963, JAAFA Box 4 Folder 21.
p. 274 'To ensure accuracy of colour, these...' For more
   on this, see Brenda Danilowitz, 'A Short History of
   Josef Albers' *Interaction of Color*', in Vanja Malloy (ed.),
   Intersecting Colors: Josef Albers and His Contemporaries
   (Amherst, MA: Amherst College Press, 2015).
'from either mixture parent.' From 'The middle mixture
   again – intersecting colors', JA, *Interaction of Color*
   (New Haven: Yale University Press, 1963).
'active–passive.' From 'Free studies – a challenge to
   imagination', JA, *Interaction of Color*.
'None of the artwork in it is his own.' As Alvin Eisenman
   recalled to Horowitz in interview (5 May 1995), this gave
   rise to misunderstanding: students often remarked
   that the images in *Interaction* were not as good as
   Albers' later work.
p. 275 'Let me describe [the picture I want]...' Letter, JA to
   Elinor Evans, 13 August 1957, JAAFA Box 3 Folder 27.
'His memory was, as ever...' So, too, his impact on Evans,
   who would teach basic design at the Rice School of
   Architecture into her nineties. In 2014, at the age of 100,
   she showed work in an exhibition called 'Some Things
   to Learn from Leaves'. She died in August 2016.
'Other letters went to the Eastman...' All in JAAFA Box 33
   Folder 9.
'Albers prevaricated.' Ibid.
'In the summer of 1962...' See p. 263.
'Mr Albers has stated that he...' JAAFA Box 33 Folder 9.
'Albers' information is relevant right...' Donald Judd,
   'Books', *Arts Magazine*, November 1963, p. 67ff.
'Every generation has...generation without ideas...'
   In Judd's 1993 Mondrian Lecture, *Some Aspects of
   Colour in General and Red and Black in Particular*;
   reprinted in Nicholas Serota (ed.), *Donald Judd*
   (London: Tate Publishing, 2004).
p. 277 'I joined the long line of those...' Edward Reep,
   review of *Interaction of Color*, *Labyrinth*, June 1965.
'If Albers "did much to rekindle an...' Kenneth E. Burchett,
   *A Biographical History of the Study and Use of Color
   from Aristotle to Kandinsky* (Lewiston, NY: Edwin Mellen
   Press, 2005), p. 53.
'The touring exhibition that accompanied...'
   'Interaction of Color: Josef Albers', Carpenter
   Centre for the Visual Arts, Harvard University,
   15 October–1 December 1963.
'For its fiftieth anniversary in 2013...' Albers' old nemesis,
   Johannes Itten, continued to haunt him. In 1961, Itten's
   Kunst der Farbe had appeared in German and English,
   preempting *Interaction of Color*. Albers denied Itten's
   claim to have taught colour at the Bauhaus, and hinted
   that the Swiss had stolen his ideas. 'I know what [Itten]
   claims in his book, the squares within squares,' he said.
   'But he did that later, after I had been in Ulm. I had
   never seen *that* before.' (JA interviewed by Finkelstein,
   tape 1, side A, track 2.)
'As one Yale student noted...' Irwin Rubin interviewed
   by Horowitz, 7 July 1997.

p. 279 'In 1969, the German-born photographer...'
   Hans Namuth and Paul Falkenberg, *Josef Albers:
   Homage to the Square*, film (1969).
'Nietzschean to his fingertips, Albers had...' For more
   on Nietzsche's anti-politicism, see Peter Bergmann,
   Nietzsche: 'The Last Antipolitical German' (Bloomington:
   University of Indiana Press, 1987).
'There are...that are pretty wild.' John Cohen
   interviewed by Horowitz, 14 January 1996.
'That art should somehow be democratic...'
   John T. Frazer interviewed by Horowitz, 30 May 1996.
'Those who did included Louise Nevelson...' For more on
   this, see Matthew Israel, *Kill for Peace: American Artists
   Against the Vietnam War* (Austin: University of Texas
   Press, 2013).
'By return came a reply from Anni saying...' Letters, Dore
   Ashton to JA, 4 March 1967, and Anni Albers to Ashton,
   9 March 1967, JAAFA Box 1 Folder 22.
'In June 1965, a telegram arrived...' JAAFA Box 5 Folder 20.
p. 280 'The poet Robert Lowell, asked to...' See Randall
   Bennett Woods, *LBJ: Architect of American Ambition*
   (Cambridge, MA: Harvard University Press, 2007), p. 642.
'In 1968, Mayor John...Albers refused.' Letter, John V.
   Lindsay to JA, 20 August 1968, JAAFA Box 41 Folder 8.
'When he explained, Albers winced...' Robert Engman
   interviewed by Horowitz, 28 February 1996.
'Other invitees included Robert Indiana...' Letter, Dr Kurt
   Martin, Edition Olympia 1972, to JA, 10 September 1969,
   JAAFA Box 44 Folder 7.
p. 282 'our idea of the eye must [today]...' William C.
   Seitz, *The Responsive Eye* (New York: Museum of
   Modern Art, 1965), p. 5.
'Seitz was quick to make this clear...' Ibid. p. 18.
'His Art Deceives the Eye...' *The Nation*, 11 November
   1965, p. 22.
'The *Herald Tribune* at least recognized...' John Gruen,
   '"Op" Pops and Their Opsprings', review of 'Abstract
   Trompe l'Oeil' at Janis Gallery, *Herald Tribune*,
   7 February 1965, p. 32.
'The piece ran under the headline...' *The Washington
   Daily News*, 5 November 1965, p. 28.
'In *Yale Scientific*, Albers argued, articulately...'
   'Op Art and/or Perceptual Effects', *Yale Scientific
   Magazine*, November 1965, pp. 5–13.
p. 283 'or textile carpeting.' JA, unpublished writings,
   JAAFA Box 80 Folder 27.
'A more useful response came in...' Pasadena Art Museum,
   17 September–27 October 1968; Henry Art Gallery,
   University of Washington, Seattle, 17 November–
   22 December 1968; Santa Barbara Museum of Art,
   25 January–23 February 1969.
'While noting that Albers...' John Coplans, *Serial
   Imagery* (Pasadena Art Museum, 1968), pp. 46–8.
'The last word was left to the artist...' Ibid. pp. 48–9.
'These would be followed by Naum and...' In JAAFA
   Box 29 Folder 10.
p. 285 'Every time he drove it home...' Engman
   interviewed by Horowitz.
'That the cook at the Hirshhorn...' Nicholas Fox Weber,
   'Seeing the Bauhaus Through a Ketchup Bottle',
   ARTnews, 1 October 2010. Many of Hirshhorn's Albers are
   now in the Washington museum that bears his name.

'In the basement, too, Albers worked...' *Wrestling* is on the courtyard wall of Seidler's Mutual Life Centre.

p. 286 'Like many wives of her day...' Danilowitz, 'A Short History'.

'The couple were in bed by nine...' 'Josef Albers, Artist and Teacher, Dies'; *New York Times*, 26 March 1976, p. 33.

'Still trim, he would wear the grey...' Mai-Tse Wu, pers. comm., 24 September 2017.

'He chatted to neighbours' children...' Brenda Danilowitz, pers. comm., Orange, CT, 20 May 2017.

'In the interim, honours had accrued...' AIA Fine Arts Medal, 1969; NIAL, 1968.

'Für einen Tag in Bottrop...' *Ruhr-Nachrichten*, 18 October 1960.

'Besides a German edition of Eugen Gomringer's monograph...' The Münster show also toured to Lübeck, Karlsruhe, Bonn and Berlin; see 'Ich war es', *Der Spiegel* 28, 8 July 1968, pp. 89–90.

p. 288 'Feted on a visit home in November...' 'Josef Albers zur 50-Jahr-Feier nach Bottrop eingeladen', *Westdeutsch Allgemeine Zeitung*, 8 November 1968.

'Two years after that, he made the city...' 'Ehrenbürger Josef Albers schenkt Stadt 127 Grafiken', *Westdeutsch Allgemeine Zeitung*, 24 October 1972.

'For all Albers' new-found celebrity...' Hunter, 'Josef Albers' Modern Icons'.

'Between January and May 1967 alone...' Sidney Janis correspondence, JAAFA Box 20 Folder 19.

p. 289 'Shortly after shooting his film...' Namuth photographed Eastman's home in July 1970: see Hans Namuth Papers, Centre for Creative Photography, University of Arizona, AG 135 Box 157.

'At his death in 1991, his collection...' See catalogue to the sale *Property from the Collection of Lee V. Eastman*, Christie's New York, November 2005.

'For Josef, Sidney Janis was...' John T. Hill, pers. comm., New Haven, 21 May 2017.

'The pair of paintings subtitled...' These, gifted by Lillian Clark, are now in the Dallas Museum of Art.

'The gallery was holding money back...' Letter, Lee Eastman to JA, 2 December 1970, JAAFA Box 16 Folder 22.

p. 290 'Two months later, Janis was ordered...' Letter, Lee Eastman to JA, 8 February 1971, JAAFA Box 16 Folder 22. This was the forerunner of the current JAAF.

'We must...proceed with the catalogue...' Letter, Lee Eastman to JA, 19 February 1971, JAAFA Box 16 Folder 22.

'Albers had had thirteen works...' See Henry Geldzahler, 'Creating a New Department', in *Making It New: Essays, Interviews and Talks* (Brooklyn: Turtle Point Press, 1994), pp. 81–92.

'Everybody wanted one.' Grace Glueck, 'How Do You Price Artworks? Let The Dealers Count The Ways', *New York Times*, 20 January 1976, p. 28.

'The next year, a Toronto dealer...' Ibid.

'The gallerist Denise René, who represented...' Letter, Lee Eastman to JA, 16 June 1971, JAAFA Box 16 Folder 22.

'A painting by Willem de Kooning hanging...' Geldzahler, 'Creating a New Department', p. 83.

'Being in a *historisches museum* meant...' Margit Rowell Noël, pers. comm., 25 May 2017.

'In his writing on...' Henry Geldzahler, 'New York Painting and Sculpture: 1940–1970', in *Making It New*, pp. 93–9.

'By 1971, the title of Albers' article...' JA, 'Historisch oder Jetzig?', *Junge Menschen* no. 8, November 1924, p. 171.

'The number and prices of Albers'...' Letter, Lee Eastman to JA, 19 February 1971.

p. 291 'The museum, sensibly, bought it.' Geldzahler, 'Creating a New Department'.

'The interviews were to lead to...' Abrams had recently published Werner Spies's *Josef Albers* (New York, 1970).

'Around five, we'd go up to the kitchen...' Rowell Noël, pers comm., 25 May 2017.

'I would...Guggenheim Museum in 1972.' Letter, Margit Rowell to JA, 26 May 1970, JAAFA Box 8 Folder 58.

'The date he proposed was autumn 1972...' Letter, Thomas M. Messer to JA, 24 September 1970, JAAFA Box 19 Folder 18.

'Albers must certainly have discussed...' Geldzahler, 'Creating a New Department'.

'It was a shame...' Rowell Noël, pers comm., 25 May 2017.

'In January 1972, Rowell published...' Margit Rowell, 'On Albers' Color', *Artforum* 10, January 1972, p. 26ff.

'Albers did not like his art...' JAAFA OS17 Folders 28–9.

'The Metropolitan exhibition opened on...' i.e., until 9 January 1972.

p. 294 'To this is added the surprising observation...' Catalogue to 'Josef Albers at the Metropolitan Museum of Art: An Exhibition of His Paintings and Prints' (New York: Museum of Modern Art, 1971).

'The show did, though, get three notices...' Grace Glueck, 'Each Day, Another Albers Pancake', *New York Times*, 5 December 1971, p. 24.

'A more intelligent response came...' 'Albers Show Is Marked by Vibrancy', *New York Times*, 19 November 1971, p. 36.

'The more one sees of his...' 'Art That Owes Nothing to "Nature", But Everything to Man Himself', *New York Times*, 28 November 1971, p. 21.

'The playwrights Edward Albee and...' Sometime in the late 1950s, Johns traded an erotic Japanese woodblock for a remade American version of the Bauhaus glass painting *Im Wasser*, owned by his then lover, Robert Rauschenberg. At Rauschenberg's request, Albers had given him the work at Black Mountain College, after it had been broken in an exhibition there. (See JA, glass notes, JAAFA Box 63 Folder 57, p. 15.) The relationship between teacher and student had clearly been less combative than Rauschenberg liked to make out.

'In this case, though, the reason...' For more on this, see 'Kanzleramt: Bammel vor dem Umzug' (Chancellery: Moving Day Nerves), *Der Spiegel* 10, 1 March 1976, pp. 33–4.

'I admire your art so much...' Letter, Maximilian Schell to JA, 30 November 1969, JAAFA Box 9 Folder 10.

p. 295 'I would...appreciate it if you...' Letter, Maximilian Schell to Conrad Janis, 22 December 1969, JAAFA Box 9 Folder 10.

'To Lee Eastman, now handling sales...' Letter, Maximilian Schell to Lee Eastman, 15 January 1972, JAAFA Box 9 Folder 10.

In February 1976, he writes...' Letter, Maximilian Schell to JA, 17 February 1976, JAAFA Box 9 Folder 10 (author's translation). In 1975, Schell had directed Voight in the film *End of the Game*. Afterwards, Voight invited Schell to be godfather to his newborn daughter, now the actress Angelina Jolie.

'From the Benedictine abbey of Gerleve…' 'Albers', Westfälisches Landesmuseum für Kunst und Kulturgeschichte, 28 April–2 June 1968.

'Albers' sister, Frau Marx, had spoken…' Letter, Father Rupert Overlack, OSB, to JA, 9 May 1968.

'Albers' warm reply directs the…' Letter, JA to Father Rupert Overlack ('Mein lieber Pater Rupert Overlack'), JAAFA Box 8 Folder 4.

'Letters came, too, from Fr Josef Tenorth…' i.e., at the Josefschule.

'Now a parish priest, Tenorth recalls…' Letter, Father Josef Tenorth, 'Albers lehrte auch an der Josefschule', *Ruhr-Nachrichten*, 26 August 1969.

p. 296 'There was something uncomfortable…' Letter, Father Josef Tenorth to JA, 13 November 1969, JAAFA Box 10 Folder 41.

'Its infinite harmony and beauty…' Ibid.

'In 1965, an Essen self-portrait had been…' These were published as *Search Versus Re-Search: Three Lectures by Josef Albers* (Hartford, CT: Trinity College Press, 1965). The book sold badly – by 1970, only a hundred and thirty copies had been bought. An accompanying exhibition, 'The Art of Josef Albers', ran at the college's Austin Arts Centre from 19 April until 7 May 1965.

'The next letter agrees the fee Albers…' Letter, Gordon Kwiatkowski to Norman Ives, 9 June 1972.

'As Alvin Eisenman recalled, Albers…' Eisenman interviewed by Horowitz.

'Mr Albers, I was so happy to have…' Letter, Gordon Kwiatkowski to JA, 29 January 1974, *ibid*.

p. 298 'Eight months before, in June 1973…' Letter, Alvin Eisenman to JA, 19 June 1973. Eisenman was then Director of Studies in Graphic Design and Photography at Yale.

'Ives, he said, had been his student…' Letter, JA to Dean Howard S. Weaver, undated (June 1973), JAAFA Box 5 Folder 12.

'But Ives-Sillman could not work…' Letter, Norman Ives to Lee Eastman, 22 October 1973, JAAFA Box 20 Folder 17.

'In November 1973, Eastman wrote sharply…' Letter, Lee Eastman to Ives-Sillman, 26 November 1973, JAAFA Box 20 Folder 17.

p. 299 'From then on, his printing would…' Tyler Graphics in Bedford Village.

'Albers' work would longer be *pro bono*…' Letter, Lee Eastman to Gordon Kwiatkowski, 8 February 1974, JAAFA Box 16 Folder 22.

'Thompson's book would finally appear…' *The Washburn College Bible* (Topeka, KS: Washburn College, 1979). Washburn was the alma mater of Bradbury Thompson, who arranged for the college to publish it.

'Now they were cut out of his life…' Letter, Lee Eastman to JA, 4 September 1974, JAAFA Box 16 Folder 22.

'They gave their lives to him.' Bernard Chaet interviewed by Horowitz, 4 March 1992.

'I feel this…should finally confirm…' Letter, Sidney Janis to JA, 31 May 1972, JAAFA Box 21 Folders 1–2.

'Dear Sidney, permit me to answer…' Letter, JA to Sidney Janis, 6 June 1972, JAAFA Box 21 Folders 1–2.

'Janis wrote again, reminding Albers…' Letter, Sidney Janis to JA, 23 August 1972, JAAFA Box 21 Folders 1–2.

'I remember [in 1948] how difficult…' Letter, Sidney Janis to JA, 8 May 1974, JAAFA Box 21 Folders 1–2.

p. 300 'In 1967, Thornton Wilder wrote…' Letter, Thornton Wilder to JA, 6 May 1967, JAAFA Box 11 Folder 46.

'While you are not my blood brother…' Letter, R. Buckminster Fuller to JA, 30 April 1974, JAAFA Box 3 Folder 49.

'In the archive of the Albers…' JAAFA Box 80 Folder 3.

'On Friday 19 March 1976…' Chester Kerr, memorial address, Yale University Art Gallery, 23 April 1976, JAAFA AA Box 5 Folder 35.

p. 301 'He was an irascible patient…' Yeng-tse Wu, pers. comm., 26 September 2017.

'He and Anni had chosen their plot…' Brenda Danilowitz, pers. comm., 20 May 2017.

'Anni apart…Hans Farman' Hans Fleischmann had changed his name on coming to America.

'The news…brought a sense of loss…' Letter, Si Sillman to Anni Albers, 26 March 1976, JAAFA AA Box 4 Folder 29.

'His presence was totally positive…' Letter, Norman Ives to Anni Albers, 26 March 1976, JAAFA AA Box 4 Folder 29.

'Hans Namuth, in block capitals, wrote…' Letter, Hans Namuth to Anni Albers, 28 March 1976, JAAFA AA Box 4 Folder 29.

'Dear Mrs Albers, I'm very sorry…' Letter, Heidi Lender (aged nine) to Anni Albers, undated, JAAFA AA Box 4 Folder 29.

'One of the last Bauhaus giants…' *The Globe and Mail*, 29 April 1976, p. 18; *Ruhr-Nachrichten*, 29 March 1976, p. 7.

'For Albers…moral function of art.' Paul Overy, *The Times*, Tuesday 30 March 1976.

p. 302 'We may assume that this, imagined…' 'Josef Albers gestorben', *Neue Zürcher Zeitung*, 29 March 1976.

'The *New York Times* quoted Albers…' 'Josef Albers, Artist and Teacher, Dies', *New York Times*.

'Josef has done his share on earth…' Kerr, memorial address.

Select Bibliography

The selection below suggests interesting (and relatively easy to find) material to supplement that contained in this book. Most is in English.

Periodicals

De Kooning, Elaine, 'Albers Paints a Picture', *Art News* 49, no. 7, November 1950, pp. 40–3, 57–8.

Rowell, Margit, 'On Albers' Color', *Artforum* 10, January 1972, p. 31.

Welliver, Neil, 'Albers on Albers', *Art News* 64, no. 9, January 1966, p. 69.

Books

Albrecht, Hans Joachim, *Farbe als Sprache: Robert Delaunay, Josef Albers, Richard Paul Lohse* (Cologne: Verlag M. du Mont Schauberg, 1975).

Arnheim, Rudolf, *The Power of the Center: A Study of Composition in the Visual Arts* (Los Angeles: UCLA Press, 1988).

Benezra, Neal David, *The Murals and Sculpture of Josef Albers*, Outstanding Dissertations in the Fine Arts (New York and London: Garland Publishing Inc., 1985).

Danilowitz, Brenda, *Anni and Josef Albers: Latin American Journeys* (Berlin: Hatje Cantz, 2007).

— *The Prints of Josef Albers: A Catalogue Raisonné, 1915–1976*, revised edition (Manchester and New York: Hudson Hills Press, 2009).

Droste, Magdalena, *Bauhaus 1919–1933* (Berlin: Taschen/Bauhaus-Archiv, 2006).

Ex, Sjarel, *Theo van Doesburg en het Bauhaus: De Invloed van De Stijl in Duitsland en Midden-Europa* (Utrecht: Centraal Museum, 2000).

Gomringer, Eugen, *Josef Albers: His Work as Contribution to Visual Articulation in the Twentieth Century* (New York: George Wittenborn, Inc., 1968).

Hamilton, George Heard, *Josef Albers: Paintings, Prints, Projects*, exhibition catalogue (New Haven: Yale University Art Gallery, 1956).

Harris, Mary Emma, *The Arts at Black Mountain College* (Cambridge, MA: MIT Press, 1987).

Horowitz, Frederick A., and Brenda Danilowitz, *Josef Albers: To Open Eyes* (London: Phaidon, 2006).

Krummel, Richard Frank, *Nietzsche und der deutsche Geist* (Berlin and New York: Walter de Gruyter, 1998).

Lamberti, Marjorie, *The Politics of Education: Teachers and School Reform in Weimar Germany* (Oxford and New York: Berghahn Books, 2004).

Lane, Mervin (ed.), *Black Mountain College: Sprouted Seeds: an Anthology of Personal Accounts* (Knoxville: University of Tennessee Press, 1990).

Lenman, Robin, *Artists and Society in Germany, 1850–1914* (Manchester: Manchester University Press, 1997).

Malloy, Vanja (ed.), *Intersecting Colors: Josef Albers and His Contemporaries* (Amherst, MA: Amherst College Press, 2015).

Molesworth, Helen, *Leap Before You Look: Black Mountain College, 1933–1957* (New Haven: Yale University Press/ICA Boston, 2015).

Oswalt, Philipp (ed.), *Bauhaus Conflicts, 1919–2009: Controversies and Counterparts* (Berlin: Hatje Cantz, 2009).

Paret, Peter, *German Encounters with Modernism, 1840–1945* (Cambridge: Cambridge University Press, 2001).

Roskill, Mark, *Klee, Kandinsky, and the Thought of Their Time: A Critical Perspective* (Urbana and Chicago: University of Illinois Press, 1992).

Seibenbrodt, Michael, *Bauhaus: A Conceptual Model* (Berlin: Bauhaus Stiftung/Hatje Cantz, 2009).

Singerman, Howard, *Art Subjects: Making Artists in the American University* (Los Angeles: University of California Press, 1999).

Stern, Robert, *Pedagogy and Place: 110 Years of Architectural Education at Yale* (New Haven: Yale University Press, 2016).

Thimmesh, Hilary, OSB, *Marcel Breuer and a Committee of Twelve Plan a Church: A Monastic Memoir* (Collegeville, MN: St John's University Press, 2010).

Writings by Josef Albers

'Historisch oder Jetzig?', *Junge Menschen* no. 8, November 1924, p. 171.

Poems and Drawings (New Haven: Readymade Press, 1958).

Interaction of Color (New Haven: Yale University Press, 1963).

Search Versus Re-Search: Three Lectures by Josef Albers (Hartford, CT: Trinity College Press, 1965).

Film

Hans Namuth and Paul Falkenberg, *Josef Albers: Homage to the Square* (1969).

Collections

This list is not exhaustive; Albers' work is also held in many smaller, lesser-known galleries and museums.

Aichi Prefectural Museum of Art, Nagoya, Japan
Albertina Museum, Vienna, Austria
Albright-Knox Art Gallery, Buffalo, New York, United States
Amon Carter Museum, Fort Worth, Texas, United States
Art Gallery of New South Wales, Sydney, Australia
Art Gallery of Ontario, Toronto, Canada
Art Institute of Chicago, Illinois, United States
Bauhaus-Archiv / Museum für Gestaltung, Berlin, Germany
Berkeley Art Museum, California, United States
British Museum, London, England
Busch-Reisinger Museum, Harvard University Art Museums, Cambridge, Massachusetts, United States
Carnegie Museum of Art, Pittsburgh, Pennsylvania, United States
Centre Georges Pompidou, Paris, France
Cincinnati Art Museum, Ohio, United States
Cleveland Museum of Art, Ohio, United States
Corcoran Gallery of Art, Washington, D.C., United States
Daimler Art Collection, Stuttgart, Germany
Dallas Museum of Art, Texas, United States
Detroit Institute of the Arts, Michigan, United States
Deutsche Bank, Berlin, Germany
Dublin City Gallery The Hugh Lane, Ireland
Fondazione Marguerite Arp, Locarno-Solduno, Switzerland
Friedrich Christian Flick Collection, Hamburger Bahnhof, Berlin, Germany
Galerie Neue Meister Dresden, Germany
Galleria Civica d'Arte Moderna, Turin, Italy
Galleria Nazionale d'Arte Moderna, Rome, Italy
Gallery of Modern Art, National Galleries of Scotland, Edinburgh, Scotland
Gemeentemuseum, The Hague, The Netherlands
Hamburger Kunsthalle, Germany
Hara Museum of Contemporary Art, Tokyo, Japan
Henie Onstad Artcenter, Oslo, Norway
High Museum of Art, Atlanta, Georgia, United States
Hilti Art Foundation Collection, Kunstmuseum, Vaduz, Liechtenstein
Hirshhorn Museum and Sculpture Garden, Washington, D.C., United States
Ho-Am Art Museum, Yongin, Gyeonggi-do, South Korea
Honolulu Academy of Arts, Hawai'i, United States
Indianapolis Art Museum, Indiana, United States
Institut Valencià d'Art Modern, Spain
Instituto Nacional de Cultura y Bellas Artes, Caracas, Venezuela
Israel Museum, Jerusalem, Israel
Josef Albers Museum Quadrat, Bottrop, Germany
JPMorgan Chase Art Collection, New York, United States
Judd Foundation, Marfa, Texas, United States
Karl Ernst Osthaus-Museum, Hagen, Germany
Kawamura Memorial DIC Museum of Art, Sakura, Japan
Kröller-Müller Museum, Otterlo, The Netherlands
Kunsthalle Weishaupt, Ulm, Germany

Kunsthalle zu Kiel, Germany
Kunsthaus Zürich, Switzerland
Kunstmuseum Basel, Switzerland
Kunstmuseum Bern, Switzerland
Kunstmuseum Stuttgart, Germany
Kunstmuseum Winterthur, Switzerland
Kunstsammlung Nordrhein-Westfalen Düsseldorf, Germany
Kurt und Ernst Schwitters Stiftung, Sprengel Museum, Hanover, Germany
Landesmuseum für Kunst und Kulturgeschichte, Münster, Germany
Leeum Samsung Museum of Art, Seoul, South Korea
Los Angeles County Museum of Art, California, United States
Louisiana Museum for Modern Art, Humlebæk, Denmark
Louvre Abu Dhabi, United Arab Emirates
Metropolitan Museum of Art, New York, United States
Minneapolis Institute of Art, Minnesota, United States
Modern Art Museum of Fort Worth, Texas, United States
Moderna Museet, Stockholm, Sweden
Morgan Library and Museum, New York, United States
Musée d'Art Contemporain Montréal, Canada
Musée d'Art Moderne, Brussels, Belgium
Musée des Beaux-Arts de Montréal, Canada
Musei Vaticani, Rome, Italy
Museo Thyssen-Bornemisza, Madrid, Spain
Museo d'Arte Contemporanea Villa Croce, Genova, Italy
Museo d'Arte di Lugano, Switzerland
Museo de Arte Contemporaneo de Caracas, Venezuela
Museo de Arte Moderno de Buenos Aires, Argentina
Museu Colecção Berardo, Lisbon, Portugal
Museu de Arte Contemporanea de Universidade de São Paulo, Brazil
Museum Boymans van Beuningen, Rotterdam, The Netherlands
Museum Folkwang, Essen, Germany
Museum Haus Konstruktiv, Zürich, Switzerland
Museum Kunstpalast, Düsseldorf, Germany
Museum Küppersmühle für Moderne Kunst, Duisburg, Germany
Museum Ludwig Köln, Germany
Museum Moderner Kunst Stiftung Ludwig Wien, Austria
Museum of Art, Rhode Island School of Design, Providence, Rhode Island, United States
Museum of Contemporary Art, Los Angeles, California, United States
Museum of Fine Arts, Boston, Massachusetts, United States
Museum of Fine Arts, Houston, Texas, United States
Museum of Modern Art, New York, United States
National Gallery of Australia, Canberra, Australia
National Gallery of Canada, Ottawa, Canada
National Gallery of Victoria, Melbourne, Australia
National Museum of Modern Art, Tokyo, Japan
Neue Nationalgalerie, Staatliche Museen zu Berlin, Germany
Peggy Guggenheim Collection, The Solomon R. Guggenheim Foundation, Venice, Italy
Philadelphia Museum of Art, Pennsylvania, United States
Phillips Collection, Washington, D.C., United States
Pinakothek der Moderne, Munich, Germany

Princeton University Art Museum, New Jersey,
United States
Robert and Jane Meyerhoff Collection, National Gallery
of Art, Washington, D.C., United States
San Diego Museum of Art, California, United States
San Francisco Museum of Modern Art, California,
United States
Santa Barbara Museum of Art, California, United States
Sara Hildén Art Museum, Tampere, Finland
Seattle Art Museum, Washington, United States
Smithsonian American Art Museum, Washington D.C.,
United States
Solomon R. Guggenheim Museum, New York,
United States
Sprengel Museum, Hanover, Germany
St Louis Art Museum, Missouri, United States
Staatsgalerie Stuttgart, Germany
Städelmuseum, Frankfurt, Germany
Stiftung Bauhaus Dessau, Germany
Szépművészeti Múzeum, Budapest, Hungary
Tate Modern, London, England
Tel Aviv Museum of Art, Israel
Ulmer Museum, Germany
University of Michigan Museum of Art, Ann Arbor,
Michigan, United States
Victoria and Albert Museum, London, England
Wadsworth Atheneum Museum of Art, Hartford,
Connecticut, United States
Walker Art Center, Minneapolis, Minnesota, United States
Whitney Museum of American Art, New York,
United States
Winnipeg Art Gallery, Manitoba, Canada
Yale University Art Gallery, New Haven, Connecticut,
United States
Zentrum Paul Klee, Bern, Switzerland

Exhibitions

This list includes a selection of significant exhibitions –
solo and group – of Josef Albers' work, from 2010 onwards.

2010, Washington, D.C., United States
Hirshhorn Museum and Sculpture Garden, 'Josef
Albers: Innovation and Inspiration', 13 February–
11 April 2010

2010, Kaohsiung City, Taiwan
Kaohsiung Museum of Fine Arts, 'Josef Albers: Minimal
Means, Maximum Effect', 3 April–1 August 2010

2010, Bottrop, Germany
Josef Albers Museum Quadrat, 'Letzte Bilder: Ad
Reinhardt und Josef Albers' [Last Pictures: Ad Reinhardt
and Josef Albers], 26 September 2010–9 January 2011

2010, Munich, Germany
Staatliche Graphische Sammlung München, 'Painting
on Paper: Josef Albers in America', 16 December 2010–
6 March 2011. The exhibition traveled to Josef Albers
Museum Quadrat, Bottrop, Germany, 20 March–19 June
2011; Louisiana Museum of Modern Art, Humlebæk,
Denmark, 1 July–31 August 2011; Kunstmuseum Basel
Kupferstichkabinett, 5 November 2011–29 January 2012;
and other venues.

2011, Waterloo, New South Wales, Australia
Dominik Mersch Gallery, 'Josef Albers: Albers and
Seidler', 10 August–20 August 2011

2012, Cork, Ireland
Lewis Glucksman Gallery, University College Cork,
The Sacred Modernist: Josef Albers as a Catholic Artist,
5 April–8 July 2012

2013, Città di Castello, Italy
Pinacoteca Comunale, 'Josef Albers: Arte come
Esperienza: I metodi di insegnamento di un maestro del
Bauhaus' [Josef Albers, Art as Experience: The Teaching
Methods of a Bauhaus Master], 19 March–19 June 2013

2013, Madrid, Spain
Galería Cayón, 'Doble mirada a España: las fotos de
Josef Albers y Robert Rauschenberg' [Two looks at Spain:
the photos of Josef Albers and Robert Rauschenberg],
4 June–20 July 2013

2013, Milan, Italy
Fondazione Stelline, 'Josef Albers: Sublime Optics',
26 September 2013–6 January 2014

2013 Milan, Italy
Accademia di Brera, 'Imparare a vedere: Josef Albers
professore, dal Bauhaus a Yale' [Learning to See:
Josef Albers as a Teacher, from the Bauhaus to Yale],
2 October–1 December 2013. Exhibition traveled to
Josef Albers Museum Quadrat as 'Kunst als Erfahrung:
Josef Albers als Lehrer–der Maler und seine Schüler'
[Art as Experience: Josef Albers as Teacher – the Painter
and his School], 15 December 2013–30 March 2014

2014, Madrid, Spain
Fundación Juan March Madrid, 'Josef Albers: Medios
Minimos–Efecto Maximo' [Josef Albers: Minimal
Means, Maximum Effect], 28 March–6 July 2014.
Exhibition traveled to Henie Onstad Kunstsenter,
Høvikodden, Norway, 18 September–14 December 2014

2014, Palma, Mallorca
Museo Fundación Juan March Palma, 'Josef Albers:
Process and Printmaking', 2 April–28 June 2014.

Exhibition traveled to Museo de Arte Abstracto Español, Cuenca, 9 July–5 October 2014; Josef Albers Museum Quadrat, Bottrop, November 2014–15 February 2015

2014, Bottrop, Germany
Josef Albers Museum Quadrat, 'Homage to the Square: First–Last, 1950–1976', 7 May–10 August 2014

2014, Palma, Mallorca
Fundació Pilar y Joan Miró Mallorca, 'Josef Albers/Joan Miró: The Thrill of Seeing', 22 May–9 November 2014

2015, Milan, Italy
MUDEC, Museo delle Culture, 'A Beautiful Confluence: Anni and Josef Albers and the Latin American World', 28 October 2015–21 February 2016

2016, Madrid, Spain
Galería Cayón, 'Josef Albers: Homage to the Square', 25 February–23 April 2016

2016, New York, United States
Museum of Modern Art, 'One and One Is Four: The Bauhaus Photocollages of Josef Albers', 23 November 2016–2 April 2017

2017, New Haven, Connecticut, United States
Yale University Art Gallery, 'Small-Great Objects: Anni and Josef Albers in the Americas', 3 February–25 June 2017

Picture Credits

All works by Josef Albers are © 2018 The Josef and Anni Albers Foundation/Artist's Rights Society (ARS), New York/DACS, London/VG Bild-Kunst, Bonn.

Courtesy the Josef and Anni Albers Foundation 1.1–1.5, 1.7–1.10, 2.2–2.3, 2.13, 2.26–2.28, 3.8, 3.13, 3.15, 3.16, 4.5, 4.10, 4.14, 4.16, 5.4, 5.6, 5.8, 5.9, 5.19, 5.22, 5.24, 6.3, 6.5–6.8, 7.6–7.9, VIII; Photo Clemens Kalischer 5.23; Photo Barbara Morgan. Barbara and Willard Morgan photographs and papers, Library Special Collections, Charles E. Young Research Library, UCLA 5.5; Photo Tim Nighswander/Imaging4Art I–V, 2–6, 8, 11, 12, 1.6, 2.1, 2.4, 2.6–2.11, 2.14–2.16, 2.18–2.22, 2.24, 2.29, 3.3, 3.6, 3.10, 4.7, 4.9, 4.11–4.13, 4.15, 4.18, 4.20, 4.22, 4.24, 4.26, 4.27, 5.2, 5.11–5.14, 5.17, 5.21, 6.9, 6.10, 6.14, 7.2, 7.10–7.12, 7.16–7.20, VII, IX–XI, XV, XVII–XXIII; Photo Claude Stoller 5.20; Photo Otto Umbehr (Umbo). © Phyllis Umbehr/Galerie Kicken Berlin/DACS 2018 4.4; Photo Walter Rüdel 6.12; Photo Ruth Wurcker 7.13; Josef Albers Museum Quadrat Bottrop 4.17; The Josef Albers Papers 4.1, 5.16; Collection of Art Gallery of Nova Scotia, Gift of Marjorie and Lauder Brunton, Guysborough, Nova Scotia, 1993. 1993.194 XIII; College of Science, Rochester Institute of Technology 7.5; Corning Glass Building, 717 Fifth Ave, New York 7.3; Harkness Commons Graduate Center, Harvard University 6.4; The Hirshhorn Museum and Sculpture Garden, Washington D.C. 3.4; The Metropolitan Museum of Art, Gift of the Artist, 1972 3.5; The Museum of Modern Art, New York 3.11; Pan Am Building, New York 7.4; Private Collection. Photo Tim Nighswander/Imaging4Art VI, 1, XII; Private Collection 2.5, 4.25, 5.18, XIV; Private Collection, Germany 2.17, 2.23; Staatsgalerie Stuttgart, Inv.Nr.3276 6.1

Courtesy the Josef and Anni Albers Foundation Archives 6.2

Josef Albers Museum Quadrat Bottrop 7, 2.25, 3.17, 5.15, 6.15; Photo Werner Hannappel 3.9

Bauhaus-Archiv Berlin 3.1, 3.2, 3.7, 4.21, 4.23; © DACS 2018: 3.12, 4.3, Photo Otto Umbehr (Umbo). © Phyllis Umbehr/Galerie Kicken Berlin/DACS 2018 4.19

bpk/Staatsgalerie Stuttgart 4.28

Bridgeman Images/Private Collection/PVDE 4.2

Centre Pompidou, MNAM-CCI, Dist. RMN-Grand Palais. Photo Georges Meguerditchian 4.6

Gebrauchsgraphik. International Advertising Art magazine, published by Druck und Verlag Phönix, Berlin, 1928 4.8

Getty Images The LIFE Images Collection/Photo Gabriel Benzur 5.10; Corbis/Photo Genevieve Naylor 5.3

Harvard Art Museums/Busch-Reisinger Museum, Gift of Walter Gropius 3.14

Courtesy John T. Hill 7.21

Magnum Photos/Photo Henri Cartier-Bresson 7.14, 7.15

Courtesy James Mai 9

Courtesy North Carolina Archives, Western Regional Archives, Asheville, N.C. 5.7

Private Collection, Germany 2.12

AP/REX/Shutterstock 5.1

Scala, Florence/Digital Image Museum Associates/LACMA/Art Resource NY 6.11

Courtesy St. John's Abbey Archives, Collegeville, M.N. 6.13

Yale University Art Gallery. Gift of Anni Albers and the Josef Albers Foundation, Inc. XVI

Yale University Library, Manuscripts and Archives. King-lui Wu papers (MS 1842) 7.1

Index

VII *Homage to the Square: Golden*, 1957. Oil on masonite, 32 × 32 in.

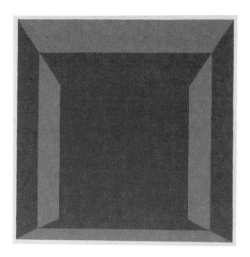

VIII *Study for Homage to the Square: Framed Sky C*, 1970. Oil on masonite, 16 × 16 in.
IX *Study for Homage to the Square: Rare Diversion*, 1959. Oil on masonite, 24 × 24 in.

x *Homage to the Square: Pasture*, 1959. Oil on masonite, 32 × 32 in.

XI *Double Homage to the Square*, 1957. Oil on masonite, 16 × 31 in.

XII *Homage to the Square: Soaring*, 1959. Oil on masonite, 40 × 40 in.

XIII *Study for Homage to the Square: Teen-Age*, 1961. Oil on masonite, 24 × 24 in.

XIV *Homage to the Square*, 1974. Oil on masonite, 24 × 24 in.

xv *Study for Homage to the Square*, 1971. Oil on masonite, 24 × 24 in.

XVI *Homage to the Square*, 1970. Oil on masonite, 23.9 × 23.9 in.

XVII *Homage to the Square*, 1971. Oil on masonite, 48 × 48 in.

XVIII *Study for Homage to the Square: Herbs*, 1962. Oil on masonite, 30 × 30 in.

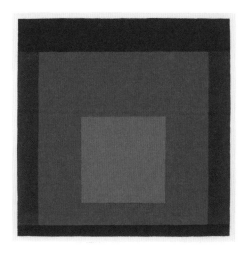

XIX *Homage to the Square*, 1962. Oil on masonite, 16 × 16 in.
XX *Study for Homage to the Square: Growing Mellow*, 1967. Oil on masonite, 24 × 24 in.

XXI *Study for Homage to the Square: Equilibrant*, 1962. Oil on masonite, 24 × 24 in.

XXII *Homage to the Square: Departing in Yellow*, 1965. Oil on masonite, 48 × 48 in.

XXIII *Homage to the Square*, 1965. Oil on masonite, 32 × 32 in.

12/18